Whispers of the Heart

Whispers of the Heart

Love Stories of Famous People

Asif Jalal

ink | OCCAM

ISBN: 978-93-6547-065-9

First published in India 2025
This edition published 2025

BluOne Ink Pvt. Ltd
A-76, 2nd Floor, Sector 136, Noida
Uttar Pradesh 201301
www.bluone.ink
publisher@bluone.ink

Printed and bound in India at Thomson Press (India) Ltd

Kali and Occam are imprints of BluOne Ink

Contents

1

Napoleon Bonaparte

Napoleon Bonaparte (1769–1821), the French army commander and statesperson, is counted as one of the greatest military generals of all times along with the likes of Alexander the Great, Hannibal Barca, and Julius Caesar. Rising from the rank of a captain in the French army, he was crowned the emperor of France in 1804.

Josephine, thirty-two, a mother of two, met twenty-six-year-old Napoleon on a September night. He saw her dancing ballet in a red fluttering gown in 1795 at a society ball in Paris. She took over the imagination of the masterful tactician Napoleon, who then held the rank of brigadier general in the French army. Just a year after this meeting, they got married at the Church of Saint-Sulpice in Paris.

Josephine was born Marie Josephe Rose Tascher de La Pagerie at the distant French colony Trois-Îlets, Martinique, an island in the West Indies. Her father was a small-time aristocrat and gambler.

Before marrying Napoleon, Josephine was married at sixteen to an abusive aristocrat, Alexandre de Beauharnais, nineteen, in Paris in December 1779. She had a son and a daughter from this marriage. Alexandre called his wife 'Josephine'.

During this period, France was a country torn by extreme tumult and violence. In 1794, the French army found Alexandre, Josephine's husband, to be involved in counter-revolutionary activities and arrested him for treason. The authorities sentenced him to death, and he was publicly guillotined at a roundabout in Paris in July 1794.

Josephine also came under the shadow of suspicion for anti-government activities and was thrown into the infamous jail Carmes Prison. She lived in a prison dress in a dark, smelly, and damp cell. She grew pale, and her health deteriorated due to a lung infection. She was also in line for execution, but the authorities found her too ill to be guillotined. They released her from jail in November 1794.

After such a crisis, Josephine made a comeback. With her husband gone and the country in the grip of violence and bloodshed, Josephine looked for security. She became the mistress of Paul Barras, a top politician of France and a man of huge fortune. At one time, he was the de facto ruler of France. He had dozens of mistresses and was the epitome of immorality in public and private lives in France.

The party where Josephine danced with Napoleon on a starry night in September 1795 was hosted by

Paul Barras. By then, this politician had had enough of Josephine, and she ceased to be an object of his desire. Barras wanted to get rid of her. He has said, 'I was long since tired and bored with her.' He encouraged Napoleon to mix with her and appreciate her charm. Napoleon did not resist the offer.

Napoleon, unlike other top generals of the world, read and wrote extensively. He wanted to leave an indelible mark and a towering legacy. Apart from conquering territories, his other work was writing; he wrote volumes of sweet words to his beloved.

In one letter, he says, 'How happy I would be if I could assist you at your undressing, the little firm white breast, the adorable face, the hair tied up in a scarf a la creole.'

Napoleon was looking for an older woman because he believed he would be more acceptable to society and would have greater legitimacy with a sophisticated lady on his arm. Within weeks, he fell deeply in love with the lady, and his infatuation grew until their marriage.

He proposed to her in January 1796 and wrote romantic love letters to her from various military posts of the French army. In December 1795, he wrote: 'Sweet and matchless Josephine, how strangely you work upon my heart.'

On 9 March 1796, Napoleon married Josephine in a civil ceremony at a town hall in Paris. In a pink-white pannier skirt of silk, Josephine looked like a fairy. The sky outside was laden with clouds, while piercing wind whispered through the trees and chilled the soul.

However, forty-eight hours after the marriage, Napoleon was given the command of the Italian army. He had no time for a honeymoon and had to leave his bride. He sprung to lead a battle against Italians and

Austrians, and reached Nice on 11 March 1796 for the war.

Napoleon's rise to power would occur in the years following 1795. By 1799, he would stage a coup d'état in France and would rule France and much of Europe.

Napoleon wanted his wife to follow him to the war posts. He wrote numerous love letters to her, expressing his deep love, fascination, and infatuation for her.

He wrote to her, 'I hope that before long I shall clasp you in my arms and cover you with a million kisses as burning as if under the equator.'

While Napoleon led his forces on the neighbours of France and conquered territories, Josephine was struck with a case of 'wandering eye' in Paris. She fell into the arms of other men in the capital. Aristocrats and elites would come to her mansion and spend time in her company.

When she did not join Napoleon, he suspected that she was in love with another man in Paris and she was not leaving the city because of her amorous relationships.

In May 1798, Napoleon boarded a ship from Toulon, France, with his army of 35,000 men to sail through the Mediterranean Sea. The weather was pleasant, and the sky was clear. His hunger for territory was insatiable, and this time, the target was Egypt.

In October 1799, he was in Paris and stood upon the precipice of power as the ruler of France. He was given the task of heading the government of France. In the winter of 1804, he was crowned the emperor, and his love, Josephine, wearing a gold silk gauze dress and diadem, was coronated as empress at the beautiful, Gothic Notre-Dame de Paris.

Even after five years of marriage, the queen could not bear a child, an heir for Napoleon's empire. An heir was necessary for his dynastic ambitions. Napoleon thought he should exercise other options and break his marriage with Josephine.

Napoleon announced at his Tuileries Palace in the winter of 1809 that he would end his relationship with Joséphine. This came as a sudden bolt from heaven for the ambitious lady. The empress of France screamed in horror. In a dress laced with gold, she collapsed on the floor. She could not stand and was carried away by the attendants to her quarters. Napoleon still loved the lady, but he was a man in a hurry and could not wait interminably for an heir.

Formal divorce and nullification of marriage came in January 1810. The reason Napoleon gave for divorce was that a priest had not presided over his marriage ceremony. Therefore, it was not legal marriage in the first place.

Two months after divorce, on 11 March 1810, Napoleon married Marie Louise of Austria, twenty, daughter of the emperor of Austria. The marriage ceremony took place in Vienna.

Despite a formal divorce, Napoleon maintained a good relationship with Josephine, and he allowed her to hold the title of empress. He said, 'It is my will that she retains the rank and title of empress.' After the divorce, the lady moved into a private residence called Château de Malmaison near Paris and spent her time there, sad and lonely.

Four years after the divorce, in 1814, Josephine suffered pneumonia. She had gone out in the open for a walk with the emperor of Russia, Tsar Alexander, at Malmaison. She died in May 1814 at the age of fifty-one.

One month before Josephine's death, everything went topsy-turvy in Napoleon's life. The emperor of France was forced to abdicate the throne in April 1814 and was exiled to the island of Elba in the Mediterranean. Napoleon's rule had come to an end in France.

Madame Bertrand, an attendant, informed him about Josephine's death. The attendant recollected, '(Hearing the news) his face did not change, he only exclaimed: "Ah! She is happy now."'

He had written a letter to her a year earlier, telling her: 'Adieu, my love: tell me that you are well. I'm informed that you are getting as fat as a Norman farmer's good wife. Napoleon.'

Napoleon wondered whether it was Josephine who brought him luck as all his achievements came to naught after the separation and divorce.

2

John Stuart Mill

John Stuart Mill, twenty-four, was invited by Harriet Taylor's husband for dinner at her residence in Finsbury, north London, in the summer of 1830. Harriet was a twenty-four-year-old poet, writer, feminist, and well-read woman with 'a complexion like a pearl'. Mill was to act as an intellectual partner and mentor to her. However, Mill fell head over heels in love with Harriet at first sight that night. Thus began a long, tumultuous romance between the two.

Harriet's husband, John Taylor, was a pharmacist and merchant and showed no interest in Socrates, Plato, or Francis Bacon. On the other hand, Harriet looked for somebody with whom she could talk about stoicism, women's rights, and liberalism.

Mill was an intellectual extraordinaire. He was going to be the most influential English philosopher of the 19th century. He would later produce seminal works on logic, economics, philosophy, and politics. He interacted with Auguste Comte, Thomas Carlyle, and others like them.

In 1831, he worked as assistant to the examiner with the East India Company. Hearing of Mill's reputation, John Taylor invited him for dinner. Mill was invited as someone who could satisfy his wife's intellectual hunger. But while he discussed Rene Descartes and Immanuel Kant with Harriet, he stole her heart and lured her away from her husband. 'They were seen everywhere together.'

Mill's love for the lady was not going to have an easy course. Harriet Taylor was a married woman with three children. As per Victorian marriage laws, if she left her husband, she would lose custody of her children and the controversy would shadow her relationship with Mill. Moreover, she did not hate her husband enough to seek separation from him. He was, after all, a rich man who gave her all the comforts of life. Moreover, Mill had no courage to take on the world, to face gossip and innuendoes, and marry her. It was an impossible situation.

However, the love between the two became intense, and their passion could hold no more. Controversies began to impact their relationship, but he would meet her at opportune moments and have supper with her while her husband was out of the house for some engagement. Taylor's husband got an inkling of the blooming romance between his wife and Mill.

At one point of time, the relationship between Harriet and Mill was on the rocks, but it soon became normal. They exchanged a pair of lengthy essays, which was published as *On Marriage* in 1833.

Harriet decided to be friends with both her husband and Mill on an alternating schedule. One day her husband would entertain his guests with her, and on another day, she would meet Mill with his friends. However, the arrangement did not work.

In 1833, Taylor agreed to a separation, as they realized they now stood on distant shores and their relationship had reached the end of the journey. Harriet and Mill visited Paris for six weeks, and under the moonlit sky on the banks of the calm Seine, they slipped into love's enchanting embrace.

In 1834, Harriet moved to her own house in Keston Heath, away from her husband. Eventually, Harriet separated from John Taylor. Now, Mill visited her house more frequently.

She wrote to him in a letter: 'Love, in its true and finest meaning, seems to be the way in which is manifested all that is highest, best and beautiful in the nature of human beings.'

Their relationship affected everybody in their circle, and it became a tale of many scandals. Thomas Carlyle, a friend to whom Mill had introduced Harriet, mentioned that in Paris they were eating grapes off one bunch, like two lovebirds.

The two faced isolation in their society; they turned away from many as people began to talk about them in hushed voices. Then in 1849, John Taylor passed away, making the course of the two lovers easier.

Mill, at the age of forty-five, eventually got married to Harriet in 1851 for the sake of decency. They had been in a relationship for the last twenty years. Mill's mother and family were outraged at the news of his marriage. Mill had married a widow. Facing assault from family members, including his mother, Mill distanced himself from them. He was by now a senior administrator at the East India Company in London.

The two moved to Blackheath in southeast London. Their house was distant from the rest of the neighbourhood at the end of the lane. It was a place away from society. People mocked them and gossiped about them all the time. Here, Mill, along with Harriet, wrote his great works *On Liberty* and *The Subjection of Women*.

A few years after marriage, Harriet was afflicted with tuberculosis. Mill had retired from the East India Company in 1857 and was not in good health himself, but the lady's health declined fast. They went to France, looking for a warm place to stay. That could have improved Harriet's condition. However, she did not recover and died in Avignon, a commune in South France, on 3 November 1858. They had been married only for seven years. Mill got a marble tombstone made for her grave with the inscription 'Were there but a few hearts and intellects like hers, this earth would already become the hoped-for heaven.'

The next year, in February, he published his magnum opus, *On Liberty*, and dedicated it 'to [Harriet] the beloved and deplored memory of her who was the inspirer, and in part the author, of all that is best in my writings'.

Mill lived for another thirteen years after Harriet's death. He was elected a member of parliament for 1865–68, from the City of Westminster. He promoted radical feminism, which he had developed with Harriet Taylor. He became the first person in the parliament to call for giving women the right to vote.

He bought a cottage at Avignon to spend his last days and indulge in writing. The cottage overlooked Harriet's grave, like Agra Fort from where Shah Jahan used to look at Mumtaz Mahal's grave at the Taj Mahal. The tall trees in the garden caused moisture and a chill in the air, which was bad for Mill's health. However, he did not want them to be trimmed as he liked to hear the nightingales sit on those trees and sing.

In 1873, J.S. Mill, one of the greatest rationalist philosophers, died at Avignon in the cottage he had bought. He was buried alongside Harriet Taylor. They had no children.

3

V.S. Naipaul

Vidiadhar Surajprasad (V.S.) Naipaul studied at Queen's Royal College in Trinidad, West Indies. In 1950, he won a Trinidad government scholarship to study English literature at Oxford University. England for him was the 'epicentre of civilisation'. In 1950, at eighteen, he travelled from Port of Spain (Trinidad) to University College, Oxford, in England.

Naipaul was the second of the seven children of Seepersad Naipaul, a journalist. Naipaul was born on 17 August 1932 in rural poverty. His grandparents had emigrated from India to Trinidad as bonded labourers on sugar plantation fields.

In Oxford, he rented a room in the house where Margaret Thatcher had lived as a student. Naipaul was short of money and had few friends. In 1952, he came across Patricia Ann Hale, a student of history at St Hugh's College, University of Oxford. She was a 'slim, small, undergraduate with a kind, pretty face'. The two met for a cup of coffee. They were mutually attracted, and the relationship deepened.

Patricia came from a humble background. Her father worked in a firm of solicitors as a managing clerk in Birmingham. She enrolled at Oxford University in 1950 on a government scholarship that was given to meritorious students. Though she studied history at the best university of the world, her heart was in the movies, and she wanted to be an actor. Her parents and sisters lived in a two-bedroom flat in Kingstanding, Birmingham.

Patricia and Naipaul met often, and after a few months, they became romantic partners. He proposed to her, and she was in awe of his genius.

In March 1952, Patricia took the bus to her parent's flat in Birmingham for a vacation. Naipaul felt her absence acutely and wrote a love letter to her. 'Yes, darling, I am missing you very much … I think of your room tonight—at St Hugh's—robbed of you, robbed of all its charm, its warmth, its coziness. I love you, my dear Pat, and I feel it grows stronger every day.'

Patricia replied to him: 'There is something very exciting about the first letter received from someone…. Vidia, you've been very good to me. Since I've been home, I've realized how much I enjoyed being with you, how interesting you make things, how you've stimulated me.'

She shared her feelings for Naipaul with her father. Her father exploded with anger and told her to choose between Naipaul and studying at the university. She felt offended and moved to her aunt's house. From there, she penned letters to Naipaul, pouring out her feelings.

Naipaul felt lonely, insecure, and depressed in England. Patricia helped him overcome this constant feeling of sinking. In September 1952, they made love for the first time. After a week, Naipaul, in a letter to Patricia, said, 'I merely wanted to tell you that I loved you completely and that Tuesday formed a lasting bond between us because you had surrendered something to me which ought to be surrendered only to the man whom you loved and who loved you and who wanted to marry you.'

Now, Naipaul was in a relationship with Patricia, but he was not sure when and whether he wanted to marry her.

In June 1953, both Naipaul and Patricia graduated from the university. Both got a second class. They were not happy with the grades they got in the final assessment.

After graduation, Naipaul required a job to take care of himself and his family. He moved out of the university area. Patricia suggested that he look for a job. Naipaul told her it was difficult for him to find work. He said he encountered racial humiliation everywhere in London. He wrote to her, 'But the people in authority feel my qualifications fit me only for jobs as porters in kitchens, and with the road gangs.... These people want to break my spirit. They want me to forget my dignity as a human being.... No fire in my room for two days and only tea & toast in my stomach.'

She told him not to worry. Everything will be fine soon. 'Just concentrate on keeping going in health and morale for the time being—and on obtaining white shirts for interviews.'

After her graduation from St Hugh's College, Patricia got another scholarship in August 1954 for further studies at the University of Birmingham.

At home, Patricia had a showdown with her father about her relationship with Naipaul. She told her father that she was going to meet Naipaul in London. Her father had brought a chicken for Sunday lunch. She thought of inviting Naipaul for lunch. Her father told her not to go to London, and if she went despite his warning, he would accompany her and tell Naipaul that he was not welcome in his family circle. He said he would take every step possible to prevent his daughter's marriage with Naipaul, but Patricia was not cowed by her father's threats.

Patricia decided to leave her parents. Her postgraduate studies at the university and love for Naipaul were her priorities. She moved out of her parents' flat to independent lodgings in a Birmingham suburb. Naipaul, a man of poor means, was of no help to Patricia. She wrote to him: 'You are the only thing wanting.' She took up work with a tax office to earn a livelihood. She found her life meaningless without him.

After graduation, Naipaul tried to get himself a one-year postgraduate degree, B. Litt., at University College in English literature in 1953. This would give him time to settle. However, he failed in the viva in 1954. His asthma attack lasted for days. He searched for jobs but could only get menial work like that of a dishwasher. He also applied for jobs in India. He sold copies of encyclopaedias from door to door. Patricia helped him emotionally and financially during this period.

Now that he had finished the course at Oxford, he left the town and stayed in the 'slum basement' of his cousin's house in west Kilburn, London. He suffered from asthma and depression. He was not sure whether he should continue in England or return to Trinidad. He thought of taking a job as a diplomat with the Indian government. He needed money to support his widowed mother and five younger siblings in Trinidad. His father had died in 1953.

In December 1954, Naipaul got a job as a radio presenter on the BBC's *Caribbean Voices*. He would stay with this part-time job for four years. After getting the job, he moved to a room in Notting Hill. He went for recording to the studio, and after returning from there he took up the work of professional writing at home. He felt good. Naipaul says he had a semblance of a household of his own for the first time in his life. Patricia cooked food for him and herself. All that she earned in her job, she spent on herself and Naipaul. Her fight with her father continued.

With security and stability in his life, Naipaul married Patricia on 10 January 1955. They were both twenty-two. There was no exchange of wedding rings during the marriage. Naipaul said, 'I had no interest in jewellery. I did not think it was important.' Neither of the families was informed of the marriage. Patricia lived in Birmingham and travelled to him to London on weekends.

Soon after the marriage, a strain developed in their relationship. Patricia felt that Naipaul was unsupportive and not giving her enough time. He was busy writing books and lived in his own world. She told him, 'You want to live in a vacuum writing your novel.'

Naipaul lost their marriage certificate. Patricia told him to look for it, and if he was unable to find it, he should collect a copy from the municipal authority. But Naipaul was not serious about it. She wondered how Naipaul could miss something so important as their marriage certificate. Patricia's parents were still unaware of their marriage. She had taken the job of a teacher at a school.

Patricia got a job at another school in Streatham, London, and kept herself busy with work. They shifted now to Streatham Hill, south London.

In his writing career, Naipaul was covering milestones. In 1957, at the age of twenty-five, he published his first novel, *The Mystic Masseur*. In 1959, he published *Miguel Street*, which won him the Somerset Maugham Award.

Naipaul tried to get a better job than what he was doing at BBC's *Caribbean Voice*. Despite his talent and a huge pile of published works, he was not able to make a break in his career in England. Then in 1960, he became part of the mainstream BBC: BBC Home Service. His remuneration was raised several times, and he also got offers from magazines to contribute articles.

In 1961, Naipaul's *A House for Mr Biswas* was published. The book received worldwide acclaim, and it was later featured in the Modern Library's list of 100 best English-language novels of the 20th century. In 1971, he won the Booker Prize for *In a Free State*. Now, he was on top of the world.

In 1962, Naipaul and Patricia travelled to India. They toured different cities. In Delhi, they met the noted writer and journalist Khushwant Singh. Naipaul's works *Mr Stone and the Knights Companion* and *An Area of Darkness: An Experience of India* (1964) came out of his tour in the country. Then he travelled with Patricia to Uganda, Kenya, Tanzania, and other countries. In between, Patricia returned to England to attend to her work. They still had no home of their own, and they shifted from one locality to another as guests or tenants.

Then, the bond between V.S. Naipaul and his wife, Patricia, drifted into uncertainty. In 1972, the *New York Review* gave Naipaul an assignment to cover the political crisis in Argentina. The country was witnessing an upheaval as the charismatic Juan Perón, who was earlier removed from the presidency in a coup, returned to the country from Spain to claim the levers of power.

Naipaul reached Buenos Aires. He met a translator, Norman di Giovanni, who organized a tour for him all over Buenos Aires. Naipaul came across experts and intellectuals with knowledge about Argentinian society and politics. During this tour, Norman introduced him to Madeline Murphy.

Madeline, twenty-six, was an Anglo-Argentine woman, married to Marshall Murphy, a British journalist. She had three children and was ten years younger than Naipaul. She was 'slender, attractive and several inches taller than Naipaul'.

Naipaul was smitten by her beauty: 'I wished to possess her as soon as I saw her.... So she came in and I was completely dazzled. I loved her eyes. I loved her mouth. I loved everything about her, and I have never stopped loving her actually.'

However, Naipaul felt he had no special talent to woo women. He felt frustrated. He wished for something intensely, but he had no talent to achieve it.

So the job of bringing Madeline Murphy close to the ace author was assigned to the translator, Norman di Giovanni. The translator agreed to work on the assignment.

Naipaul, with the translator's aid, invited Madeline to Bariloche, a resort in the foothills of the Andes Mountains. Madeline reached there and the two met as two wandering souls drawn by the unseen hands of time. In the quiet embrace of time, they shared laughter and their thoughts. When it was time to leave Bariloche, Naipaul was happy. He found the experience 'staggering'.

Naipaul returned to Trinidad from Buenos Aires in June 1972. Patricia received him at the airport. At home, Patricia felt he was a different man.

Naipaul writes: 'I felt good for the first time.' He further says, 'The books stopped being dry after Madeline, and it was a great liberation. Nothing was missing. The world was complete for me.' She was a woman who was a pure fantasy.

The relationship with Madeline would provide Naipaul a continuous flow of creativity to write fiction. He says, 'I feel a lot of my creative energy has come from that.... It would have been terrible to have died without it.' However, his meetings and interactions with Madeline devastated Patricia. She was not able to bear the development.

Located in two different continents, Madeline and Naipaul started writing letters to each other. She travelled from Buenos Aires to Casablanca, Morocco, to meet Naipaul. They spent time together beneath the blue sky, under gentle shades of trees, and in the quietness of a hotel. Then he met her in Trinidad. In one of the letters, she wrote to him, 'Love is the disease most worth having, for its opposite is the doleful serenity of death in life.'

'Madeline was addicted to Vidia: She loved him, was caught by him, amused by him and liked to be dominated by him.' She wanted to leave her husband and come to

Naipaul permanently, but Naipaul was not ready to accept her as his wife.

In October 1973, Naipaul told Patricia about Madeline and his relationship with her. Naipaul says, 'I told Pat, as I might have told my own mother. I was lying down in my little bed in my own little room and she (Patricia) wondered what was wrong with me.' He told her everything as if she was his confidant, not his wife. She listened and restrained her emotions.

The revelation destroyed Patricia. She felt she could not bear anymore. She wanted solitude to cope with Naipaul. She had recently shifted to another flat at Queen's Gate Terrace Street in Kensington, London. She started writing a diary, detailing her grief and Naipaul's indiscretions. She took sleeping pills to keep herself sane.

However, Naipaul approached her to return to his house and help him in writing. He relied on her guidance and support. He said, 'I cannot imagine writing anything if you are not sitting near me.' Patricia relented and returned to him. She cooked food, washed his clothes, and read books to him. She also recorded the way she felt being near him: 'On Saturday night Vidia told me he has not enjoyed making love to me since 1967.'

During the winter of 1973–1974, she worked with him on his novel *Guerillas*. She wrote in her diary in February 1974 that the intimate relationship between her and Naipaul was revived. Then one day, he told her that they were at the end of their relationship.

The relationship with Naipaul had a crushing effect on the trust and bond between Madeline and her husband. Her husband told her she was not welcome in their home. He denied her access to their children. She became rootless and got a temporary job in a telephone company to survive.

In May 1974, Naipaul again planned a tour to Argentina. This time, there was no assignment from a newspaper or magazine. He was perhaps missing Madeline and wanted to be with her. After writing the first draft of the novel *Guerrilla,* he flew to Buenos Aires. Patricia felt humiliated and lonely. Her husband had gone to meet someone, leaving her alone. She wrote in her diary, 'All of London knows he is going back to her (Madeline).' Naipaul met Madeline in Buenos Aires and spent two months with her. From there, they went to Cordoba in Spain to spend time in the hills and on the beaches.

Then in the autumn of 1974, Naipaul came up with something new. He told Patricia that he wanted to end his relationship with her. Patricia was shocked to hear this statement. She was completely dependent on him, and leaving him meant she would have no future and no support system. Naipaul was the fulcrum of her life. She had left her parents for him, and she had no child out of the marriage. She had invested in him, emotionally and financially. She did not know how to react.

On Naipaul's proposal, she moved to another flat in London. She thought she could live alone and take care of herself. When Patricia left the house, Naipaul felt things were not good at home. Apart from being his wife, she had also helped him write the tomes that brought him acclaim and repute. He could not bear her absence and called her on the phone to tell her that he had a recurring dream of a human head exploding. Patricia melted and came back to him. However, after helping him overcome the sense of desolation caused by her absence, she returned to her flat again.

Madeline attempted journalism to make her life meaningful, but it did not work out. She came to meet Naipaul in England and joined him on his tour for lectures, research, interviews, and the like. She accompanied him to India also, and the Emergency had been declared. The result of the tour was the book *India: A Wounded Civilisation*. Patricia felt deprived of her husband's love and care. She was lonely in England.

Naipaul often thought of breaking up with Patricia and living with Madeline, but he was not sure what he wanted to do. Sometimes he would waver between Madeline's beauty and Patricia's love and would think of leaving Madeline for Patricia.

In the early autumn of 1977, Naipaul started writing *A Bend in the River*. He wanted Patricia's presence to work on this book. Patricia was happy with the opportunity to live with her husband and returned to Wilsford. *A Bend in the River* is considered Naipaul's greatest novel. Now, Naipaul had money coming from the sale of his books. He was counted among the probable candidates for the Nobel Prize in literature.

In 1978, he got an invitation for a teaching assignment at Wesleyan University in Connecticut, USA. Madeline joined him there. He returned to England after the end of the contract. In 1980, *Newsweek* magazine put him on the cover with the headline 'The Master of the Novel'. He bought a house in Salterton village near Salisbury. The family moved into this house, Dairy Cottage, in February 1982.

Then Naipaul went to Brazil to meet Madeline. Patricia was broken from the inside because of his closeness with the lady. Everyone in their social and professional circle knew that Patricia did not enjoy Naipaul's love and respect. She wrote in the diary: 'He has just left for Gatwick on his way to Brazil. We did not touch or embrace—I just touched him on the side of his shoulder.'

In 1989, Naipaul had returned from India. He was working on his book *India: A Million Mutinies Now,* when Patricia learnt that she had breast cancer. Naipaul went with her to a Southampton hospital for a biopsy. Naipaul remembers, 'I had to go back in the afternoon to pick up Pat.... She was in a wheelchair, obviously terribly stressed, very unhappy and obviously in pain.... When I saw her, I became so ashamed. It was very upsetting.'

She underwent mastectomy at the hospital, where her right breast was removed, but after the treatment, she was fine.

Shortly afterwards, she fell ill again. She received chemotherapy to control the disease, but her situation did not improve.

In July 1995, Naipaul was in Indonesia, working on the book *Beyond Belief: Islamic Excursion among the Converted People*. Madeline accompanied him to the field, while Patricia was seriously ill in London.

While Patricia was hospitalized with an advanced stage of cancer, Naipaul felt a sort of intense emotion for her, a longing akin to the first bloom of their love. He sent love-laden words across the distance from his room in Hotel Hilton, and Patricia from her hospital bed in London answered with words carrying the same yearning. Madeline commented on this development between Patricia and Naipaul: 'It is almost like an affair.' This angered Naipaul. A surge of bitterness rose within him, and he told her that her words displeased him. Madeline became upset and left Indonesia for London.

After Indonesia, Naipaul went to Iran. From there, he reached Pakistan on 24 October 1995. He attended a party at the US consul general's house in Lahore where the who's who of Pakistan had come. Nadira, a forty-two-year-old journalist, was also invited to the party. She was a 'tall, feisty, and energetic woman'.

Nadira saw him picking at the food on his plate. She asked him, 'Are you V.S. Naipaul?'

He said, 'Yes'.

Looking into his eyes, she said, 'Can I kiss you?'

Then she kissed him and said, 'A tribute to you.'

Naipaul and Nadira met again. Naipaul shared stories about Patricia, Madeline, and his family with Nadira. He told her that his wife was dying, and Madeline had expectations from him which he could not fulfil. Nadira listened to him patiently. They went on a tour to Uch, a city founded as 'Alexandria' on the Indus River by Alexander the Great during his invasion. Nadira told him the story of her life. He told her, 'I have never wanted children, and if I did, I would want you as their mother.'

Nadira was born in Kenya in 1953, and before meeting Naipaul, she had been married twice. She divorced her second husband, Iqbal Shah, in 1980. She worked as a journalist for the Pakistani newspaper *The Nation* for ten years.

Naipaul returned to England in January 1996. Patricia's condition had deteriorated, and she only had a few days to live. She stayed at Dairy Cottage, Salterton in Wiltshire, and was taken care of by a nurse. He sat beside her and spoke about love, music, and stars, while she lay in bed. Naipaul told her he had met a lady named Nadira in Pakistan. He read *Pickwick Papers* to her, and they both laughed about the misunderstanding between the protagonist and his landlady.

Patricia died on 3 February 1996. After her cremation, he photographed her shoes, spectacles, and other belongings. The couple had no children.

The same day, he told the housekeeper Angela to buy food items to be prepared for Nadira. Angela understood that immediately after the cremation, he had invited Nadira to Dairy Cottage, the home where Patricia had lived with him. 'How could he do that? His wife had just died,' Angela thought.

Nadira came to London from Pakistan on 9 February 1996. He went to Heathrow airport to receive her.

On 14 May 1996, two months after Patricia's death, Naipaul, sixty-nine, and Nadira, forty-eight, got married at the Chelsea register office in London. Naipaul invited close family members and friends to a reception party at a local restaurant. 'I began to feel protective towards her as soon as we met,' he said about Nadira. Naipaul went with Nadira to scatter Patricia's ashes in Cooper's Hill, Surrey.

Naipaul had no child from the marriages. He legally adopted the twenty-five-year-old Maleeha, Nadira's daughter. He won the Nobel Prize in literature in 2001 for *Half a Life*. His last work was *The Masque of Africa: Glimpses of African Belief*, which came out in 2010. He died at his home in London on 11 August 2018.

4

Amrita Pritam

Amrita Pritam (1919–2005) is one of the most significant poets of Punjabi literature. Her magnum opus, *Sunehade* (Messages), a long poem inspired by her love for the poet and lyricist Sahir Ludhianvi, won her the Sahitya Akademi Award in 1956.

Amrita Pritam née Kaur was born in Gujranwala in Pakistan in 1919. Her mother, Raj Bibi, died when she was eleven. Her mother's death shattered her faith in God. She grew up in Lahore and started writing poetry in her teens under the influence of her father, Kartar Singh. She was famously beautiful. Her house was full of books, mostly on religion and meditation. When she was sixteen, in 1935, her father got her married to Pritam Singh, the son of a hosiery merchant, who was much older than her.

After marriage, the couple lived in Lahore. Soon after the marriage, the joy in their relationship withered.

Writing and her love for literature led Amrita, then twenty-five, to a literary function, a *mushaira*, in 1944 at Preet Nagar, a village between Lahore and Amritsar. Sahir Ludhianvi, twenty-three at the time, a budding Urdu poet, also came to the function.

The very first meeting was fatal for Amrita. She says, 'I do not know whether it was the magic of his word or his silent gaze, but I was captivated by him.'

The next morning, the poets were supposed to go to the nearby township of Lopoki by a bus and from there to Lahore. However, they could not ride the bus because the road was muddied by rain, and they covered the distance by walking.

Amrita remembers: 'Walking at some distance from Sahir, I noticed that where his shadow was falling on the ground, I was being engulfed by it entirely. At that time, I didn't know I would spend so many years of my life in his shadow, or that, at times, I would get tired and seek solace in my own words.'

They interacted more and talked about poetry, literature, love, and sweet songs. Slowly, the two became closer. When they met, they did not speak much to each other. They preferred to be silent and absorb the wondrous spell of the eyes. Amrita says there were two obstacles between them—one of silence and the other of language. She wrote poetry in Punjabi, while Sahir wrote in Urdu. She says whatever she wrote was inspired by his shadow, an unseen force. She gave flesh and blood, a vague mass, to the unspoken love for him.

She says, 'When Sahir would come to meet me in Lahore, it was as if an extension of my silence had occupied the adjacent chair and then gone away.... He would quietly smoke his cigarettes, putting out each after having finished only half of it. He would then light a new cigarette. After he would leave, the room would be full of his unfinished cigarettes.... I would keep these remaining cigarettes carefully in the cupboard after he left.... When I would hold one of these cigarettes between my fingers, I would feel as if I was touching his hands.'

She adds, 'That was how I got into the habit of smoking. I used to feel his presence from the aroma around.... And from the smoke curling up I would see his form emerging like a genie.'

Amrita also gives Sahir's side of the story: 'Sahir also told me, much later in life, 'When both of us were in Lahore, I would often come close to your house and stand at the corner where I would sometimes buy a paan or light a cigarette or hold a glass of soda in my hand. I would stand there for hours together watching that window of your house which opened towards the street.'

During the Partition, she was devastated by the scale of violence. While on a train from Pakistan to India, she called on the Sufi poet Waris Shah to speak out from his grave:

From the depth of your grave
Waris Shah
Add a new page to your Book of Love
Once when one daughter of Punjab wept
You wrote a million dirges
A million daughters weep today

And they are looking up to you,
Waris Shah.

Shah had written the story of Heer-Ranjha, the love story that ended in the death of the lovers. He bewailed the loss of one Heer. 'But who could lament the plight of millions of Heers today?'

Amrita Pritam's father died in 1946. She arrived from Pakistan with her husband in May 1947 in Dehradun. Her son, Navin, was born. Later, she settled in Delhi. She joined the Punjabi service of All India Radio in Delhi in 1947 and worked there till 1961. She says, 'By sheer chance, I met M. S. Randhawa, who wrote to the station director of All India Radio and got me a job.... I stuck to it a full 12 years, the first few of which were on a daily contract of Rs 5.' Then she left it to take up writing full time.

Sahir had established himself in Bombay a few years after the Partition.

She started writing and produced several works inspired by the love and loss of Sahir. Sahir sometimes became a character in her poems and stories, and the plots of several of his works were woven out of her experiences with him. Perhaps that was one of the ways of being in love and in touch with Sahir, who was away from her in Bombay, making his career, penning songs of love and separation for the films.

She composed *Sunehre* (Messages), a long poem, in his love. She says writing it was like leaping into flames every day. The work fetched her the Sahitya Akademi Award in 1956. She started writing it after she received a letter from Sahir: 'When someone telephoned me saying he wanted to give me the news of the Academy Award in 1957, my first thought was: "Lord I did not write *Sunehre* for an award! If one who had inspired me had not read the book did it matter at all to me if this entire world had?"'

She further says, 'Late that evening, came a reporter and a photographer from the press. The photographer wanted me to pose as one engrossed in the act of writing. I ... began writing in a trance the name of the one for whom I had written *Sunehre*. "Sahir, Sahir, Sahir..." I had completely filled the sheet with that name.... When the pressmen had gone and I was alone, it struck me: "What if, in the photo that would appear in all the papers the next morning, the incantation 'Sahir, Sahir, Sahir' would show?"'

An Urdu weekly magazine, *Aayeena*, was launched in Delhi in 1955. The editor requested Amrita to write a story for them. She penned a story, 'Aakhari Khat' (Last Letter), in 1956 about her first meeting with Sahir. The story reached Sahir, but Amrita had no idea about that.

One day, Amrita ran into him. He said, 'When I read the story "Aakhari Khat", I was so delighted that I wanted to take the magazine to each of my friends and tell them—look this has been written for me, but I decided to keep quiet. I thought if I told friends like Khwaja Ahmad Abbas and Krishan Chander, they would chide me and threaten to take me to the asylum.'

Amrita had a turbulent, loveless marriage, and it ended with divorce in 1960. Her relationship and experiences during marriage fed her works. In her world, a woman was meant to live out her desires with dignity. She had one son, Navin Khurana, and a daughter, Kavya, from her marriage with Pritam Singh.

She says, 'The distance between the way our minds ticked, and our nerves reacted was immeasurable. We could not work out a living together. Yet, must we carry on because it was the socially acceptable thing? There had to be another course. Between the two, after due deliberation, I thought it better, and so chose in all honesty, the second. Neither of us had any grievance against the other. The decision was reached after long discussions in a friendly fashion.'

Amrita met Imroz (born Inderjeet Singh), a visual artist and poet, at All India Radio in 1957 to discuss designing her book cover. He was six years younger than her. Born in Faisalabad in Pakistan in 1926, he had come to Mumbai to work with Guru Dutt as a poster designer.

She says, 'The curse of my lonesome state has been broken through … by Imroz.' She started the publication of a Punjabi literary magazine, *Nagmani,* with Imroz in 1966. Imroz worked as an illustration artist for the magazine. He brought calmness to her chaos. He became her anchor and support in her life as the years unfolded. He moved into her house at Hauz Khas, and they lived together.

Amrita Pritam believed in magic, spells, and astrology. She learnt that during pregnancy, the child would get the face and features of the person whom she thought about. So, she chose Sahir. She hoped her baby would look like Sahir: 'I had read about how a child develops and how his mind is shaped by his mother's thoughts…. My imagination drew me away from the world around me and I said to myself: If you always have Sahir's face in your mind's eye, he'll grow to resemble him…. In this state of crazy love, when my baby was born on July 3, 1947, and I first looked upon his face, it was the face of Sahir in my mind.'

She says, 'Navin [her son] was about thirteen when he too said, "Mamma! Can I ask you a question? Will you tell me the truth?"

"Certainly!"

"Am I Uncle Sahir's son?"

"No."

"If I am, do tell me. I like him."

"So do I, son! But if what you think was the real truth, I would really and truly have told you."

My son was convinced of the truth.'

She described 1960 was the saddest year of her life. She had gotten a divorce, and she did not know what to do next. She wanted to talk to Sahir: 'I had just about stretched my hand to pick up the phone to put a trunk-call through to Sahir, when I was flabbergasted at finding myself glaring at a page in *Blitz* magazine. It blared forth the news—supported by a picture of him and his newly found friend. My hand stood suspended in the air inches away from the dial.'

Amrita brought closure to her relationship with Sahir with a dream. She says, 'There was a white marble statue right in front of me. I kept looking at it, staring at it, and then I said to it, "What do I do of you! Neither do you speak, nor do you breathe. Today I will destroy you, break you into pieces. You have wasted all my life, my imagination, my principles," and then when I hurled that statue with all my strength, I woke up under the influence of my own fury.'

Imroz addressed her as 'Madam'. She drove her on his scooter to her workplace. Sometimes he addressed her with the name of a character or heroine in a novel he read. They wrote letters to each other.

She wrote to Imroz: 'Yesterday, (the Prime Minister) invited Khrushev (Nikita) for lunch. I went there.... I was happy for a while but all of a sudden the fact of being away from you seized me intensely and everything became meaningless—the day, the routine, the socializing, everything.'

Imroz wrote to her in a letter: 'Gulzar [poet and filmmaker] had come yesterday. "I heard that you aren't well, so I came to check on you. What happened?" I told him, "I am more or less fine but the moment the sun goes down, the pain begins." Gulzar started laughing. 'In the older times, someone had tied kaal to a peg; why don't you tie the sun to a peg. Don't let it drown. I told him, "I have already tied it. When Jeet's letter comes in the evening, that's the sun only."'

Amrita and Imroz lived together for the next forty years: 'With Imroz, it has certainly not been roses, roses, all the way. Our association has had its troughs and its heights ... two beings oscillating between merging and clashing ... merging like the water of streams and clashing like rival peaks. Imroz's personality is like the flow of a river, uncontrolled by rocks and sluices. Should he be restrained, Imroz would impetuously divert his course. A relationship with him can last only so long as there is nothing to bind it.'

In her last poem dedicated to Imroz, she wrote, 'I will meet you yet again... I know not how and where ... but I will meet you for sure.'

Amrita died in her sleep on 31 October 2005 at the age of eighty-six. Uma Trilok, author of the book *Amrita Imroz: A Love Story*, describes Amrita's love for both Sahir and Imroz in her book: 'She expressed her views on love saying that there was one kind of love like that of the sky, and there was another, which was like a roof over one's head. Sahir Ludhianvi was "like the sky" for her. A woman seeks both, she had said, and the roof eventually opens to the sky. It was chance and circumstance that she chose the roof. The sky was very distant.'

5

Mirza Ghalib

Mirza Ghalib was born in Kala Mahal, Agra, in India on 27 December 1797. His ancestors occupied important positions in the armies of the Mughals. His father, Mirza Abdullah, was killed in a war in 1803 when Ghalib was five. His uncle took care of him, but he also died three years later in 1806. Ghalib started composing poetry at the age of eleven.

Mirza Ghalib did not receive any systematic education. On 8 August 1810, at the age of thirteen, he married Umrao Begum, the daughter of a nawab. Ghalib moved to Delhi in 1812 and rented a haveli in the walled city near Chandni Chowk. He described his marriage as the second imprisonment after the initial confinement that was life itself. The struggle for freedom from life would end with man's death. One of his couplets translate as: 'The prison of life and the bondage of sorrow are the same. Why should man be free of sorrow before dying?'

He advised a friend about marriage, saying that a wise fly is not caught in a single honey pot; it runs from one pot to another.

Ghalib's wife carried a baby boy in her womb in 1812, but the baby was born dead. This broke Ghalib's heart, and a shadow of grief fell upon the family. He wrote,

> Not all, but a few soul,
> manifest themselves
> in the form of the beautiful flowers
> after death.

Ghalib's second child was born next year in 1813, but the joy was cut short as the baby died after a few months. His wife, Umrao Begum, cried, and her eyes shimmered with tears all the time. Ghalib could not tolerate seeing her drowned in despair.

The financial condition of the family was also bad. Ghalib had no regular source of income, and he looked to patrons for help. He lived on borrowed money. To make matters worse, he loved drinking and gambling and played chausar. His addictions and revelry demanded money. He was depressed and spent his time at a bookshop with his friend.

He wrote about his condition:

> Sorrow brims over greatly,
> then sorrows cease,
> My woes weighed on me so much that
> by burden, they were eased.

However, his poetic genius, his words, and his glistening verses earned him name and recognition. He participated in a mushaira in Delhi and floored the elite and the people with his words that soared on the wings of imagination. In 1850, Emperor Bahadur Shah Zafar bestowed upon him the title of Babir-ul-Mulk (secretary of state). Zafar also gave him the additional title of Najm-ud-daula (star of the state). With these titles, he was now part of the nobility of Delhi. He also got the title of 'Mirza Nosha', which enabled him to add 'Mirza' in his name.

Ibrahim Zauq, the court poet of the Mughals, died in 1854. Then the emperor appointed Ghalib his Ustad. Mirza Farukh, the heir apparent, became his pupil. This meant he would get an additional salary of 33 rupees.

One day, while returning to his home from the place of his friend Mir, a book seller, he heard a courtesan singing his couplets at her Mahalsara. He climbed the wooden stairs and went to see the beauty whose voice wove dreams. Dressed in glazed cotton in a big, decorated hall with ember light, she was singing Ghalib's writings in her silvery voice. Ghalib said he came to her on hearing the beautiful rendition of ghazals.

She stopped and asked him, 'Do you know whose ghazal this is?'

Ghalib said, 'My friend Mirza Ghalib has written this.'

He kept his identity secret and posed to her as a friend of Ghalib's. Ghalib was fascinated by her charm, her sparkling eyes, and the honeyed words that fell from her lips. She was a professional singer, and her name was Nawab Jaan. Her house was crowded with her admirers. He dished out more ghazals to her to sing in her seductive voice. She was also awed by this 'friend of Ghalib'. She wanted to know more about Ghalib, but he walked down the steps thinking about the grace and the melody of her voice.

She resumed singing Ghalib's compositions. At home, the thought of her charming grace disturbed Ghalib. He kept thinking about her. He opened his notebook and wrote:

> Again this heart of mine is somewhat restless.
> My chest searches for the deep wound.
> The season of red flowers has arrived.
> The spring stirs up desire and agitates me
> as if my fingernails are cutting deep into my liver.

Ghalib's wife, Umrao Begum, was a religious woman, and kept herself so much devoted to prayer and fasting that Ghalib called his home the Fatehpuri Mosque. She got a whiff of his affair with the woman. She asked him, 'Why are you lost in thought all the time? Who is the one separating you from me?'

He told her, 'That woman was a professional singer.' She did not protest. She knew that falling in love several times was a routine thing for a writer, poet, and artist.

On one occasion, he dressed himself in a shervani to meet Nawab Jaan. His wife told her he was not looking smart in that dress. He should wear another dress. He asked his wife, 'Do you know whom I am going to meet?'

For Nawab Jaan, waiting for Ghalib was becoming difficult to bear. She wrote a letter to Ghalib and sent it to his residence through a messenger. In the letter, she had written: 'I met your friend at my place. He gave parts of the incomplete ghazals to me. If you could give me more ghazals to sing, I would be grateful to you for life.'

Nawab Jaan had collected Ghalib's address from Mir's bookshop, where Ghalib used to go, sit, and share his poetry. She asked the shopkeeper whether he had published a collection of Mirza Ghalib's poetry.

The shopkeeper said, 'Ghalib's work has not been published yet. But whenever he comes to me, he shares his ghazals with me.' He showed her some poetry written by him from his notebook.

Nawab Jaan requested him to give her the ghazals. Just then, Ghalib reached there. She requested Ghalib to give her his ghazals. Mir told her, 'This gentleman is the poet for whose poetry you are going mad!' She was amused. She left the bookshop crooning Ghalib's verses.

She kept on sending messages to him through a messenger on one pretext or the other. One day, she wrote to him to come to her Mahalsara where she would sing his composition for him. She told him not to decline her offer.

However, Ghalib told the messenger, 'Tell her that I have been arrested before I could fly. My feet are in chains. Nobody loves custody, but now I am accustomed to it.'

Nawab Jaan readied herself in anticipation of the visit of her love, Mirza Ghalib.

She sang Ghalib's words:

Someone should ask my heart about
the half-drawn arrow one fired at me.
Had the arrow passed through my heart
and killed me,
I would not have been in such pain.

To whom should I say what it is,
this night of grief is a distressing experience.
Why would I complain of dying,
if it had occurred to me only once.

Ghalib's financial condition was getting worse, and those who lent him money were hounding him. Shopkeepers who gave him food without payment asked him to shell out money. People queued in front of his house seeking repayment. Some went to court to file suit against him. There was no hope of pension coming from the British rulers. His income from the pension through some sources had declined from Rs 10,000 to Rs sixty-two.

Ghalib pursued his pension case. The British officials in Delhi told him that his request for pension was sent by the Delhi commissioner Thomas Metcalfe to the governor general in Calcutta. His lawyer Harilal advised him to go to Calcutta to pursue his matter. Ghalib's wife, Umrao, was pregnant again.

Nawab Jaan was upset because he gave her no time and did not come to her Mahalsara for days. She sent a letter to him again, complaining and asking what was wrong if he could talked to her while he attended the affairs of the world. Nawab Jaan was swept away by love's current; she became obsessed with Ghalib's compositions, the beauty of the words, and the depth of their meaning.

Nawab Jaan had other lovers as she was a courtesan and had several visitors. Her guests wanted a piece of her beauty and melody. One of the lovers was a thanedaar, a police officer. However, Nawab Jaan spurned everyone for the poet. The thanedaar did not like her devotion for Ghalib and warned her of consequences.

Nawab Jaan came to know about Ghalib's financial distress and loan burden. She sold her jewellery to pay his loans, but Ghalib did not accept her assistance.

She met him at a Sufi dargah and asked him why he did not come to her place. Ghalib did not reply directly. His was a life of uninterrupted affliction, suffering, and grief. He was living in poverty and penury, and his drinking habits, gambling, and the death of his children had made his life difficult. His wife was living like a corpse; the tragedies of her life had stolen the light from her eyes. He did not want to visit a courtesan and add pain to his life.

He told her that a guest was to be born at his home, and he had come to the dargah to pray for his life. She said she had prayed to the Sufi that Ghalib would wear a crown of fame. He would be a star among the poets of Delhi. He would be called by the emperor for his service. Ghalib said he would make an offering of a gift to her if her prayers were answered.

She gave a tune to his lines:

Don't break the relationship between you and me.
Even if nothing remains between us, then let there be enmity.
Why are you showing displeasure in my presence?
If you don't like it here in the presence of the public,
then meet me at some lonely place.
If this is my trial, then tell me what is torment?
If you have chosen my rival,
what is the need to test and cause me pain?

Ghalib was invited by the emperor Bahadurshah Zafar to his court in a mushaira to present his couplets. He was on the verge of being a celebrated poet of Delhi. His poems were on the lips of all sections of society—beggars, people in the bazaar, courtesan, saints, and artists in cultural functions. Nawab Jaan's prayers had come true.

A son was born to Ghalib, and he was happy. He went to the house of Nawab Jaan to meet her, but she was gone. The thanedaar had played spoilsport and made her life difficult in Delhi. She was in love with Ghalib and did not want to yield to anyone else. She had gone to Benares.

Ghalib walked through her Mahalsara. He read his ghazals written in her handwriting on the wall of the hall:

> If you cannot give me love,
> I am okay with madness for you.
> Let me roll into insanity,
> and you embrace the fame.

Ghalib was shocked. His ladylove and the melody of her laughter were gone. He did not know where she was. He said:

> Thousands of desires,
> each desire worth dying for.
> We have heard of the dismissal of Adam from the heaven,
> But with a greater humiliation,
> I am leaving the street in which you lived.

Now he planned to go to Calcutta to meet Governor General Charles Metcalfe to sort out his pension issue. He hired a horse. On the way, he was welcomed by literary men and the public in different cities as he was a big name. He stopped at Benares for a break and interacted with poets and authors. He stayed there for about four weeks in a rented haveli.

He came across Nawab Jaan's mother. He asked her about Nawab Jaan. He said, 'I went to her house in Delhi to meet her and present her a gift of doshaala (shawl).'

The mother said, 'We had to leave Delhi because of the thanedaar who was after her life.'

Ghalib said, 'Anyway, I would like to meet her. I have to give her something.'

Then her mother sobbed and said she was no more. 'She was remembering you till her last breath. Somebody's thought and loss were eating her from inside. She had stopped singing.' It was 1849.

Mirza Ghalib was broken after hearing that. He went to her grave with the shawl he wanted to gift to her and broke down in front of the white gravestone. Nawab Jaan lay there, sad, incomplete, asking for his love. He placed the shawl on the grave of the woman whose only wish in life had been to meet him. The words inscribed on the marble stone on her grave were:

> I lived on your promise knowing that
> the promise was false.
> I would have died of happiness
> if I believed that your promise was serious.

He remembered her saying that one day her poet (Ghalib) would be the crown-poet of Delhi. He had told her that if her prayer was accepted by God, he would gift her a shawl.

6

Camille Claudel

Camille Claudel, born in north France on 8 December 1864, was a sculptor. Among the sources and inspirations for her work were Donatello, Cellini, and Greco-Roman mythology. Being a female artist in the mid-19th century was a difficult task. She faced prejudice and gender-related restrictions in her artistic training. She was the beloved of the legendary sculptor, the progenitor of modern sculpture, Auguste Rodin.

Camille Claudel wanted to be an artist from her teens. She was fascinated with stone and soil and started working with clay, making human forms from the age of twelve. She refined her skills as she grew older. Her father supported her efforts and showed her works to the artist and sculptor Alfred Boucher, who was her neighbour in a village near the town of Nogent-sur-Seine. She made busts of historical figures like Napoleon and Bismark and biblical themes like David and Goliath.

Seeing her works, Boucher said Claudel was an extraordinary artist and she should be given all support for her learning and training. He encouraged her father to move to Paris for better education and training.

In 1881, Camille travelled to Paris with her parents. Her father got her enrolled at the Académie Colarossi, an art school in Paris. It was a private art academy that admitted girl students and allowed its disciples to work with nude human forms. The best art school of France, École des Beaux-Arts, barred the entry of female students.

Claudel shared a studio with three girls from England and worked there. Alfred Boucher came to the studio once a week (in 1883) as an adviser and became her mentor. He depicted her in his sculpture *Camille Claudel lisant* (1883), showing Claudel in a reading pose. She also created a bust of her mentor.

However, Boucher had to go to Florence, Italy, for three years after winning the Grand Prix du Salon. The prize allowed an artist to tour Italy. He told Auguste Rodin, a fellow artist, to take care of Claudel and guide her and his other disciples at his studio in the Rue Notre-Dame-des-Champs.

Camille Claudel reported to Rodin in 1884 and joined his studio—a dusty, labour-intensive place of creation. She was then nineteen and Rodin, forty-four. He found Camille to be talented, young, and beautiful. He saw that the girl was passionate and possessed ideas for making great pieces of art. On the other hand, Camille saw that Auguste Rodin was a genius of the highest order, his talent forged in heaven's fire. He was getting work orders from the French government, and working with him would get her exposure and opportunity to create immortal works of art. She was determined to make the best out of his tutelage.

Thus, it was a confluence of professional interests and genius. They grew closer. She achieved the status of the principal disciple at his studio and blossomed under his shadow. On the other hand, Rodin saw in her raw beauty, a romantic story etched in bones. He cast his masterpieces in her shape. The proximity, long hours of work, and the meeting of minds sparked love's sweet flame between their souls. One stormy night, all the barriers between the two were swept away, and they became lovers.

Like all love stories, this love story also faced a challenge. Rodin had been in a relationship with a seamstress, Rose Beuret, for the past twenty years. He had started living with Rose Beuret in 1864. She lived in the village with their son. She had no interest in art and sculpture. Claudel filled the vacuum as his intellectual, romantic, and artistic partner. With Claudel, he got 'the happiness of always being understood, of always being exceeded in his expectations'. However, he had no intention to abandon Rose for Camille.

The productivity and the romance between the two bloomed. In a letter in 1886, Rodin wrote: 'But, in an instant, I feel your terrible power. Have pity, cruel girl. I can't go on. I can't spend another day without seeing you. Otherwise the atrocious madness. It is over, I don't work anymore, malevolent goddess, and yet I love furiously. My Camille be assured that I feel love for no other woman, and that my soul belongs to you.... Ah! Divine beauty, flower who speaks and loves, intelligent flower, my darling. My dear one, I am on my knees facing your beautiful body which I embrace.'

Genius that she was, apart from working under Rodin, Claudel sought recognition as an independent artist and displayed her work in the exhibition at the Salon des Artistes Français between 1882 and 1889.

Rodin modelled several portraits on his love and disciple, Claudel, and titled them *Claudel with Short Hair* (1882), *Mask of Camille Claudel* (1895), *I Am Beautiful* (1880), and *Eternal Springtime* (1881). These works were intended originally for *The Gates of Hell*, a monumental bronze sculptural work containing 200 figures. The young girl, on the other hand, contributed complex pieces for his famous works, including *The Gates of Hell*. She worked with him on his masterpieces like *The Burghers of Calais* (1884–1889), a work on French heroism. In *The Waltz* (1893) and *The Wave* (1897), she helped him capture a fleeting moment in motion. She also sat before Rodin for his *Danaid* (1885), a nude figure of a woman curled up with her face down.

She went to England in 1886 to meet her friends who studied with her at Academie Colarossi, Paris. After a week, she came back to France. Rodin was happy to see her in his studio. After the return, during the same year, she demanded from Rodin that he would not accept any other or new student at the studio, and he would marry her. This was a difficult proposal for Rodin, but on her insistence, he signed a contract to this effect without any intention to honour it. She sculpted *Bust of Rodin* in 1886, which became a famous portrait.

She conceived in 1886 a model called *The Abandonment*, which depicted the reunification of two lovers. For shaping this piece of art, she drew inspiration from the Indian legend in which the protagonist was separated from her husband due to a dark spell. The sculpture captured the moment when the lady was reunited with her husband.

In 1888, Claudel left her father's house and moved to an apartment with a studio rented for her by Rodin. During this period, she assisted Rodin in making *The Gates of Hell*. Rodin modelled his sculpture *Thought* after her; Claudel appears pensive in this work.

She worked for two years on *Sakuntala* in 1888, a large marble of a male nude figure kneeling at the feet of a female nude figure and encircling her torso with both hands. American scholar Angelo Caranfa described *Sakuntala* as 'Claudel's desire to reach the sacred, the fruit of the lifelong search of her artistic identity, free from Rodin's constraints'. In 1888, she created *The Abandon,* depicting an erotic moment of two nude lovers reuniting, and *The Waltz,* a dancing couple in a close embrace. Rodin carved *The Kiss,* two naked lovers fused in passion, between 1888 and 1895.

Though Claudel was a genius and produced phenomenal pieces of art, she was not married and lived her life as Rodin's beloved. The stigma of living as a friend of someone was monumental and brought disrepute to the family. Her brother Pierre and mother felt uncomfortable with her status. For a young woman, being a sculptor was abnormal, and living with someone without marriage was a fate unworthy of a soul born of honour.

In the art world, while working with Rodin, Claudel's standing and reputation was mainly that of a disciple of Rodin and not that of a prodigy in her own right. She had no financial independence. She did not get any credit for her contributions to the works that were attributed to Auguste Rodin's genius. Success brought more success, more work, and fame to Rodin, but her status remained that of nothing more than a disciple, an apprentice.

Claudel became pregnant in 1892. Rodin was not ready to accept the child she carried in her womb and told her to undergo an abortion. As a dependent woman without financial wherewithal, she had no choice but to follow his wishes. The abortion wrought a mighty transformation in her personality. She felt that the intimacy with Rodin was not worth it. He did not accept her as his wife, and she did not receive due credit and recognition for the work she was doing in partnership with him. She should seek solace elsewhere.

Finally, Claudel, twenty-eight, after working for ten years as Rodin's disciple, his model, and his muse, unfettered herself from his shadow. She would now concentrate on her work and work hard to make her name as a sculptor and become financially secure.

Rodin did not like this separation. He thought it was a temporary burst of anger and Claudel would return to him. He tried to help her professionally and financially.

He helped her to get work from the director of fine arts. *The Age of Maturity,* which she created, was a work commissioned by the government in 1895 and exhibited in 1899. It showed the love triangle between Claudel, Rodin, and Rose Beuret—a man being pulled by an old woman and a maiden in the bloom of youth. The young woman was naked.

When the work took shape, Rodin did not like the sculpture. The old woman represented Rose, and the nude young woman stood for Claudel. The work shocked and angered him, and it damaged his reputation. He stopped his support for Claudel.

Now, Claudel looked at Rodin as a villain who was out to destroy her and her work. Breaking with Rodin, however, drained her emotionally. It also destroyed her financially and professionally. She got other works from the government, but they could not fructify to the final stage. Rodin's intervention was suspected as he was unhappy with her for taking liberties with his reputation and personal life.

She got no further work from the government. The well of creativity that was brimming with ideas soon ran dry. Socially, she became a recluse. Her world had fallen apart. She no longer interacted with people in the art world. One additional reason for her not getting work was that her proposal was a tapestry woven with the threads of boundless nudity.

A friend of hers, Eugene Blot, supported her and bought her work to make her financially secure. He also tried to get her assigned works through non-governmental sources and make her stay connected with a wider circle. However, she believed that Rodin and his circle were conspiring to ruin her. She refused to participate in any gathering, saying that she had nothing good to wear. Her last masterpiece *Perseus and the Gorgon* was completed in 1906.

After 1905, Claudel became mentally ill. She plunged into despair and went missing for long stretches. Her mother took her to doctors when she saw that things were not normal in her life. Doctors diagnosed her with schizophrenia. The situation slowly became worse.

She showed signs of 'systematized persecution delirium'. She accused Rodin of stealing her ideas and leading a conspiracy to kill her. At home, she began to destroy her works. Sometimes, she was found wandering the streets dressed in beggars' clothes.

Her father, Louis-Prosper, supported her and encouraged her through all her pursuits, but he died in 1913. After his death, no one was there to take care of her. In 1913, her mother planned to get her hospitalized. She concluded that Claudel was a danger to herself. However, a medical certificate was required to send the artist to an asylum. A doctor living in the Claudel family's neighbourhood and her mother signed a certificate authorizing the mental asylum authorities to confine her in an asylum. They cited evidence of her mental disorder. They gave as reasons her not leaving her room during the day, coming out of the house at night, being 'badly dressed and absolutely filthy', and living in terror of Rodin's 'gang'.

The officials of the mental asylum at Ville-Évrard came to take her from her apartment to their care. She was then forty-eight, exhausted and dishevelled. She was uncomfortable with the new arrangement. Her wings were clipped and her spirit bound. She lost half her weight after being interned.

She wanted to leave the place. She tried to convince the world that she was fine, sane, and healthy and that she loved life and freedom and should be allowed to live as an ordinary person. She wrote to her cousin Charles Thibault in 1913: 'At this moment, M. Rodin has persuaded my relatives to have me locked up. They are all in Paris because of that. The scoundrel will then, as a result of this suit, take possession of my life's work.'

She further wrote: 'If you wish to come and see me you can take your time, because it will be long before I get out of here; they have me and they are not going to let go.'

In September 1914, the authorities shifted her from Ville-Évrard to the Montdevergues asylum near Avignon in Provence due to the outbreak of the First World War. She appealed to her brother Pierre to get her released. She also requested her mother and sister to get her out, but nothing worked. Her brother came to see her once in a while to see her, but her mother and her sister did not consider it necessary to go to her. Rodin made no effort to renew his bonds with her.

The caregivers at the asylum found that Claudel became quieter and more docile. She was a threat to no one. She could have stayed at home with her family. In 1920, the asylum doctor proposed that she be discharged on a trial basis. 'Mademoiselle Claudel is calm,' the doctor wrote to her mother.

The asylum authorities told the family members that she should not stay in the asylum. The hospital staff regularly proposed to Camille's mother and her brother Pierre Claudel that she be discharged, but they said she should remain there.

In 1929, Jessie Lipscomb, one of the English women who had shared the Rue Notre-Dame-des-Champs studio in the 1880s with Claudel, found her way to the asylum. The two artists sat and talked about their lives. Lipscomb realized that Claudel was not insane. Instead, she was stuck in a kind of living death.

Claudel wrote to her friend Eugene Blot: 'I have fallen into a void.... I live in a world that is so curious, so strange. Of the dream that is my life, this is the nightmare.'

She wrote to the asylum doctor in 1915: 'It is terrible to be so abandoned. I can't help but succumb to the grief that overwhelms me.'

She did not taste freedom after entering the asylum. She could not touch clay ever again.

Rodin married Rose Beuret fifty-three years into their relationship on 29 January 1917. Beuret died two weeks later. Rodin himself was ill that year. In January, he suffered weakness from influenza and died on 17 November 1917 at the age of seventy-seven.

In September 1943, the asylum officials informed Claudel's brother, Pierre, that his sister was terminally ill. The Second World War had engulfed Europe in its violence. Pierre crossed occupied France to see her. Camille died on 19 October 1943 after suffering for thirty years in the asylum. She was then seventy-eight. Pierre was not present at the time of her death or her funeral. Some nuns attended the funeral, and the officials interred her body in a communal grave at the asylum. Later, her body was shifted to an anonymous public grave. A movie, *Camille Claudel,* was made on her life in 1988.

7

Karl Marx

Karl Marx and Jenny von Westphalen met each other regularly as young children in Trier, a city in south-western Germany, and were close friends as teenagers. During her adolescence, Jenny developed interests in French socialism and German romanticism. Jenny's brother, Edgar, was a good friend of Marx. Her father liked Marx. They went on long walks and discussed philosophy, politics, and literature.

Karl Marx, born on 5 May 1818 in the kingdom of Prussia, was the son of Heinrich Marx, a lawyer. Jenny was born in 1814 to Prussian aristocracy. Her father, Ludwig Von Westphalen, was a government counsellor and a civil servant in Trier.

Jenny saw in Karl Marx all the features of the romantic characters. He was the man of her dreams. On the other hand, Marx liked Jenny deeply and wrote love poetry for her.

Marx enrolled at the University of Bonn in October 1835 to study humanities. In 1836, Marx, eighteen, came home to Trier on leave from the university and got secretly engaged to Jenny. He thought his parents would not approve his marriage as Jenny was four years older than Marx, and the girl's father may not like his daughter marrying a non-conformist.

When he returned to the university to study after the leave, the thought of Jenny tormented him all the time. He wrote to his father about her on 10 November 1837: 'Please give greetings from me to my sweet, wonderful Jenny. I have read her letter twelve times already, and always discover new delights in it. It is in every respect, including that of style, the most beautiful letter I can imagine being written by a woman.'

Marx had moved from Bonn to the law faculty of the University of Berlin in October 1836 and graduated in law from there in 1841.

On 19 June 1843, Karl Marx, twenty-five, and Jenny von Westphalen, twenty-nine, married at a Protestant Church in Kreuznach, 50 miles away from Trier. Jenny's mother and brother Edgar and a few friends were the guests on the occasion. Jenny wore a green silk dress and a garland of pink roses. In their native town, marrying a Jewish radical like Karl Marx was outside the norm, and Jenny's relatives opposed the union. After the marriage, they went for their honeymoon to the towns and villages along the

Rhine River. Marx carried luggage containing more than forty books on this trip.

Back at Kreuznach, they would stroll down the river in the evening, listening to the nightingale singing in the distance. He also worked on his political theory and read books extensively. The fathers of both did not live to see the marriage. Marx's father, Heinrich Marx, fifty-seven, passed away on 10 May 1838, and Jenny's father, Westphalen, died in 1842. With the death of their fathers, the couple lacked financial support. They had to take care of themselves.

After marriage, the young couple moved to Paris in October 1843 to start their life. Marx was going to be a writer, a full-time revolutionary, and a communist ideologue. Jenny was also steeped in the socialist and communist ideology. Paris was going to be an ideal place for the new couple as it was a centre of thought and experiment in ideas. For him, it was the 'new capital of the new world'. Marx was also to join the newspaper *German-French Annals*, which was proposed to be published from Paris, as a co-editor. Jenny was worried about getting a steady income for running the house, something that would always elude her. The couple freely mingled with radicals and debated with the best minds. The German poet Heinrich Heine was their family friend. Their first child, Jenny Caroline, was born on 1 May 1844. The child had bouts of severe illness. Jenny once went to Trier to meet her mother and felt worried about the air of 'unfaithfulness' in Paris.

In August 1844, Karl Marx met the German socialist Friedrich Engels, twenty-three, in Paris while he was returning from a ten-day visit to London and Germany. Jenny had then gone to Trier to spend her days of pregnancy.

Marx hadfirst met Engels at the office of the German newspaper *Rheinische Zeitung* in Cologne two years earlier. After this meeting in Paris, they would become lifelong friends and start an intellectual collaboration. While Marx lived in penury and chaos, Engels's family was wealthy and owned cotton textile mills in Prussia and England.

Jenny kept herself engaged and busy with political activities. She organized communist meetings and provided shelter and relief to the refugees. She helped Marx write philosophical and economic works. She came from a privileged background, but after marriage, she walked along with him through the tempests and the triumphs of life.

In February 1845, the French authorities told Marx to leave Paris. He had been indulging in radical political activities that would threaten the stability of the political system in France. In his writings and speeches, he was critical of the reputation of the French government and the political system of France. The government of adjoining Prussia too wanted to make him taste the bitter fruit of his labours and to dislodge him from the comforts of Paris. He had flayed the Prussian government in his book *The Holy Family* (1845), which touched a raw nerve with the authorities there.

Marx was a professional and full-time revolutionary and was not earning a salary. Jenny had no money to run the house and was always in acute financial distress. She was running their home by selling their furniture and borrowing. With the orders of the French government to leave, they left Paris in the winter of 1945. Jenny was pregnant with their second child, Jenny Laura. She had to pay rent and buy food to feed the daughter and buy medicine for her.

From Paris, they moved 300 km north and found refuge at Brussels in Belgium. Jenny did not want to leave the enchanting city of Paris. They had no permanent house in any town and shifted from one location to another. Jenny told Marx to make things a bit stable for her at the new place and left for her mother's home. She returned to him, and after a few days, in September 1845, their daughter Jenny Laura was born.

In Brussels also, Marx became busy in writing and political activities, though he was not supposed to write on political issues. Jenny supported her husband and defended his work and politics. She also chipped in to his writing work. She copied Karl Marx's manuscripts for publishers and colleagues as Marx's handwriting was not legible.

Jenny wrote a letter to Marx while she was at her mother's place: 'My dearest, unique Karl, you cannot believe, my darling, how very happy you make me by your letters, and how your last letter has once again restored calm and peace to your poor lamb.' She added, 'The dark feelings of anxiety and fear, the real menace of unfaithfulness, the seductions of a capital city ravaged my mind all the time.' Marx was then in Paris.

Jenny's mother, considering her daughter's difficulties and her pregnancy, sent a maid named Ellen Dermuth, twenty-five, to their home in Brussels in April 1845. Ellen had been working at Jenny's mother's place since she was seven. A round-faced woman with blue eyes, she was to help Jenny with chores and cooking during the pregnancy.

Marx, leaving his family in Brussels, went to London in August 1845 with Engels. Among other things, he wanted to explore London to see whether it would make a better place to stay. Things were not good for him in

Brussels also as he was facing the heat of the authorities for his views and activism. Besides, London was also an active centre of the working class. He and Engels would explore the industrial slums of Manchester to study capitalism and gather data for writing books and political activism.

Marx, in collaboration with Friedrich Engels, wrote *The Communist Manifesto* in January 1848, which would give a new strength to the communist movements across Europe.

While Marx was away in London, Jenny visited her mother, Caroline von Westphalen, along with their housekeeper Ellen Dermuth in Trier in 1845. After a short period, she returned to Brussels and looked forward to the publication of Marx's work. She was careful that their second child, Jenny Laura, did not disturb Marx's intellectual activity.

This time, Marx stopped writing. Perhaps, he suffered from writer's block; the wellspring of his genius became dry. However, Marx did not share this problem with his wife as this would distress her. She knew Marx was an extraordinary genius and nursed high hopes for him and his publications. She hoped his books would sell and bring a mountain of gold and happiness. The financial woes she was faced with would end.

Marx worked in partnership with Engels in London and further developed their ideas about communism. While poverty and scarcity wrecked the life of the family, Marx seemed to be okay scribbling notes in the British Museum Library in London or indulging in drinking. Marx co-authored with Engels *The German Ideology* (1846), and before that, he wrote *The Holy Family* (1845) and *Theses on Feuerbach* (1845).

Jenny gave birth to their third child and son, Edgar, in 1847. The Belgian government expelled Marx in February 1848 for participation in political activities. From there, he, along with his wife and children, went to Cologne in Germany and started editing and publishing a radical newspaper. After a few months, he moved to England with his family. He had already done a survey of London with Engels and found it suitable for his mission. In London, Marx, Jenny, and Friedrich Engels established a political bulletin. They looked for ways to generate money to continue their enterprise.

In London, their fourth child, their six-month-old son, Henry Edward, suffered convulsions. The baby slept at most for two hours in a day. It sucked its mother's breast so hard that blood spurted into its mouth. Finally, continuous ill health claimed its life in the winter of 1850.

However, the baby's death was not the only reason for the family's distress. Jenny faced harassment from her landlady and two bailiffs for overdue rent. When she could not pay the rent, they stripped her home of all her belongings. Her young children had no cradle, and they shivered in the room in the extreme cold.

Jenny looked for help from her family members. She was the daughter of a civil servant; however, with her father's demise, she had become poorer. She went to Holland to meet her uncle, an industrialist, and requested him to aid her financially. He offered no succour to her, and the lady returned empty-handed. However, while she was away, a romance was kindled between Karl Marx and the maid, Ellen Dermuth.

Ellen was then thirty and Karl Marx thirty-one. This romance saw a serious development. Ellen conceived.

Marx knew that if Jenny learnt of his infidelity, she would wreak havoc and leave him. The love and support of the woman who stood by him in joy and in sorrow would be withdrawn, and the anchor that Jenny and their children provided him would be shattered.

Marx turned to Engels to take responsibility for Ellen's child. Engels, thirty, agreed to take the brunt, and Marx's marriage was saved. Ellen gave birth to a baby boy, Harris Dermuth, on 23 June 1851 at Marx's house in Soho. The boy was sent to live with a foster family in East London, and when he grew up, he worked hard to prove that his father was Karl Marx.

On this event, years later, Jenny wrote: 'In the early summer 1851 an event occurred which I do not wish to relate here in detail, although it greatly contributed to increase our worries, both personal and others.'

During this period in London, Jenny had to deal with the creditors and take care of her family. She once told Marx, 'I sit and go to pieces. Karl, it is now at its worst pitch.... I sit here and almost weep my eyes out and can find no help. My head is disintegrating. For a week I have kept my strength up and now I can no more.'

In the spring of 1853, Marx's eight-year-old son (third child), Edgar, died while asleep in his father's arms. He was the third child the couple lost.

In November 1853, Jenny was stricken with smallpox and was left disfigured. When she recovered, her children returned home to the mother as they were kept away for fear of infection. Her daughters Caroline and Laura looked at her face and were horrified to see what the disease had done to their mother's face. They sat with her on the bed and cried.

Through all these years, Marx's love for Jenny did not diminish. He wrote, 'There you are before me, large as life, and I lift you up in my arms and I kiss you all over from top to toe, and I fall on my knees before you and cry: "Madame, I love you." And love you I do, with a love greater than was ever felt by the Moor of Venice.'

In 1867, Marx's magnum opus, *Capital: Critique of Political Economy*, was published in London. Marx had been working on this book for fifteen years. The family members expected that the book would be a stunning success, and all their financial woes would be a thing of the past. But nothing of that sort happened, and the book went unrecognized. Jenny and Karl's hopes were crushed.

Jenny was tired of poverty and the difficulties of life. She began to lose faith in Marx and his ability to give her a good life. She became hopeless and disillusioned. She now craved distance and independence from Marx's 'burdensome shadow'. Persistent poverty and illness had devoured four of her children. She did not want her surviving daughters Jenny Caroline, Jenny Laura, and Jenny Eleanor to face the kind of deprivation she had suffered.

Jenny was diagnosed with cancer in early 1881. By the middle of 1881, her condition deteriorated. On 30 November 1881, Marx sat beside her and read a positive review of his book *Capital* in the newspapers and magazines. This was good news as the hard work of a lifetime had failed to evoke the expected response from the intellectuals. Lying on the bed, Jenny liked the development and smiled at her husband's success. However, she did not stay long to rejoice. She died two days later on 2 December 1881 at the age of sixty-seven. She was buried in Highgate cemetery in London. Marx was sick and could not attend her funeral.

Marx did not live long after his wife's death. About one and a half years later, he died at the age of sixty-four on 14 March 1883. He had developed breathing problems immediately after Jenny's death. Marx was buried in Highgate cemetery, the place where his wife lay, in London on 17 March 1883. Engels, Ellen, and Marx's two daughters, amongst others, attended his funeral.

8

Margaret Mead

Margaret Mead, born in 1901, was an eminent American cultural anthropologist. She studied South Pacific and Southeast Asian traditional cultures and is the author of classics like *Coming of Age in Samoa* (1928) and *Sex and Temperament in Three Primitive Societies* (1935), which reshaped the understanding and attitude of the Western culture to sex and adolescence and influenced a sexual revolution in the West in the 1960s. What Albert Einstein was to physics, Margaret Mead was to anthropology.

As a child, Mead read 'hundreds of books a year and every magazine, allowed or forbidden, that came into the house'. At eighteen, the young lady joined De Pauw University, known for liberal arts education, in Indiana in 1919. From there, she moved to New York City to study

English and psychology at Barnard College. She graduated from there in 1923.

Margaret Mead, twenty-one, met the famous anthropologist Ruth Benedict, thirty-five, at Barnard College, New York, in 1922. Benedict took classes at the college there as a teaching assistant of the renowned anthropology scholar Franz Boas. Ruth persuaded Mead to enrol in the anthropology programme of the college.

Mead enrolled herself at Columbia University, New York, after her graduation in 1923. The university was a happening place, and the discipline of anthropology, which focussed on the study of tribes and non-White cultures, was in its inception. She decided to pursue anthropology after attending Franz Boas's lectures.

After a brief interaction, the two women became intimate friends. They met at each other's place, went for long walks, and discussed anthropological theories overnight. The friendship between the two bloomed into love.

Ruth Benedict was married to Stanley Benedict, a professor of economics at Columbia University, in 1914. She entered the graduate programme at Columbia in 1921 and joined Columbia University as a regular faculty in 1931. For the students of sociology and anthropology, she is known for her seminal book *Patterns of Culture,* which became one of the best-selling works of academic anthropology ever written. She stood among the most important intellectuals of the century.

Mead remembers Ruth kissing her on her neck. Mead writes that Ruth's love gave her strength, joy, and excitement in life; it made her life worth living. She says Ruth's love was bread and wine for her.

Mead married a fellow anthropologist, Luther Cressman, in 1923. She had been engaged to him for six years. Cressman was studying theology and went to Europe for further studies. Later, he changed his area of study and received a doctorate in sociology from Columbia University, New York City, in 1925. He joined the University of Oregon as a sociology faculty in 1929.

Cressman was the brother of Mead's school teacher and had met Mead at a social gathering.

Mead, twenty-three, earned her master's degree in 1924. In August 1925, she sailed to Samoa, an island located between Australia and Mexico, for her field study. This was a radical departure from the norm as, at that time, a woman did not travel far away from her home by herself. Franz Boas, the 'father of modern American anthropology', was her guide for this field study.

This study would help Mead produce an influential work, *Coming of Age in Samoa* (1928). The book is said to be one of the most famous anthropological books ever and sold 100,000 copies in the 1960s. It became basic reading for introductory social science courses.

While going to Samoa, she left a farewell letter for her husband: 'I'll not leave you unless I find someone I love more.'

On the way to Samoa, Ruth Benedict accompanied her from New York to New Mexico, where she was to study myths and rituals in the Zuni Pueblo. 'The journey took them through Ohio to Illinois, across the prairie, then south toward the deserts. It was the longest the two of them had ever spent together, certainly the longest without their husbands in tow.'

They parted near Gallup, New Mexico. The separation weighed heavily on Mead's heart. She wrote, 'For the first time in my life, I expect defeat.' She wept in Benedict's arms and boarded a train to travel further west.

While Mead left for Samoa by ship, she missed her mentor and love, Benedict. The journey was long, and her vessel sailed on the disturbed ocean through humid days and moonlit nights. On her fourth day at sea, she sat and scribbled on a piece of paper: 'Ruth, dear heart ... five letters from you—and, oh, I hope you may often feel me near you as you did—resting so softly and sweetly in your arms. Whenever I am weary and sick with longing for you, I can always go back and recapture that afternoon out at Bedford Hills this spring, when your kisses rained down on my face, and that memory always ends in peace, beloved.'

As the days passed, her yearning to meet Ruth intensified. She wrote more letters. A few days later, she jotted down: 'Ruth, I was never more earthborn in my life—and yet never more conscious of the strength your love gives me. You have convinced me of the one thing in life which made living worthwhile.... You have no greater gift, darling. And every memory of your face, every cadence of your voice is joy whereon I shall feed hungrily in these coming months.'

After reaching Samoa, she wrote to Ruth, 'In my dreams I bury my face in your hair.'

Mead did field work in Samoa for nine months and studied the lives of Samoan girls. She returned to New York in August 1926 and was offered a position as assistant curator at the American Museum of Natural History, New York City, the same year.

Mead's marriage with Luther Cressman, with whom she had a long courtship, ended in 1928. Mead called her union with Cressman as 'my student marriage'. Cressman, after the divorce, married Dorothy Loch in London in 1928.

Then came Reo Fortune, a New Zealand academician, in Mead's life.

Reo Fortune was two years younger than Mead. She met him near American Samoa, a place near Samoa, in 1926, while she was doing field study there on a rainy day in a boat. She had completed her field work and was now on her way back to the USA. The young man was going to Cambridge to study psychology. In a white shirt and tie, she fascinated the lady anthropologist. The two took in the glorious view of the ripples on the surface of the South Pacific Ocean. At that time, she was married to Cressman.

After divorcing Cressman, she married Reo Fortune in Auckland, New Zealand, in 1928.

In 1931, the two went for fieldwork to Papua New Guinea, an island north of Australia. She published *Sex and Temperament in Three Primitive Societies* in 1935 on the basis of this field study. This book also sold like hot cakes.

Mead's marriage with Reo also did not last long. Fortune was 'uncaring, volatile and physically abusive'. He competed with his wife in scholarship and felt jealous of her standing and influence in academia and public life. He also suffered from Victorian morality and believed that a man was inherently superior to women in academic intelligence.

While Mead and her husband Fortune were on joint field work in New Guinea in December 1932, Mead met Gregory Bateson, an eminent British anthropologist, who had arrived there to celebrate Christmas. He was doing field work on the nearby Iatmul island.

A few days later, Mead and Fortune again met Bateson and made a trip on Sepik River in Bateson's canoe. They spent the night at a government guesthouse. Mead and Bateson stayed up all night, talking about anthropology, environment, and colonialism, while Fortune slept off after a heavy dose of local liquor.

Mead and Fortune separated in 1933, and their marriage was dissolved in 1935. Later, Fortune felt distressed over the failure of his marriage. He faced difficulty in finding employment and returned to New Guinea for further fieldwork. He got short-term academic assignments and settled finally as a lecturer at Cambridge. His talent, dynamism, and work ethic were gone after separation from his anthropologist wife. He was not able to write any anthropological work of significance.

Mead said after her divorce, 'Anthropological marriages are like theatrical marriages. They add more of a strain to the relationship.'

Mead's effort to look for love and innocence was rewarded in her relationship with Gregory Bateson. Gregory's father, a naturalist, coined the word 'genetics' and named his son after Gregor Mendel, an Austrian monk and the father of Genetics.

Bateson's grand theory corresponded with Mead's prolific field work, and the two complemented each other academically. She found Bateson lovable and admirable. He was somewhat the man she was looking for.

She married Bateson in Singapore in 1936 while both were on the way to Bali, Indonesia, for field work. They spent time together living and interacting with the tribals and developed a photographic analysis of the culture.

Their daughter, Mary Catherine, was born in 1939 in the United States. Mary graduated to become a faculty at Harvard and wrote several monographs and books, including *A Memoir of Margaret Mead and Gregory Bateson*. She was Mead's only child from three marriages.

Mead once said that Bateson was the husband she loved the most. In 1947, Mead became a faculty member in the Department of Anthropology at Columbia University.

Mead's third and last marriage also saw some strain in the relationship. After thirteen years of marriage, she felt it was time to move on. The Second World War kept them separated, and their interests varied. Finally, she snapped the marital tie in 1950.

However, deep within, she liked Bateson. They continued to collaborate for research and professional work. She treated him like a friend and kept his photograph by her bedside.

After the divorce, Gregory Bateson married Elizabeth in 1951 and had a son, John. Then he divorced Elizabeth and married a therapist and social worker, Lois Cammack, in 1961 with whom he had a daughter, Nora.

Through all these, Mead's relationship with her teacher and mentor, Ruth Benedict, continued and deepened. Ruth lay awake at night and remembered the nights they spent on the train to New Mexico—'making love, kissing Mead's fingers, trailing her lips across the palm of her hand'.

Ruth Benedict suffered from arthritis affecting her spine. She faced health issues throughout her life. She succumbed to a heart attack in 1948. Mead would live another thirty years.

In 1959, Mead wrote *An Anthropologist at Work*, an anthology based on Ruth Benedict's letters, diaries, notes from studies that Ruth had collected throughout her life, and unpublished manuscripts.

While Mead broke new grounds in anthropology, she also became the voice of liberalism in the US. She wrote on issues ranging from sex and gender to nuclear policy and the environment and argued to legalize marijuana. She spoke at public forums, and her lectures overflowed with crowds. Her book *Coming of Age in Samoa* talked about the way adolescents overcame change in their body, which was in contrast with the stress that American young boys and girls underwent. She lectured about sexual liberation at a time when a woman could not talk about sex in the society.

Mead contributed to *Redbook*, a popular magazine for women, read by millions. She declined US President Lyndon Johnson's offer to become the secretary of health, education, and welfare in 1963. *Time* magazine, in its 1969 issue, published her as a personality with the title 'Mother to the World'.

In 1970, Mead joined the faculty of the University of Rhode Island, USA, as a distinguished professor of sociology and anthropology.

Mead's health deteriorated, and she was hospitalized in New York Hospital on 3 October 1978. On 15 November, she died at the age of seventy-six and was buried in Pennsylvania.

She was then at the zenith of her reputation. President Jimmy Carter mourned her death, saying she had 'brought the humane insights of cultural anthropology to a public of millions'. In 1979, Carter awarded her the Medal of Freedom. The citation said she was awarded the honour for her struggle to show 'that varying cultural patterns express an underlying human unity'.

9

Edward Gibbon

Edward Gibbon, the British author and historian, best known for his *The History of the Decline and Fall of the Roman Empire*, was born in Putney, a suburb of London, on 27 April 1737. As a child, he had no interest in games, and he read books on a wide variety of subjects. He entered Magdalen College, Oxford, at the age of fifteen in 1752, where his major complaint was that his instructors were indifferent to his intellectual curiosity.

During this period, he came under the influence of Roman Catholics and converted to Catholicism. This troubled his father, who was a Protestant. The senior Gibbon immediately dispatched him to a Protestant clergyman named Daniel Pavillard at Lausanne, Switzerland, just after fourteen months of his stay at Oxford.

Edward Gibbon, sixteen, came to Lausanne on 30 June 1753. He liked the ambience and social atmosphere of the place. He had to study and return to Protestantism as per his father's expectation. He travelled and studied Latin literature and the works of great minds like John Locke, Blaise Pascal, Pierre Bayle, and Pietro Giannone. On 25 December 1754, he reverted to Protestantism.

In 1757, four years after his arrival in the town, he came across a Swiss man, Georges Deyverdun, who became his study companion, and Suzanne Curchod, a bright lady. She was the daughter of a Swiss clergyman and an ambitious girl.

Gibbon was deeply impressed by Suzanne from the first meeting itself. He came home after meeting her and scribbled in his journal on a summer evening in 1757: 'I saw Mademoiselle Curchod. "*Omnia vincit amor, et nos cedamus amori.*" (Love conquers all; let us, too, yield to love!)' He swore to the girl an attachment beyond the assaults of time.

Suzanne was born in 1737 at Crassy, a village in Switzerland. Her parents had moderate means. Her father, Louis Antoine Curchod, gave her an education far superior to that of the daughters of noble houses of that time. Suzanne's charm and accomplishments made her an especial object of admiration in the society. She had the fresh beauty of youth. She was chosen president of a local literacy society, and its meetings were held in a valley near Lausanne.

Suzanne, too, was fascinated by Gibbon. She drew his portrait and described him: 'He has beautiful hair, a pretty hand, and the air of a person of quality. His expression is "spirituel" and peculiar, and excites a constant interest.

He knows the respect that one should pay to women, and he is polite without being familiar.... He dances poorly.'

In 1758, Senior Gibbon called Edward Gibbon, twenty-one, back home from Switzerland. He had married again, this time to a woman named Dorothea née Patten, and wanted to discuss inheritance and property distribution with his son. He aimed to reduce and limit Gibbon's inheritance to £300 a year for life. This was a small amount, and Gibbon would have to live hand to mouth. When Gibbon came home to Surrey, his father put the proposal before him. Gibbon agreed to it.

Then Gibbon told his father about Suzanne and his love for her. He told him that he wanted to marry her. His life would be good in her company. She was beautiful as well as intelligent, and the two had shared tastes. He should permit him to marry her.

However, Gibbon's father was an insecure man; he did not want his son to bring an unknown foreign girl to his home. He also did not want his son to leave him and settle abroad with his wife. Senior Gibbon withheld his permission for marriage to Suzanne. To emotionally blackmail Gibbon, he reminded Gibbon at the dinner table of his duty as a son. 'If you did not listen to me and pursued the lady, you would hasten my movement to the grave.'

The senior Edward Gibbon was a Tory member of parliament, a London Alderman. He had seven children of which Edward alone had survived. His first wife, Judith, had died in 1747 during the birth of their seventh child.

Gibbon was shocked by his father's demand and expectation. If he accepted his proposal, he would lose his dream girl. What kind of proposal was this from a father who thought of his own interests and not of the wishes and happiness of his child? He stopped eating, stood up, and shut himself in a room. He thought over the issue. On the one hand stood his obligation as a son and his heart's desire on the other hand. His father had put him in a difficult situation, and he had to make a choice.

He came out of the room and told his father, 'Dear Dad! I will do as you desire.'

For a year, he sent no message to the lady except a copy of his *An Essay on the Study of Literature*. Then he sent her a letter, saying that his father had played spoilsport and forbade the match. He wrote: 'The decision is pronounced.... My heart laments, but before my duty, all else must be silent.' He told her that he would remember her 'as the worthiest and most charming of women'. But he could not move forward in the relationship.

Suzanne was devastated. She wondered, 'You made up your mind in two hours,' referring to the time he had shut himself in the room to decide his fate.

Even without such a letter, Suzanne would have been convinced that Gibbon had forsaken her as he did not write to her from England for a long time. But the quiet life of a Swiss village, the lakes, and the mountains kept her hope alive.

When Suzanne understood that his father did not want his son to settle abroad with a girl, she thought this was not such a big stumbling block, and that this could be addressed. Gibbon could spend a few months in Switzerland with her and return to his father for the rest of the time till his father was alive. After his death, Gibbon could come to her permanently.

However, Gibbon was not very enthusiastic about pursuing his relationship with her. When he heard this proposal, he did not respond positively to her. He wrote in his diary: 'The personal attractions of Mademoiselle Suzanne Curchod were embellished by the virtues and talents of the mind. Her fortune was humble, but her family was respectable.... In her short visits to some relations at Lausanne, the wit, the beauty, the erudition, of Mademoiselle Curchod were the theme of universal applause. The report of such a prodigy awakened my curiosity. I saw and loved. I found her learned without pedantry, lively in conversation, pure in sentiment, and elegant in manners.... She listened to the voice of truth and passion, and I might presume to hope that I had made some impression on a virtuous heart. At Crassy and Lausanne I indulged my dream of felicity, but on my return to England I soon discovered that my father would not hear of this strange alliance. After a painful struggle I yielded to my fate. I sighed as a lover, I obeyed as a son. My wound was insensibly healed by time, absence, and the habits of a new life. My cure was accelerated by a faithful report of the tranquillity and cheerfulness of the lady herself, and my love subsided into friendship and esteem.'

Suzanne's parents favoured the match with Gibbon. They said they would pursue the matter with his father. However, Suzanne said she would not like them to implore anyone.

Between 1758 and 1763, Gibbon spent time in London in the company of the Francophile Lady Hervey and the poet and philosopher David Mallet and visited theatres. He was also commissioned in the South Hampshire Militia, one of the armed units to defend England in

1759. He contested an election for the parliamentary seat of Petersfield in 1761 but did not win. He visited Lausanne again in 1963. He busied himself reading books and enjoying the beauty of the lakes, the blue sky, and the majestic Alps. In his memoir of the tour, he did not mention the lady he had once loved.

After that, when he met the lady at Ferney (near France) in 1963, he treated her as if he was meeting her for the first time. Suzanne did not expect that kind of treatment from a person whom she loved with all her heart. She was hurt. She wrote one final letter to him: 'I blush for what I do but for five years I have sacrificed myself to a chimaera. My mind is convinced of its error. Release a foolish heart, sign the avowal of your indifference, and the certainty will produce the tranquillity for which I sigh. You are the most despicable of men, if you refuse this act of frankness.'

She ended her letter with the sentence: 'A thinking soul is punishment enough, and every thought draws blood.' That was a strong statement.

A clergyman named Moulton was observing the complex situation and Gibbon's apathy. He tried to play cupid in the matter. He requested the philosopher Jacque Rousseau to talk to Gibbon and persuade him to marry Suzanne. As per a plan, Gibbon was to meet Rousseau during this visit to Switzerland. Rousseau could then have pleaded Suzanne's case.

But when Rousseau understood the whole story and Gibbon's attitude, he was appalled. He said, 'M. Gibbon is not the man for me, and I do not believe he is the man for Mademoiselle Curchod. He who does not feel her value is unworthy of her, but he who could feel it and abandon it is a man to be despised.'

However, on repeated requests, Rousseau agreed to talk to Gibbon on the issue. Unfortunately, Gibbon could not meet Rousseau on this tour, and the issue did not move further from there.

In 1760, Suzanne's father died, and in 1763, her mother also passed away. She was lonely and depressed and left with meager means to eke out a living. She supported herself by teaching. She was in a difficult situation, and she would have to find a husband fast to escape poverty.

She went to her friend Madame de Vermenoux's house in Paris in 1764. There she came across one Jacques Necker, a thirty-two-year-old Swiss-born banker. Necker was courting Madame de Vermenoux, who was a beautiful young widow, but the woman was not well disposed to the idea of marrying Necker. Necker then tried his luck with glamorous and witty Suzanne and courted her. Suzanne, lonely and uncertain of the future, accepted the offer from the bright and rich young man. This proposal was an extraordinary piece of good fortune for her. The two married in the same year.

Gibbon's father died in 1770. He felt lonely, and overcame his troubles by friendship, study, and writing. Soon, he took up writing full time and wove words into tome upon tome. The first volume of *The History of the Decline and Fall of the Roman Empire* appeared on 17 February 1776. The book sold like hot cakes. Then came the second volume in June 1776, a third in 1777, and the fourth in 1781. Gibbon's work was on every table in Europe.

Jacques Necker's political star shone bright in the otherwise disturbed firmament of French politics, and in 1777, he was sworn in as the finance minister of France in the government of Louis XVI. Suzanne, with a palatial home in Paris, was a great hostess and gathered the leading writers and learned men of the day at her home. Gibbon was one of her famous guests.

Gibbon remembers one of his visits: 'She was very fond of me and the husband, particularly civil. Could they insult me more cruelly? Ask me every evening to supper! Go to bed, and leave me alone with his wife! It is making an old lover of mighty little consequence.'

Suzanne could feel that now the parts were reversed, and her position was better. She wrote to a friend that the man who had discarded her now appeared abashed. She treated him with frank cordiality.

10

Catherine of Aragon

Henry VIII, king of England from 1509 to 1547, married Princess Catherine of Aragon on 11 June 1509. He was seventeen, and his father, Henry VII, had just died two weeks earlier.

Catherine, twenty-four, was a princess of Spain, six years older than Henry VIII. She was a woman of ethereal beauty and elegance and was the widow of his elder brother, Prince Arthur. Arthur had died of an unknown illness seven years earlier at the age of fifteen in 1502.

Henry VIII decided to marry his brother's widow Catherine, as marrying the princess of Spain made good political sense. Spain was the most powerful country after France in Europe. Marriage with Catherine would bring him wealth, repute, and more power.

Two weeks after the wedding, on 24 June 1509, Henry and Catherine were crowned as the king and the queen of England at Westminster Abbey in London. The archbishop of Canterbury William Warham anointed them with holy oil and crowned them in an elaborate ceremony. The coronation was followed by a magnificent banquet in Westminster Hall. Henry VIII was now the second king from the famous and powerful house of Tudors.

Henry VIII loved Catherine and showed his care and passion for her publicly. They were two bodies, one soul. After seven months of their marriage, in January 1510, the couple had a stillborn daughter. Now, silence sat upon the the palace where sweet melody danced in the air, but the royal family took the tragedy in its stride and moved ahead.

In January 1511, the queen gave birth to a son, but the baby died after two months. Then the family had a stillborn child in 1513. The journey of losses continued. Catherine again gave birth to a prince who died after a short period in 1515.

The cruel twists of fate singed the powerful king, but the relationship between Henry VIII and Catherine continued to be warm. In medieval times, stillborn babies, infants dying, and women losing their lives during childbirth were not uncommon.

While Catherine waited to give Henry VIII an heir to the throne, she continued assisting him in the governance of the kingdom. When Henry launched a joint invasion against France along with the all-important Holy Roman Emperor Maximilian I, in 1513, Catherine was the regent in his absence. She had administrative experience as she had been the Spanish ambassador to Britain before her marriage to Henry. People liked her as a queen and loved her for her intelligence, strength, piety, and devotion to the people.

Then on 18 February 1516, Catherine gave birth to a daughter, Princess Mary. She survived to adulthood. Henry VIII loved his daughter madly and treated her like a celestial jewel. The girl filled the emptiness of the palace, and the king called her 'my pearl in the world'.

But despite his love for Mary, Henry VIII wanted a son, and by 1520, after more than ten years of marriage, Catherine's failure to produce a boy started oppressing Henry VIII. The king was now twenty-seven and Catherine thirty-three. The time left for her to conceive and give birth to a baby was short. Catherine's spell over Henry VIII started waning. In 1518, she gave birth to a child, but it was a stillborn daughter. Henry VIII's requirement was still unfulfilled.

By 1525, Catherine was nearing forty. Several pregnancies had wreaked havoc on her body. She had gained weight and had lost her elegance. Her hold on the king's heart was gone. She was now past child-bearing age.

Then, in 1526, Anne Boleyn, the nineteen-year-old daughter of the ambassador to France, came to the king's court and disturbed the family life of the royals. She was to be a maid of honour to Queen Catherine but later came to erode her position and authority.

Anne had returned to England from the French court with her father, Thomas Boleyn. At Henry VIII's court, she captivated everyone with her wit, style, polished beauty, and charm. She was fashionable and attractive. Henry VIII, bored with his middle-aged wife who had failed to give him an heir, fell for the ravishing young lady.

Anne's instant hold over the king was noticed by everyone, and their affair became a matter of public knowledge. Catherine, of course, did not like it as Anne threatened her position. However, till then, the thought of divorcing Catherine had not come to the king's mind. He wanted to have a love affair with Anne and requested her to become his mistress. But Anne aimed higher. She was not someone who would fall for the good words and smiles of the king of England. She said she would give love to the one who married her. The position of mistress was not acceptable to her.

This was a difficult situation for Henry VIII, but he did not stop wooing her. Henry wrote love letters to her and drew an image of a heart on the letters. He loaded her with gifts, jewels, and trinkets.

In 1527, Anne left the king's court and went to her parents at Hever Castle. She was torn by the king's love for her and his inability to leave his wife, Catherine. Henry was enamoured by her and now looked at her as someone who would provide a son to succeed him. He wrote letters to her and told her that he missed her and loved her.

In one letter, he wrote, 'In turning over in my mind the contents of your last letters, I have put myself into great agony, not knowing how to interpret them … beseeching you earnestly, to let me know expressly your whole mind…. It is absolutely necessary for me to obtain this answer, having been for above a whole year stricken with the dart of love, and not yet sure whether I shall fail of finding a place in your heart and affection.'

Henry sent many more letters to Anne. Anne responded to his pursuit with letters and gifts in return. After some time, she returned to the court, and the king became more open in expressing his love and admiration to her.

By 1527, a year after Anne's return to the court, Henry decided to divorce Catherine and start a new life with Anne as his wife. However, casting off his wife Queen Catherine in the medieval world was no easy matter. There was no law providing divorce to one's wife. The Bible said, 'Everyone who divorces his wife and marries another commits adultery.'

When Henry had first married Catherine in 1509, he had done so against convention. There had been objections to this marriage. The Bible said a man must not marry his brother's widow as marriage with her would be incestuous. However, teenaged Henry VIII had been in love with the beautiful princess, and he had his way.

To allow himself to marry Catherine in 1509, Henry VIII came up with a two-point solution. One, Catherine claimed that her marriage to Arthur lasted only for six months, and during that period, Arthur was continuously ill, and their marriage could not be consummated. Secondly, Pope Julius II issued a special dispensation to allow him to marry Catherine.

Now, in 1527, when Henry VIII wanted to throw Catherine out of his life, he argued that he had no son because his current marriage was a sin against God. Catherine was his elder brother's wife and, therefore, not lawful for him in marriage. Divorce was the only solution. He appealed to Pope Clement VII of Rome to give him a remedy.

Henry VIII's path to divorce was tricky. In 1527, Charles V, the Holy Roman Emperor, sacked Rome and took Pope Clement VII as his prisoner. Charles V was Queen Catherine's nephew (son of her sister), and he did not want his aunt to be divorced. The pope, who was under his custody, did not dare to grant the divorce.

Henry VIII then turned to Cardinal Thomas Wolsey of England. Wolsey owed his status to the blessings of the king. He was not born into nobility and was the son of a butcher. Henry made him bishop, archbishop, and cardinal in quick succession. The king wanted a return of his favours. Wolsey ideally should have sorted out the issue, but he did not handle the challenge tactfully. He set up a legatine court to look into the matter and give a judgement. The court, instead of giving the king a solution, referred the matter to the College of Cardinals in Rome. This further complicated the matter and widened the scope for everyone's intervention.

The king was not happy with the mismanagement, and Wolsey fell out of his favour. Henry VIII stripped him of his government titles and dispossessed him from his palace. Wolsey was the government's chief advisor and wielded a lot of influence, but he was now no one. After falling from the king's grace, Wolsey thought to focus on studies and meditation on God. Henry VIII, however, was not going to forget him after sacking him from the office. He put him on trial for treason and called him to London to answer to the charges. Thomas Wolsey died on the way in November 1530.

Anne moved into Henry's London palace, but she kept the king at a distance. Henry VIII had no hope of any positive result regarding the annulment of his marriage to Catherine from the College of Cardinals or the pope in Rome. He had to now look for other avenues.

He approached the theologians at Europe's universities and requested them to study his issue and pronounce a verdict. However, to his consternation, these theologians gave a verdict against annulment and thus did not help the king in any way.

With the doors closed on all fronts, Henry VIII and his advisors came up with an innovative idea: repudiate the authority of the Roman Catholic Church over England. The bishop and the king of England would not be guided by the dictate of the pope of Rome. This was going to be a big leap.

Thomas Cromwell, the king's most powerful minister, put himself on the job. He worked to bring Thomas Cranmer, a theology professor at Cambridge, to the king's camp. The objective was to establish the supremacy of the court over church and find a resolution to the king's problem.

Cranmer and Cromwell argued in favour of the king's supremacy over the bishop. He said a king is anointed by God, and therefore, he is answerable to God only. The king was sovereign over the church. Henry VIII should not have to petition the bishops and cardinals for a petty issue like divorce.

This argument was something that Henry VIII yearned to hear. He realized he was now in control of the situation, and the parliament legislated a law to break the subordination of the English Church to the Catholic Church of Rome. By 1532, Henry VIII had the power of both king and pope. He ruled earth and the heavens. Funds being sent to Rome were stopped.

Now, his matter would be decided by the Church of England. Henry VIII wanted his man as the head of England's top church, and no one was a better candidate than Thomas Cranmer for that post. Cranmer was appointed the archbishop of Canterbury in March 1533.

Shortly after his appointment as the archbishop of Canterbury, Cranmer pronounced Henry's marriage with Catherine invalid in 1534. Catherine said she had been cast aside 'without cause at the instigation of an enemy completely without scruples [Thomas Cromwell]'.

However, Thomas More, Henry's chief minister and author of the famous book *Utopia,* did not like the king's dirty works. He refused to accept King Henry VIII as the head of the church. This was a small problem for Henry VIII. He imprisoned More for a year in the iconic Tower of London along the Thames River. Henry VIII expected that during the imprisonment, More would mellow down and accept the reality. More showed no change and held on to his convictions. Henry VIII thought his stubbornness was insubordination. The king got More convicted of treason and executed him in July 1535. His head was severed from his body at the Tower of London.

The matter which Henry VIII had pursued from 1527 was thus resolved. Henry VIII showed urgency and married Anne in a secret ceremony on 25 January 1533, four months before the order of annulment by the church and crowned her as queen on 1 June 1533. After seven months of marriage, Anne gave birth to Elizabeth I of England, who would rule England for forty-four years as a monarch.

Catherine was now banished from the court. She lived far from London. She lost her royal status and lived under house arrest. Her old rooms were given to Anne Boleyn. Her world had turned ugly. She died a lonely death at Kimbolton Castle, Cambridge, in January 1536.

However, Anne Boleyn, the woman who spun traps for Queen Catherine, soon found herself in the most undignified position. As the queen of England, she meddled with affairs of state. She opposed an act of parliament that provided for the suppression of the lesser monasteries, as she thought this was incorrect. Chaplains under her instruction spoke against the law. Slowly, the issue became more complicated, and court politics worked to discredit her. One day, the king accused Anne of infidelity and adultery with five men. One of the men accused was the queen's brother.

On 15 May 1536, Queen Anne and her brother stood trial. Four other accused persons had already been condemned to death. On 17 May 1536, Thomas Cranmer, who had declared Catherine's marriage to Henry VIII invalid, repudiated Henry VIII's marriage to Anne. Two days after that, Anne was executed on the lawns of the Tower of London.

11

Winston Churchill

Winston Churchill (1874–1965) was a British statesperson, an army officer, a journalist, and an author. He served as Britain's prime minister twice and as its Home Secretary. He was awarded the Nobel Prize in literature in 1951.

Churchill graduated from the Royal Military Academy, Sandhurst, in 1895. Thereafter, he joined the Queen's Own Hussars regiment of the British Army as a second lieutenant.

Churchill, twenty-one, came to India in October 1896 as a major in the army and joined British expeditions to Hyderabad and the North-West Frontier Province (now in Pakistan). He stayed in India for three years till 1899. These were productive years of his life as he extensively studied Western literature and history, wrote the book

The Story of the Malakand Field Force, and worked as a war correspondent for the *Pioneer* and the *Daily Telegraph*.

The high point of his visit was meeting Pamela, the daughter of Sir Trevor Plowden, the British Resident at Hyderabad.

Plowden was an Indian Civil Services (ICS) officer and served as the British Resident in Hyderabad state during 1891–1900.

In Hyderabad, Churchill stayed at the Secunderabad cantonment. In a dinner party in November 1896, he met Pamela Plowden at the cantonment. Pamela, with 'seductive gray eyes, porcelain complexion and glossy dark hair', enchanted him over a glass of chilled red wine. After this meeting, he visited Pamela at her residence and went for an elephant ride with her in Hyderabad. He wrote to his mother: 'She is the most beautiful girl I have ever seen.'

Winston Churchill wrote letters to Pamela from wherever he was on duty or travelling in India. He shared his feelings for her and praised her beauty. He also sent her the manuscript of his novel *Savrola: A Tale of the Revolution in Laurania* to impress her.

He always thought sufficient wealth was one of the pre-conditions of his eligibility to marry Pamela Plowden, and he thought he had not enough money.

However, Churchill was not a boy from England's middle class. His father was a member of parliament in 1874 (the year he was born), and his mother, Jennie, was the daughter of a rich American businessperson. Still, he thought he was not rich enough to wed Pamela.

In March 1899, he wrote to her from Calcutta: 'My dear Miss Pamela … I have lived all my life seeing the most beautiful women London produces.... Never have

I seen one for whom I would forego the business of life. Then I met you.... Were I a dreamer of dreams, I would say ... 'Marry me—and I will conquer the world and lay it at your feet.' For marriage two conditions are necessary—money and the consent of both parties. One certainly, both probably, are absent. And this is all such an old story.'

Churchill left India in October 1899 to join the British forces in South Africa during the Second Boer War. He was to cover the war for a British newspaper. He carried Pamela's portraits in his pocket. He was then twenty-five.

In South Africa, during his work as a journalist, the Boer troops captured him at Natal in December 1899. They detained him in Pretoria as a prisoner of war. While in detention, he wrote to the lady, 'Among new and vivid scenes, I often think of you.'

His mother, Jennie, wrote to him in South Africa: 'Pamela is devoted to you and if your love has grown as hers—I have no doubt it is only a question of time for you to marry.'

In December 1899, Churchill managed to escape from prison. He reached neighbouring Mozambique, and from there, he appeared in Britain as a hero.

In England, he met Pamela at the castle of Daisy Greville, the countess of Warwick. Daisy was known for her beauty and social connections. She invited them to spend the weekend at her castle.

In 1900, Churchill was elected as a member of parliament at the age of twenty-six from Oldham constituency.

He took Pamela for boating in the river Avon, passing through the hills covered by forests. The boat man served them grilled fish. He held her warm hand and asked her again if she was interested in him. She said no.

Churchill still believed that she was the only woman in the world he could live happily with.

He went to Canada and the United States in December 1900 to deliver lectures and earn some money. That would raise his marriage prospects with the lady of his love.

On this tour, he met Pamela, who had come to Canada to visit her friend Lady Minto, wife of the governor general of Ottawa. He proposed marriage again. The answer was still no.

Back in London, they continued meeting at parties and social gatherings.

Finally, in 1902, any possibility of a marriage with Pamela ended. Pamela was engaged to Victor Bulwer-Lytton, who served as the governor of Bengal, India. Victor was the son of Edward Lytton, viceroy of India (1876–1880).

It was a painful time for Churchill. He was heart-broken. Six years of courtship and hope had come to an end. Perhaps his fear that he was not rich enough and thus could not marry Pamela came true.

Churchill congratulated Victor and Pamela and wished them 'all the happiness and good fortune which wit & beauty deserve when they combine to share the inheritance of the future'.

With Pamela gone from the scene, he looked for other women who could be his wife. He saw the American actor Ethel Barrymore, an extraordinary beauty, performing plays in London. Churchill, twenty-nine, fell for her charm in 1903. An admirer of Ethel described her as 'a pretty creature, with dangerously expressive eyes, luxuriant dark hair, and highly captivating manner'.

Ethel remained busy with her assignment, and Churchill had no opportunity to interact with her at length and impress her. She moved frequently between New York and London for her work.

Churchill wrote letters to her, expressing his love and admiration for her beauty and persona, but she was not impressed.

Ethel came to London again in 1904 for a performance, and this time, Churchill did not hold himself. He told her he was deeply in love with her and wanted to marry her. Ethel was then preoccupied with her work and performance. She did not know how to respond to this proposal. She returned to the US without giving him an answer.

A year later, Ethel fell in love with an American businessperson and married him in 1909.

Later, Churchill confessed, 'I was so in love with her. And she would not pay any attention to me at all.'

Then in 1904, Churchill met Muriel Wilson, (b.1884), the daughter of a British businessperson and politician. 'With her delicate mouth, large eyes and rich mass of wavy dark hair, Muriel was dubbed "Great Britain's most beautiful girl" by the American press.' She had a large mansion near Buckingham Palace in London.

By September 1904, Churchill was sure that their friendship was ripening into something more serious. But Churchill was mistaken. Muriel was not aware of what was cooking in young Churchill's heart. Churchill told her: 'My love burns brighter than the sun for you. I seek your solace. I want to start a new life with you.' But she turned down his proposal. Churchill wanted her to think and not take a decision in hurry. If he was not up to her mark, he would change. He would refine himself. He wrote to her: 'Perhaps I shall improve with waiting.... Why should not you care about me someday?' He thought she may have a change of heart with the passage of time and come to like him.

During this time in 1905, Churchill's career took an upswing. He was posted as under-secretary to the colonial office. He was now a minister in the British Government with Henry Campbell as the prime minister. But Muriel was not interested in marriage with Churchill. She was nearing thirty and had a large set of admirers.

Churchill still pursued her. In September 1906, he persuaded her to spend a week with him in Venice, the city of love. She agreed. They spent time on a gondola in the waterways of Venice. From there, they drove on to Tuscany, the central part of Italy, famous for art, wine, sunsets, and the countryside. Still, she did not relent. With a refusal to marry him, they reached a dead end.

Thereafter, in March 1908, he met twenty-two-year-old Clementine Hozier at a dinner party hosted by the American-born socialite Lady St Helier. Daughter of an army officer, '(Clementine) did have that air of mystery that Winston liked, and there was a touch of exotic in her almond-eye beauty'.

After this party, meetings between the two continued. He invited her to the family's ancestral home, Blenheim Palace in Oxfordshire County, with beautiful gardens on 11 August 1908. They met there and went for a long walk amidst gusts of wind and light downpour.

Here, Churchill again took the risk of proposing marriage to a woman. This time, however, he did not suffer disappointment. Clementine agreed to his proposal.

He was happy. He wrote to Muriel that he was engaged to Clementine.

Churchill arranged for their marriage after a month lest something went wrong, and Clementine changed her mind. They got married on 12 September 1908.

12

Steve Jobs

Steve Jobs, thirteen, enrolled at Homestead High School, Cupertino, California, in 1968 and passed out in 1972. There, he met 'a green-eyed bohemian girl', Chrisann Brennan, in January 1972. She was one year junior to him. Chrisann had three sisters, and her father worked at an electronics multinational company. Her father named her Chrisann after the flower chrysanthemum.

She remembers about Steve Jobs, 'He was wearing blue jeans that were full of big holes.... I was drawn to him immediately.... He was tall and beautiful and intentional, a study in contrasts, something like a fine prince in shabby jeans.... Then he reached into his pocket and gave me a copy of Bob Dylan's song *Sad Eyed Lady of the Lowlands*.'

Chrisann and Jobs started a passionate romance. Jobs was shy, and Chrisann was the one who initiated kissing when she met him. She says, 'I was his "North Country Girl," the one from the Dylan song who was a true love, the one he would know before fame and wealth came, the one hit by heavy winds.'

After graduating from school, in mid-1972, Jobs and Chrisann rented an accommodation in Cupertino. They lived together as a couple. Jobs played guitar for her in his bedroom. He had told her on their first date that he would be a millionaire someday.

In September 1972, Jobs went to Reed College in Portland, Oregon, 1000 km north of Cupertino, California, to study. It was a private school 'known for its free spirits and hippie vibe' and one of the most expensive colleges in the country. Jobs had the option to apply to Berkeley and Stanford, but he did not go there as he was not interested in traditional college education.

He studied psychology and philosophy as Reed College. Steve Wozniak, a friend from high school, came there to meet him. However, by the end of the first semester, he dropped out of college. Jobs says, 'After six months, I couldn't see the value in it...I had no idea what I wanted to do with my life and no idea how college was going to help me figure it out. And here I was spending all of the money my parents had saved their entire life. So I decided to drop out.'

Jobs hung around Reed for another six months, taking a class in calligraphy. 'I didn't have a dorm room, so I slept on the floor in friends' rooms.' He got free meals at a Hare Krishna temple. Daniel Kottke, who met him in 1972 at the college and who also dropped out of college, became his friend.

At Reed, Jobs was introduced to the teachings of Neem Karoli Baba, an Indian guru. He spent time reading eastern philosophy and religions. He also came across Kobun Chino Otogawa, who practised Zen meditation in California. Jobs went for a retreat with him.

Daniel Kottke and Steve Jobs rented a house in Portland, Oregon, and welcomed Chrisann Brennan as their third roommate. The three often went for long drives in a Volvo minibus. Jobs watched art movies and wrote poetry. He hung a poster of Bob Dylan on the wall adjoining the bed. Both Chrisann and Steve Jobs were happy and felt blessed. They had very little money and no foreseeable prospects. Chrisann enrolled herself in painting classes at a local community college.

In the mid-1973, Jobs, eighteen, moved south 1000 km, from Reed College to the San Francisco area. He rented an apartment there. Then in February 1974, Jobs returned to his parents' home in Los Altos about 60 km further south and began looking for a job. He was soon hired by Atari Inc. in Los Gatos, California, as a computer technician. He dreamt of starting his own business. The job at Atari gave him the money for a trip to India.

He and Daniel Kottke embarked on a pilgrimage to India in 1974 to meet Neem Karoli Baba at his ashram at Kainchi near Nainital, but the guru had passed away shortly before they arrived. Jobs says about the experience: 'For me it was a serious search. I'd been turned on to the idea of enlightenment and trying to figure out who I was and how I fit into things.' They lived in a one-room cement hut on a potato farm. They spent about seven months in India and then returned to California.

Chrisann and Steve Jobs had 'an on-again, off-again romance over five years'. They lived together for parts of that time. In 1975, Brennan was also introduced to zen meditation practice in Los Altos and went into periodic retreats. After losing contact with Jobs for a while, she again came back to him. Jobs began to spend more time with her, but he was not as passionate in the relationship with her as before. She enrolled at Foothill College, California, and pursued a degree in art. She lived for some time again with Jobs in the summer of 1976. Daniel Kottke worked in the Apple garage, testing circuit boards, and mediated between Jobs and Brennan during the fights.

Chrisann became close to Greg Calhoun, Jobs's former classmate at Reed College. She moved to the All One Farm, a farm near McMinnville in Oregon established by Jobs's friend Robert Friedland, who was also a student at Reed College, and lived there for a while with Greg Calhoun. They also planned to make a trip to India to dive into spirituality. They moved to the San Francisco Bay Area to work and earn money for a trek to India. Finally, they pooled some money and left for India in March 1976. They travelled for a year through India, visiting spiritual gurus and religious centres in Uttar Pradesh and Himachal. At one point, they ran out of money, so Calhoun hitchhiked to Iran to teach English in Tehran. Brennan stayed in India, and when Calhoun's teaching stint was over, he turned towards India. Chrisann proceeded north-west and received Calhoun in Afghanistan. But their relationship ended by the time she returned to the United States in 1977.

In 1976, Steve Jobs, Kottke, and Steve Wozniak designed the Apple-I computer. Apple was incorporated by Jobs with the help of his friends, including the venture capitalist Mike Markkula, in 1977. Apple Inc. unveiled Apple II computer at a computer fair in San Francisco in 1977. It became a bestseller product as one of the first mass-produced microcomputers. With its sale, Jobs became a millionaire at twenty-three, an icon of entrepreneurialism and capitalism.

In 1978, Chrisann became pregnant, despite birth control measures. The news destroyed Jobs's mood and upended his career plan. Chrisann became upset with Jobs's response to the news. They had regular fights, and one night, she threw plates at him. Robert Friedland invited her to his place. She left Jobs and went to the farm. She wrote, 'Little by little, Steve and I separated.... We never talked about breaking up or going our separate ways and we didn't have that conversation where one person says it is over.'

At that time, in 1978, Steve Jobs started working on the desktop computer Lisa. Apple launched it on 19 January 1983. It was the precursor to the Macintosh personal computer. However, this computer turned out to be a commercial failure, its production was discontinued, and the unsold computers were buried.

Their daughter, Lisa Brennan-Jobs, was born at the All One Farm on 17 May 1978 with the help of two midwives. Jobs, twenty-three, arrived there to see the child a few days later. 'My parents took me out into a field, laid me on a blanket, and looked through the pages of a baby-name book,' says Lisa. He and Chrisann named the baby Lisa Nicole Brennan.

Now Jobs and Wozniak were working on early versions of what would become the Macintosh. This would be the first personal computer to use a graphical user interface, built-in screen, and a mouse.

Chrisann left the commune in Oregon and shifted 1,000 km south to a house at Menlo Park in California. She was alone with her baby without any financial support from Jobs. She received welfare payments from the government and worked as a server to supplement her income. She took the job of babysitting at a day-care centre inside a church. In 1978, Jobs had launched Apple and was a wealthy man.

In 1980, the district attorney of San Mateo County, California, sued Jobs for child support payments. Jobs denied paternity and swore that he was sterile. He underwent a DNA test for paternity. The test established that he was the father of the child. On 8 December 1980, the court ordered Jobs to pay Chrisann US$385 per month for child support. In 1980, Apple went public, raising US$110 million in the initial public offer.

When Lisa was three, in 1981, Jobs bought a house for her and Chrisann. They now lived a comfortable life. However, Chrisann's relationship with Jobs was broken.

Steve Jobs bought an apartment at the San Remo building in Central Park West, New York, in 1982. He was busy trying to make the Lisa computer a successful venture. His neighbour at his San Remo apartment was the famous Hollywood actor Diane Keaton. Jobs sent her a request, saying that he wanted to meet her. Keaton, thirty-three, had built her reputation with a career spanning over a decade with Academy Awards and acting in films like 'The Godfather' trilogy. She was at the height of her career and eight years older than him. She went to his massive apartment to meet him.

She remembers her meeting with Jobs: 'I really didn't go out with him … no, I did not kiss him, but here's what happened: I lived at the San Remo in New York City, and it was a building with two towers. And Steve Jobs had just bought the top three floors of the north tower. So this was after Annie Hall and he was interested in meeting me. Granted, he was younger than me. He'd be about 8 years younger than me or something like this, but he wanted to meet me. So I go over to his tower and it's like amazing … and he says, he starts talking, but all he's talking about is this thing. The computer thing, you know? How the computer was gonna take over the world. I'm sitting there going "Okay, right". And he's talking about how everybody was going to have a computer for their world and their life and their homes and I'm going "Yeah, right right." And I never saw him again, ever. Because, obviously, I just wasn't prepared for that for even a second. I thought 'Is he nuts?'

Steve Jobs, twenty-seven, met famous folk singer Joan Baez, forty-one, through her sister Mimi Farina in 1982. After a few weeks, he and Baez had lunch in Cupertino, California. She was a world-famous celebrity. Jobs asked her if she would teach him how to play the piano. Baez told Jobs that she didn't know how to play the piano well. Jobs persisted, saying she should still come over to help him. Soon they became close friends. Jobs found her to be beautiful and funny.

Joan had appeared on the cover of *Time* magazine in 1962. She was lauded as the queen of folk. 'She (had) a genius for harmony, reflecting an agility to listen, collaborate and adapt swiftly onstage.' She was a hero of protest folk. Dr Martin Luther King Jr and the Czech president

Vaclav Havel were her friends. Her father, Albert Báez, was a pioneering physicist. She had once been arrested for protesting against the Vietnam war.

Baez had once been Bob Dylan's lover. She had shared the stage and toured places with Dylan as a part of a music team. Dylan said she was a voice straight from God. However, she had a split with him in 1965 while she was on a tour with him. Dylan was one of Jobs's all-time heroes. Baez's connection with Dylan was one of the reasons for his fascination for the singer.

Baez married anti-war activist David Harris in 1968, but the couple divorced amicably in 1973. 'I was designed to live alone,' she says. She had a son, Gabriel Harris, born in 1969 from the marriage with David Harris. Jobs gave her son an Apple II to use.

Jobs once drove her to a clothes store to buy her beautiful clothes. He asked his friends whether he should marry her. 'Both were intrigued by each other's creativity and influence, which fuelled their intense connection.'

Jobs wanted a family with children, but she did not. He thought there was no point wasting time with her if she did not want a family with him. 'We disagreed on almost everything,' she says. After three years, they ended their relationship and became just friends. She wrote a memoir, *And A Voice to Sing With*, in 1987.

When Jobs was on his deathbed, Baez asked him, 'How does it feel to have changed the world?' He said, 'Ok.'

Jobs went to a dinner party in Silicon Valley in 1983. Jessica Logan, an undergraduate student at the University of Pennsylvania, sat next to him. She was on a week's vacation to San Francisco from Philadelphia. Jobs was fascinated by the young girl. She was working on a weekly magazine in San Francisco, California. She remembers: 'I kept saying, "What, exactly, do you do?" And he would only mention specific tasks. Because he looked so young, I thought he was trying to hide the fact that he had a very lowly job.'

Later, Jobs tracked her down. He called her and invited her for lunch. He took her to Jacqueline Cafe near Telegraph Hill in San Francisco. They dated for a year.

Jobs came to meet Logan in Philadelphia (University of Pennsylvania). Located in the east of the USA, Philadelphia is 4500 km away from San Francisco. When he went to New York, she travelled 130 km from Philadelphia by train and stayed with him in the evening. They went to theatres and restaurants. While apart, they spoke on the phone for hours in the day and night. She says: 'It was very fun to have him be so in love with me, honestly. I would call him at his office from the pay phones at the Pennsylvania University library, and, no matter what he was doing, he would always come to the phone. We would have these long conversations, and then he'd say, "Well, I can see some reporters waiting for me outside my office so I probably should go."'

He discussed with her the Buddhist teachings of his zen teacher Kobun Chino. He showed no interest in materialism and meditation. She flagged the apparent contradictions in his belief and his conduct: passion for meditation, Buddhist philosophy, and working relentlessly to develop computers and sell them to the whole world.

Logan came to stay with her mother in San Francisco during the winter break at the university. That time, in January 1984, Macintosh computers was launched in the market. Steve Jobs came to her house with a box of Macintosh computers.

Jobs told her he wanted to marry her. Logan thought over his proposal. She felt she was too young to be married to him. She says, 'I grew up saying, "I'm not going to be the wife".' She felt overshadowed by him. Jobs would talk about going to the White House, mentioning the names of the top men of the Reagan administration. She felt dwarfed by that. 'That was a lot to have in my head as a college student.' She told Jobs she was not ready for marriage with him. Jobs said, 'It is alright.' He moved ahead while Logan went to Cambridge University to study English literature.

Just after a sort of break-up with Jessica Logan, Steve Jobs met Tara Redfield, twenty-six, a computer consultant. He was going to attend a meeting in early 1985 at his Cupertino office campus. He stopped at the office of a guy who worked with the Apple Foundation. Tara Redfield was on duty in her cabin in that office. She 'combined a hippie aura of natural purity with a solid sensibilities of a computer consultant'. Jobs described her as one of the most beautiful women he had ever seen. He called her the next day and asked her out for dinner. She told him that she was living with her boyfriend and could not go out with him. A few days later, he took her on a walk to a park and again asked her out to dinner. She told him to wait. Tara talked to her boyfriend and informed him that she wanted to go for dinner with Steve Jobs. The boyfriend said It was okay. Then she went for dinner with him, and after finishing the food, she began to cry. She knew her life was going to be disrupted.

Jobs says about her: 'She was the first person I was truly in love with.... We had a very deep connection. I don't know that anyone will ever understand me better than she did.'

Tara had a disturbed childhood like Jobs. She told Jobs that her past was scarred. The interaction between them turned into an all-consuming romance. They could be seen lost in love in open spaces, office corridors, and parks. Violent disagreements, loud shouts, and sporadic suspicions also characterized their relationship. They fought in movie theatres, cafes, offices, and other places.

On 31 May 1985, Steve Jobs was stripped of all authority at the company he had co-founded. He was thirty. John Sculley outsmarted him and took over Apple as its new CEO. Jobs went home and spent hours talking to his friends on his phone.

Relieved from the busy schedule of the work at Apple, he travelled to Europe with Tara Redfield. He met heads of state, university presidents, business honchos, and creative people. Jobs and Tara contemplated settling permanently in Paris, but then Jobs could not finalize the idea.

They returned to the USA. Jobs lived at Jackling House, a mansion in Woodside, which he had bought in 1984, in California. Tara lived with him at first and then moved out to her house in Palo Alto after an argument with him. She felt he was neglecting her and that he was a self-centred person. Tara persuaded him to spend more time with Lisa.

There was a conflict of personality between Tara and Jobs. She was loving and caring in general. Anyone who came across her benefitted from her money, generosity, and kindness. However, she was not ambitious and competitive like Jobs, which perhaps Jobs did not like. When they were together, they fought, and when away, they craved each other.

Jobs, ousted from Apple Inc., was thinking of starting something new. He had a meeting with Nobel laureate Paul Berg, who told him that the country needed personal computers for research and modelling. After this conversation, he founded NeXT Inc., a new computer company, in 1986. He also bought Pixar, a company that made computer-animated feature films, from George Lucas, filmmaker and creator of Star Wars.

He kept himself busy trying to come up with the best personal computer that the whole world would buy. His friend Steve Wozniak came to him from Apple Inc. to work on his vision.

Jobs, finally, in the summer of 1989, told Tara he wanted to marry her. However, she did not want to marry him, considering his temperament and behaviour. She thought she would go crazy if she lived with him. She would not be able to take his unkindness. They broke up. She founded ClearVision, a mental health resource network in California. She later married and had two children.

Steve Jobs married Laurene Powell in 1991. They were together until his death in 2011. They had three children together.

Steve Jobs had gone to Stanford University to deliver a lecture on the topic 'View from the Top' in 1989. He had an invitation from the students of the university. Before the talk started, Jobs sat next to Laurene Powell and chatted with her. She won a raffle to take Jobs for dinner after the speech. Jobs told his sister on the phone about Laurene: 'There's this beautiful woman and she's really smart and she has this dog and I'm going to marry her.'

A few days after the evening talk, the two went for dinner. It was a beautiful fall evening, and they walked to a vegetarian restaurant in Palo Alto. She was twenty-five and Jobs thirty-four. They departed after an hour.

Laurene was born in New Jersey in 1963. Her father was a Marine Corps pilot. She graduated from the University of Pennsylvania and worked at Goldman Sachs. Later she studied at Stanford Business School. The relationship between the two deepened. Jobs liked her intelligence and manners. In December 1990, Jobs proposed going on a vacation, and the two went to Hawaii.

Immediately thereafter, Jobs proposed marriage to her on 1 January 1990. She accepted the proposal. However, Jobs was still not clear whom to marry: Tara Redfield or Laurene Powell. He thought he was still in love with Tara Redfield.

Jobs remembers, 'There were only two women in my life that I was truly in love with, Tara and Laurene. I thought I was in love with Joan Baez, but I really just liked her a lot. It was just Tara and then Laurene.'

Finally, Steve Jobs, thirty-six, decided to marry Laurene, twenty-seven. The wedding was held at the Ahwahnee Lodge in Yosemite National Park, California, in 1991. Steve's father, Paul Jobs, his sister, Mona Simpson, and about fifty others attended the marriage. That day, it snowed. The ceremony was conducted by his Zen teacher Kobun Chino. After the marriage, the couple moved into a two-storeyed house in the Old Palo Alto area.

Laurene gave birth to a son, Reed Paul Jobs, in 1991 after a few months of marriage. Erin Jobs, the second child, was born in 1995, and the third child, Eve Jobs, was born in 1998.

His daughter Lisa joined the family and stayed with them. She enrolled at Palo Alto High School. She stayed with them through all the four years of her schooling. Her name was now changed to Lisa Brennan-Jobs. After graduating from the school, she got admission at Harvard in 1996 and shifted from her father's place to the university.

In 1997, Jobs returned to Apple as its de facto head. He set foot for the first time in Apple's Cupertino office campus on 2 December 1996 after leaving it in 1985. He was invited by Gil Amelio, CEO of Apple, to join the company. Apple Inc. was on the verge of bankruptcy. Jobs worked to revive the company. In 1998, Apple returned to profitability and unveiled the iMac computer. In 2000, he became its CEO again.

Jobs died at his home in Palo Alto, California, on 5 October 2011. He was laid to rest at the Alta Mesa Memorial Park in Palo Alto. Apple was then the world's most valuable company. He had transformed seven industries: personal computing, animated movies, music, phones, tablet computing, retail stores, and digital publishing.

13

Amrita Sher-Gil

Amrita Sher-Gil, born on 30 January 1913 in Budapest, Hungary, is known to be one of the greatest avant-garde artists of her oeuvre. A woman with beauty carved by the angels, she spent most of her time painting or playing the piano.

Her father, Umrao Singh Sher-Gil, born near Amritsar in 1870, was a Sikh aristocrat. He lived in Lahore and was friends with the poet Mohammad Iqbal and top litterateurs and intellectuals of his time in India. He was a scholar of Persian and Sanskrit and is credited as India's first modern photographer. He loved cricket, chess, and stargazing. His younger brother, Sundar Singh, was a member of the Viceroy's Imperial Legislative Council.

Umrao Singh met Marie Antoinette, an opera singer from Hungary, at a dinner party in Lahore in 1912. Marie had come to India accompanying Princess Bamba Sutherland, a member of the royal family of the erstwhile Sikh Empire in the Punjab. She hailed from a middle-class family of Hungary.

After a brief interaction, Umrao Singh proposed marriage to Marie. She agreed, and they married in Lahore in 1912. She became his second wife. The couple left for Budapest, the capital of Hungary, for their honeymoon. Amrita was born there and grew up on Hungarian folk tales and European classical music. The family stayed in Hungary till February 1921 because of the First World War. Their house was a beacon for the intellectuals, authors, and artists of Budapest.

The Umrao family lived an unconventional life. They had connections with the rich and famous, and they mixed with royals and political bigwigs. They were a a gathering of luminous souls with a life dedicated to art, literature, theatre, and intellectual pursuit.

The family finally returned to India in 1921 and settled in Shimla. They purchased a house, The Holme, from a Swedish family, at Summer Hill. Amrita started learning art from the age of eight and mixed with high society. She was educated there and displayed her paintings at the famous Gaiety Theatre in Shimla, a rendezvous of creative and talented minds. She painted *Self-Portrait*, a smiling teen with bare shoulders and thick red lips, in 1928.

On 19 April 1929, Amrita, sixteen, moved to Paris to study art at the prestigious École des Beaux-Arts. Paris was the Mecca of modern art at that time. Amrita's maternal uncle, Ervin Baktay, told her parents that their child was a prodigy, and her talent should not be wasted in India. India; Paris was a crucible where a genius was forged. Her parents placed their trust in the journey that awaited her.

Amrita reached Paris in 1930. There, besides learning art, she lived with an untamed spirit, embracing life with an unyielding thirst for experience. She embarked on the limitless journey of the heart, unshackled by convention. Her friendship with the fellow artists was a sky without a horizon, and in its embrace, she moved with freedom, untroubled by the judgments of the world. She 'plunged into everything Paris had to offer'.

Seeing her vibrant circle of artist friends, her mother searched for a suitor for her and got her engaged to Yusuf Ali Khan, a man from an aristocratic family of Uttar Pradesh. However, Amrita's engagement with him was broken after a short while. She painted Yusuf's portrait in 1931.

In the gathering of these artists and poets, she found uncharted realms of her own soul. From these interactions, a current of inspiration emerged, which shaped her art in ways she had not foreseen. She said, 'How can one feel the beauty of a form, the intensity or the subtlety of a colour, the quality of a line, unless she is a sensualist of the eyes?'

She was believed to be friends with Boris Taslitzky, a fellow student at Ecole des Beaux-Arts and two years senior to her. Boris called her 'his first passionate love'. She drew his portrait in 1930. Their letters fell in the hands of Amrita's mother and were burnt in 1938.

Her mother feared she was in a relationship with her art school roommate Marie-Lonise Chassan. She asked Amrita about the nature of her bond with Marie. Her mother's suspicion angered Amrita. She replied to her in February 1934: 'My dear Mummy, do you know that I am of age now? So please do respect me, my dear clever and understanding mother.'

After finishing her studies at École, she set up a studio with Marie and painted her portrait.

Her mother came to know about her meetings with the famed pianist Edith Lang. Amrita was not amused with her mother's concern about her relationship. She told her mother: 'Mother, sexuality cannot be channelised through art and spiritualism. Such superstition is only invented for the brainless.'

She painted *Young Girl* and received a gold medal at the 1933 Paris Salon. She was only nineteen, and by getting this top prize, she became the youngest member of Grand Salon. This painting depicted her sister Indira sitting with a friend named Denise Proutaux.

She painted several nude pictures, such as *Sleeping Woman,* a bold painting of a sleeping young girl, modelled by her sister Indira, in 1932. She produced *The Little Girl in Blue,* a painting of her cousin, in 1934. It was displayed in an exhibition in Mumbai in 2018 and sold at a huge price. She also created self-portraits that showed her 'grappling with her own identity'. She used red colour for lips and garments, suggesting sensuality.

Amrita planned to return to India. Her teacher at Beaux-Arts told her that she would be more creative and successful in the East. She wrote a letter to her parents in 1934: 'Dearest Mummy and Paddy (Papa), ... I have decided to return to India... I wish to return primarily in interest of my artistic development.' She wanted new sources of inspiration.

After five years of study, learning, and fulfilling experiences in Paris, Amrita returned to India, though her father did not want her to leave Europe.

She reached India in December 1934. She said, 'Europe belongs to Picasso, Matisse and Braque and many others. India belongs only to me.' At another place, she said, 'There are such wonderful, such glorious things in India, so many unexploited pictorial possibilities, that it is a pity that so few of us have ever attempted to look for them even (much less interpret them).'

She spent her first few years in her ancestral home at Amritsar, and then she embarked on a cross-country journey. The women in saris and blouses, smiling girls with dimpled cheeks, dusty towns, and village courtyards started to appear on her canvas. She painted *Mother India* in 1935. On seeing the poverty and condition of women, she wanted to be the voice of India's poor. She painted *Group of Three Girls* (1935), a portrait of three women in red and green. She was awarded a gold medal by the Bombay Art Society for this piece of work.

While in India, her journey of discovery and encounters with artists, painters, musicians, and writers continued. And by her mid-twenties, they became familiar with her unconventional spirit.

In 1935, she formed a deep bond with Malcolm Muggeridge, a British journalist at Shimla. Muggeridge was working for the *Calcutta Statesman*. He was ten years older than her, and they came across each other at the Gaiety Theatre in early 1935 in Shimla. She painted his portrait, shaping his image with the quiet echoes of her heart.

She painted his father and called the painting 'Tulsi'. Like her mother, her father was also worried about her, for the path she walked was uncharted.

In 1938, Amrita, twenty-five, decided that she should get married. Her parents were happy that their daughter would have a stable life at last. However, their happiness did not last long when they realized that Amrita had chosen her maternal cousin Victor Egan to marry. Victor, twenty-eight, was a doctor in the Hungarian army, and Amrita and Victor had known each other from childhood. One of the first paintings she had done had been of Victor.

Her parents did not want this marriage to happen, and they opposed her proposal. Marie wanted her daughter to marry someone from an Indian royal family, a man having wealth and privilege. Victor was a youth without experience in medicine. But Amrita's parents had no choice before her insistence.

She left for Hungary in June 1938 and got married to Victor in District VIII of Budapest on 16 July 1938. 'It is a pleasant, trusting relationship and I feel it will continue to be so. We know each other so well!' she wrote to her parents.

After their marriage, they lived in Hungary for about a year. She painted Hungarian rural areas, village churches, peasants, and women. She drew a portrait of Victor Egan in 1939, a parting gift to Egan's family. The Second World War was on the horizon, and a dark cloud was to swallow the whole of Europe. So they decided to board a ship from Hungary to India in 1939.

After the marriage, the couple came to India in July 1938. A studio was built at her house in Shimla to allow her to tap into her creative genius, while she would stay in Amritsar.

However, they finally shifted to Umrao Singh Sher-Gil's ancestral mansion in Saraya village in Gorakhpur District, Uttar Pradesh. Umrao Singh owned a sprawling estate and sugar factories there. Victor accompanied her and worked there at the village hospital, while she absorbed the atmosphere of the East and fed her canvases with raw emotion and vitality.

During this time, she appears to have been sad and melancholic. She wrote a letter to her sister Indira: 'I and Victor are tremendously fond of each other and yet we seem to have nothing, absolutely nothing whatsoever, to say to each other, when we are alone together, we sit by the hour in silence. He begins to yawn and I sink deeper and deeper into a depressed and depressing silence, and we weigh intolerably on each other, till unable to bear it longer. One of us gets up and suggests a game of patience or chess.'

At Saraya, Jawaharlal Nehru came to see her during his tour to Gorakhpur. She was impressed by Nehru, and they began to correspond regularly. She never painted him as she found him to be 'too good looking' to be painted. She came to see off Nehru at the railway station.

At Saraya, she worked continuously, and her canvases were painted with vibrant colours. She painted *Woman and Charpai* in 1940. Her paintings from this period show the influence of Mughal miniatures. After a while, Amrita realized that the estate at Saraya, though comfortable and lavish, did not provide the ambience and the creative fire a painter needed. After all, it was a village, not Paris.

Her melancholy tormented her. She wrote to her sister on 14 March 1941: 'There seems to be elemental forces at work, disturbing, throwing things out of equilibrium. The chaos and darkness of the lives of the individuals, in the wars, earthquakes, floods, all seem to be indefinably interconnected. We are not alone. I see it everywhere.'

Finally, she thought she should shift from there to a happening place. She chose Lahore, a centre of art and culture.

She reached Lahore in September 1941 and rented a house, Ganga Ram Mansions, on the Mall. Victor opened a surgery ward on the ground floor, and Amrita's studio was on the top floor. Lahore was a city of dreamers, poets, and merchants fuelled by raw energy and ambition. She hoped the place would give wings to her ambition and energy. She revived her social life and prepared to show her pictures on 14 December 1941.

From her studio at the house, she saw a milkman with his buffaloes and painted the scene.

However, only about a month later, she felt a pain in her stomach. Her condition worsened. Her husband Victor treated her and called a few doctors to assist him to cure her. But that did not work. Amrita died on 6 December 1941 at the age of twenty-eight. She was cremated on the banks of the river Ravi at Lahore on 7 December 1941. Victor lit the pyre. The couple had no children.

On her death, her father Umrao Singh wrote in a magazine: 'Those fingers which had painted and that brain which had conceived works, receiving inspiration from the deathless spirit, were dissolving into their elements before our eyes.... She had entered the prenatal world at Lahore and death seemed to have conspired with life to release her spirit from its physical chrysalis in the same city.'

Her mother, Marie, accused Victor of murder. Victor did not inform Amrita's parents about her condition during her last days. Marie went into depression after this incident. She tried to kill herself several times, and ultimately, she succeeded in committing suicide with a gun at home in 1948.

Victor returned to Saraya and practised medicine there. He remarried and had children. He retained his portrait with himself but gifted the rest of Amrita's paintings to the Modern Art Gallery, New Delhi. He died in 1997.

14

Marie Curie

Marie Curie was born Maria Sklodowska. At the age of twenty-three, in November 1891, she boarded a train from Warsaw, Poland, and travelled 40 hours to reach Paris. It was winter, and Paris was 1600 km west. Snow had covered much of the railway track, and it was all white as far as her eyes could see. She was a penniless student and was going to Paris for college education. Warsaw University in Poland did not admit women for studies. She travelled in the fourth-class compartment, which meant she carried her own food and a stool to sit.

Marie stayed with her elder sister Bronya, who was studying medicine there. Marie gained admission to the prestigious Sorbonne (University of Paris) in the end of 1891 and rented a garret close to her place of study. She studied science, that is, physics, chemistry, and mathematics. Her life was difficult. She had no money, no access to good food, and not enough clothes to protect herself from the cold in Paris. She studied by day and tutored teenagers in the evenings to earn her livelihood. For her, the first principle was never to let oneself be beaten down by persons or by events.

After three years of labour, she earned her master's degree in physics in the summer of 1893 from the university and then took up new courses and research work in Paris.

While doing research, in the spring of 1894, Marie, twenty-six, met Pierre Curie, thirty-five, the head of the Municipal School of Industrial Physics and Chemistry in Paris. Marie was looking for laboratory space for research work and experimentation. She was investigating the magnetic properties of steel. For her a scientist in his laboratory was a child confronting natural phenomena that impressed him as though they were fairy tales. A Polish physicist working at the Municipal School took her to Pierre and introduced her to him. Marie remembers meeting Pierre for the first time: 'As I entered the room, Pierre Curie was standing in the recess of a French window opening on a balcony. He seemed to me very young, though he was at that time 35 years old.... I was struck by the open expression on his face and by the slight suggestion of detachment in his whole attitude. His speech, rather slow and deliberate, his simplicity, and his smile, at once grave and youthful, inspired confidence.'

Pierre finally found some solution for her requirement. He appointed her at his laboratory as his student, and

Marie was able to begin her research work. He allowed her to use a piezoelectric device that he had invented.

Marie and Pierre grew ever closer. Pierre Curie was a French physicist and an extraordinary scholar. He earned a master's degree in physical sciences at the age of eighteen from the Faculty of Sciences at the Sorbonne. He could not pursue a doctorate immediately after his master's degree because he was short of money. Instead, he worked as a laboratory instructor at the Municipal School in Paris.

Pierre had no interest in women or marriage. He had loved a woman, but she died about fifteen years earlier. After that, he forgot about women and marriage and kept himself busy with studies and research in science. He believed that women were a distraction to scientific and serious work. The women he came across in the campus and the locality where he lived showed no interest in science or studies; thus, he built no relationship with them. However, an interaction with Marie was an exception.

Pierre Curie proposed marriage to Marie. However, she said she was not ready. She wanted to go back to her home to Poland and settle there.

Pierre Curie told her that if living in Paris, where he was settled, was a problem, then he was ready to move with her to Poland. She and the marriage with her was his priority. He was ready to sacrifice his career and go with her to Warsaw, even if that meant leaving a career in physics and teaching French in a school in Poland. But Curie did not budge.

In the summer of 1894, Marie took a train from Paris to Warsaw. At home, she met her family, ate home-cooked food, and felt good being with family members. She looked for an employment opportunity there and tried a faculty position at Kraków University, in Kraków town, about 300 km south of Warsaw. She submitted her degrees and appeared for an interview, but she was not found suitable. She was rejected for being a woman.

Pierre kept pursuing Marie. He told her to return to Paris and do a PhD on magnetism for a better future. There was no reason to be disappointed. Paris would provide her more career opportunities. Discouraged by the development at Warsaw, she agreed to return to Paris by the end of 1894.

Marie was back in Paris. Earlier, she had persuaded Curie to research magnetism. Pierre could not focus on one domain of science and wasted his time researching in several fields simultaneously. Following Marie's advice, he completed his PhD and, in 1895, was awarded a doctorate. After earning his doctorate, he became a professor of physics at the Municipal School. Then in 1900, he joined the Faculty of Sciences at Sorbonne as professor.

After returning from Poland in 1884, Marie married Pierre on 26 July 1895 at Sceaux, a southern suburb of Paris, in a small function. The lady wore a dark blue outfit instead of a bridal gown. She explained: 'I have no dress except the one I wear every day.... If you are going to be kind enough to give me one, please let it be practical and dark so that I can put it on afterwards to go to the laboratory.'

This marriage brought together two talented scientists with complementary minds and personalities. While Pierre was a slow thinker who framed scientific conclusions and cared little for fame, Marie moved quickly from experiments to bold hypotheses. They went for their honeymoon on bicycles to the French countryside.

In 1897, their daughter, Irène, was born, and two years after that, Marie enrolled herself at the Sorbonne for a doctorate in physics. She needed to choose a research project for her dissertation. She chose Becquerel rays for study. The French physicist Henri Becquerel, while looking for X-ray sources, found that uranium compounds emitted weaker rays. Curie decided to search for other substances that emitted these rays. She worked for hours in the poorly ventilated hall in summer and in freezing winter. Pierre understood the significance of Marie's research and started helping her with his expertise. Marie named the element polonium and called this phenomenon radioactivity.

The scientific community and leading scientists recommended the names of Pierre Curie and Henri Becquerel for the Nobel Prize for physics in 1903 for discovering radioactivity. Pierre learnt that Marie had not been nominated with him for the prize, though she was a leading contributor. This perturbed him and he took up the matter with the Swedish Academy of Sciences. He wrote to the members: 'I very much wish to be considered together with Madame Curie with respect to our research on radioactive bodies.' Finally, Marie, along with her husband Pierre and Henri Becquerel, won the prize in 1903. In 1904, Curie's family was blessed with another daughter, Eve.

Marie Curie lost Pierre in a road accident in Paris on 19 April 1906. He was run over by a heavy horse-drawn wagon while walking on a street in Paris. Marie was then thirty-eight. She was deeply distressed, and she became lonely. She wrote about Pierre: 'So perished the hope founded on the wonderful being who thus ceased to be.

In the study room to which he was never to return, the water buttercups he had brought from the country were still fresh.'

Marie had to start life afresh after this loss. She had two young daughters and had to take care of them. She said, 'We must keep our certainty that after the bad days the good times will come again.' On 13 May 1906, the Sorbonne invited her to take up Pierre's academic post. Marie accepted the offer and became the first woman faculty at the Sorbonne. Artists, journalists, and fashionable ladies joined students on 5 November 1906 to hear her lecture.

By the end of 1911, about five years after her husband Pierre died, the forty-three-year-old widow had an affair with Paul Langevin. Langevin, thirty-nine, was a scientist and student of her husband and had obtained his PhD under him. He was serving as a professor of physics at the Collège de France. Marie and Langevin rented a flat near Sorbonne to meet in private. However, rumours of an affair started circulating.

Langevin was a married man and the father of four children. His wife discovered the love letters Marie had written to him; she parcelled them out to the press. One newspaper published the excerpts of a letter Curie had written to him. They portrayed her as a woman who was destroying a home. Langevin did not like his name to be sullied. He challenged the editor of the newspaper, Gustave Tery, for a duel. The two exchanged fists in the fight, but neither was hurt.

The publication of the letters scandalized France. Marie's proximity to Langevin was not just an infatuation. She was thinking of marriage with him and asked him to divorce his wife to marry her. Paul Langevin's status during his romance with the Nobel laureate was that of a married man. However, after the embarrassment, he arranged a legal separation from his wife.

While all this was happening, Marie received a telegram at her home in the evening that she had been conferred a Nobel Prize for the second time, this time for her contribution in chemistry. This award was for the discovery of radium and polonium by her in 1898. She named the new element polonium, for Poland, and radium, for its ability to emit rays.

After the news broke, Svante Arrhenius, a member of the Swedish Academy of Sciences, wrote to Marie Curie, suggesting that she should not come to Stockholm to accept the Nobel Prize until her name was cleared of the scandal.

Curie did not buckle. She replied: 'The prize has been awarded for the discovery of radium and polonium. I believe that there is no connection between my scientific work and the facts of private life. I cannot accept ... that the appreciation of the value of scientific work should be influenced by libel and slander concerning private life.' She told the Nobel committee that she would come to Sweden to accept the prize in 1911. Finally, she went to Stockholm with her sister Bronya and daughter Irène.

The publishing of her private affairs damaged Madame Curie's scintillating reputation. Then during the First World War, she threw herself into humanitarian work and travelled to the French battlefront to teach military doctors how to use X-rays. This won the heart of the people and intelligentsia.

Marie Curie died on 4 July 1934 of leukaemia. Overwork and long-term exposure to radioactive materials destroyed her health. In April 1995, the bodies of Pierre and Marie Curie were moved from their family cemetery and were enshrined in the crypt of the Panthéon in Paris, the national sepulchre for eminent French citizens.

While the relationship between Marie Curie and Paul Langevin could not bloom, Marie's granddaughter Hélène and Langevin's grandson Michel married in 1948.

15

Muhammad Iqbal

In 1907, in London, a woman with an Aligarh connection, Miss Beck, invited the poet Muhammad Iqbal for a dinner party. There he met Atiya Faizi, a twenty-nine-year-old lady, and felt he had met the fairest of all creation.

Atiya was born in Istanbul to an Indian-origin merchant and had earned a scholarship in 1906 to pursue higher studies in England. She was also invited to the party at Miss Beck's apartment. Her father ran a business of cloth and spices in Turkey.

Atiya, enrolled at the Teachers' Training College in London, was a writer and a critic. Iqbal had heard about this modern, pretty-faced woman who wore no veil. He had read her literary works. During the party, while Atiya left him fascinated with her grace and class, Iqbal charmed her with his wit and humour.

The two departed the party with the promise to meet again. Then Iqbal invited her for lunch, and she arrived happily. Iqbal invited her to dinner, and she readily accepted the request. Iqbal got spicy Indian food prepared for her, and she was floored by his gesture. They met in Cambridge, London, and Heidelberg and discussed philosophy, life, music, painting, love, poetry, metaphysics, and history. After lunch and dinner, they went for long walks and picnics, and visited museums and poetry sessions.

However, Iqbal was not free to love Atiya.

In 1893, when he was sixteen, his parents had married him to Karim Bibi, the daughter of an affluent Gujarati physician, Khan Bahadur Ata. Karim joined Iqbal at Sialkot to start a new life, but Iqbal had no place for her in his life. He did not want to solemnize this marriage with her, but his parents gave him no choice. He surrendered but did not open his heart to her.

Karim Bibi spent the first two years of marriage with Iqbal in Sialkot with ups and downs. Iqbal was then doing an FA course (equivalent to plus two).

Thereafter, Iqbal moved to Lahore in 1897 for graduation. The gap between the couple widened. Then he went to Europe in 1905 to study philosophy at Cambridge and law at London's Lincoln Inn. Iqbal had, by then, established himself as a poet of repute in India. His words and couplets moved millions of hearts.

Karim Bibi, spurned by her husband, went to her parents in Gujarat. She would feel less lonely in her father's house.

Their children, Miraj Begum and Aftab Iqbal, accompanied Karim Bibi and held her spirit aloft.

In Europe, Atiya Faizi lit up Iqbal's life. She fitted Iqbal's conception of a woman and a partner. However, like all good things, Iqbal's time with Atiya and his study period in England and Germany came to an end. Now it was time for him to return home. In 1908, Iqbal landed in Delhi at the age of thirty-one. He remembered his days in Europe as the best days of his life.

In India, Atiya Faizi occupied his mind all the time. The beauteous flame had burnt the poetic genius. He wanted Atiya Faizi to become his life partner. However, he could not propose marriage to her, nor did he know what was on her mind.

Social life in Sialkot and Lahore and his wife, bound in tradition and complexity, intensified his disenchantment with life. During this time, Atiya wrote letters filled with fragrance of unshared wishes to Iqbal , and the letters kept the embers of separation alive and ruined any possibility of reconciliation between Iqbal and Karim Bibi. Ironically, Atiya gave him tips on how to deal with challenges in life. In return, Iqbal told her about his longing for true, romantic love. He told her about his wife: 'I am quite willing to support her, but I am not prepared to make my life miserable by keeping her with me.'

Then, Iqbal, convinced that he would not be able to move the cart along with his wife, decided to divorce Karim Bibi, and in 1910, he separated from her. Now, he looked for a new partner.

In 1910, Iqbal saw the photograph of nineteen-year-old belle Sardar Begum with the help of his clerk. Sardar Begum was a poor orphan who was brought up by her aunt in Mochi Darwaza of the walled city of Lahore. Blossoming Sardar Begum was literate but without school education. Her brother sold carpets, slung over his shoulders, in the streets of the city.

Iqbal was instantly drawn to the photo. His mother said she had no objection to that proposal. The nikah (marriage ceremony) was performed by a maulvi (priest) in the winter of 1910, and the girl was to come to Iqbal's house in Lahore to start a new life.

Then everything went topsy-turvy. A series of letters landed at Iqbal's house and said that Sardar Begum had affairs with men and her chastity was doubtful. Iqbal was scandalized. He did not know what was happening.

He asked his friends and relatives what to do. He said he wanted to repudiate the marriage as it was a bad choice. They told him to hang on, but Iqbal did not want to waste time on nonsense. As the girl's character was sullied, he felt there was no point wasting time on her. He decided to break off the marriage with Sardar Begum and marry another woman.

Iqbal's love interest, Atiya Faizi, on the other hand, kept travelling to new destinations. Iqbal did not figure in her scheme of things. She married a Christian painter named Samuel Rahmin in 1912, who took the name Rahmin Faizi after his marriage with her. She started her life with her husband and lost contact with the man in whose heart she had stirred a storm. She met the author of 'Saare jahan se achha' again much later in Lahore, but by then, the passion in Iqbal's life had ebbed. The circumstances of life had broken his spirit.

With the help of a friend, Muhammad Iqbal came to know about a girl called Mukhtar Begum from a rich Kashmiri family in Ludhiana. Iqbal's sister went to see Mukhtar Begum at the city and told Iqbal that the girl was no less than a fairy. Iqbal decided to wed her. He married Mukhtar in 1914 and brought her to his house in the Anarkali locality in Lahore. However, when the new bride arrived at his home, Iqbal realized he had been deceived. The lady he married was not the one his sister had seen and approved. This Mukhtar Begum was an orphaned niece of a friend and looked less than ordinary. Iqbal decided to bear the deceit and move ahead.

Then Iqbal came to know about the source of the letters on Sardar Begum's character. A Lahore-based lawyer, Nabi Bakhsh, who wanted Sardar Begum to marry his son had spread the malice. Iqbal's friends also told him that the allegations against the girl's character were unfounded.

Poor Sardar Begum had suffered the ignominy for a long time. She wrote to Iqbal, 'I am married to you now and I cannot imagine another nikah with another man. I will spend my entire life rejected like this and will put you on trial in the court of God on the day of judgement.' A man of such standing and a poet who talked of lofty things, such as winds of the heavens, running brooks, the light in the heart, and the secrets of the universe, had judged the enchanting lady based on street gossip and wild rumours.

Iqbal realized he had been unjust to Sardar Begum. He told his wife Mukhtar Begum how he had abandoned a poor, homeless young woman after promising her a new life. Mukhtar Begum said there was no need to worry. She would welcome Sardar Begum if she was brought home.

Iqbal felt this was an opportunity to undo his mistake. He went through a nikah one more time with Sardar Begum four years after the first one and brought the girl to his home. She lived with Mukhtar Begum in peace at the poet's house at Anarkali.

In 1924, Sardar Begum gave birth to a son, Javed Iqbal, who later became a judge of the Pakistan Supreme Court. However, the other wife, Mukhtar Begum, died along with the first baby during childbirth in 1924 after ten years of marriage.

Love between Iqbal and Sardar Begum faded with time. Sardar Begum saw that though Iqbal had earned repute as a poet and philosopher, he was a failure as a husband. He did not even earn enough money to get her a decent house and kept himself busy writing poetry sitting on a charpoy.

Sardar Begum died in 1935 after a prolonged illness and was buried in Lahore. Iqbal hired a German governess for their son Javed and daughter Muneera to teach and take care of them. The children called the lady Aunt Doris. She stayed with Muhammad Iqbal's family and took care of his children.

Iqbal died in 1938 at the age of sixty from a throat illness and was buried near Badshahi Mosque built in Lahore. Atiya came to see his grave, built in marble stone with tulips in relief. She lit incense sticks and prayed for the peace of his soul.

16

Pelé (Edson Arantes do Nascimento)

The football superstar Pele was born Edson Arantes do Nascimento in Três Corações, Brazil, on 23 October 1940. During his childhood, he played the game barefoot with rags rolled into a ball. He was given the nickname 'Pelé' in school when he kept calling a soccer player named Bile 'Pelé'. He signed his first professional contract with Santos Club of Santos city in Brazil at the age of fifteen.

Pelé is one of the greatest soccer players. He earned the nickname O Rei ('the king' in Portuguese) after he won his first FIFA World Cup as part of Brazil's national team in Sweden in 1958. He travelled on a plane for the first time for this match. He scored two goals in the final match, and his team won the world cup.

After the 1958 World Cup, he led his country in the 1962 and the 1970 World Cup tournaments, both times Brazil coming out on top. In the 1966 tournament, he was injured during a match, and Brazil failed to make any breakthrough.

Pelé had multiple marriages and affairs with women. When he was seventeen, in 1958, he came across nineteen-year-old Rosemeri Cholbi during a women's basketball match. Pelé was to play a match against the Corinthians team the next day. Rosemeri told him, 'Don't beat Corinthians too badly tomorrow.'

Pelé was floored by her beauty. He says, 'I kept watching her, looking at her lovely brown hair, thinking what a beautiful girl she was.'

Pelé returned with his friends to the changing room but kept thinking about her. Rosemeri worked in a shop as an assistant. She was a White woman from the Santos area and he a Black male. She did not like football but recognized Pelé as he was a football star.

He went to her house one day and met her parents, who were friendly to him. Her father, Guilherme Cholbi, worked at the Santos docks and was a supporter of his football team (Santos). One day, Pelé cajoled her into going to a movie. He joined her in the theatre when the lights were off and sat next to her. He has said about that experience: 'What an amazing feeling to be near her! Despite the very restricted nature of our relationship, I knew how I felt, and I started to think about the day when we could get married.'

In 1965, he thought he should get married to her. He told her he was going to ask her father's permission. He went out on his fishing boat with her father and told him that he wanted to marry his daughter. Her father consulted his wife and gave him the go-ahead. They married on 1 February 1966. Pelé was then the heartthrob of the nation.

After the marriage ceremony, the couple went to Europe for their honeymoon. They travelled to France, Switzerland, Austria, and Italy. Pelé was happy marrying his sweetheart: 'I felt like all the pieces of my life were in place.'

Their first child, Kelly Christina, was born in January 1967, and their son, Edinho, was born on 27 August 1970.

During the birth of their third child, Jennifer, in 1978, Pelé was not present with Rose to support her. She became distraught and told him that she would not accept his perpetual absence for commercials and meetings. She said she wanted a divorce. Finally, they announced a separation after twelve years of marriage. Pelé expressed his regrets, saying that marriage with Rosemeri at the age of twenty-six was too early.

Two years into his marriage with Rosemeri, Pelé met a sports journalist named Lenita Kurtz and started dating her. The woman was a rose in full bloom. She covered Santos Futebol Clube, the club for which Pelé played, for her newspaper. Kurtz was born in 1940 and came from the place where Pelé was born. Her relationship with Pelé became intimate, and in 1968, a daughter, Flavia Christina, was born out of this relationship. Because the girl was born outside wedlock, Pelé did not acknowledge the child as his daughter till 2002. However, when Pelé's mother saw the baby girl, she immediately recognized her as her son's child. Later, Lenita got married and maintained her relationship with Pelé as a friend.

Rosemeri knew about his extramarital relationships but tolerated him. About such relationships, Pelé has said, 'My first wife, my first girlfriend, knew about it.' Pelé understood that being his wife was difficult for Rosemari. He had to travel a lot for games and commercial and advertising projects, and meeting and working with new, gorgeous women was part of the work.

The couple bought a house in New York, USA, in 1975 and shifted there from Brazil. Rosemeri maintained a distance from him and lived more or less the life of a separated woman. However, when her anger and frustration subsided, she entertained him, sat with him, chatted with him, and exchanged stories with him. But at last, she realized that she could not carry the burden of the relationship any longer with a man who was not trustworthy in the relationship. She concluded: 'I should snap ties with him. Permanently.' In 1982, the couple broke off.

Pelé also waited for this relationship to end. He said, 'The passion one feels when one is madly in love with someone was not there.'

Pelé, twenty-nine, played the 1970 World Cup and scored the opening goal against Italy in the final match in Mexico. Brazil won the World Cup. This was his last and final international game. He retired from Brazilian soccer in 1974 at the age of thirty-four after playing for eighteen years. After retirement from football, he became busy with commercial offers and advertisements. His star value was at its peak.

While still married to Rosemeri Cholbi, Pelé, forty, had an affair with a seventeen-year-old model of German ancestry named Maria da Graca Xuxa. The relationship started in 1981 and continued till 1986.

Pelé crossed Maria's path when he visited a studio of *Manchete* magazine for a photo shoot with four models. Maria was one of them. The photo was to be used by the magazine for the cover page. When Pelé saw Maria, he was melted by the power of her gaze, and he immediately invited her for dinner and a date.

She told him, 'Sir, I cannot come. I am a minor and I live far away from here. I have to go home early.'

Then Pelé called her father and said, 'Sir, would you mind if Maria came with me for dinner tonight?' Pelé was a superstar, and an invitation from him for dinner was a privilege one could not have rejected. Maria's father permitted her to go with him.

Maria remembers his encounter with Pelé: 'I was already known as a sex symbol, and I was actually a virgin.... I would come home crying and tell my mom that I wanted to lose my virginity. She would say, "Don't worry, the right time will come." I wanted to lose my virginity right away....

Maria admitted that her relationship with Pelé was not easy. He was in a relationship with other women when he was dating Maria.

She became disenchanted with Pelé. 'I said: "Why am I doing this with a guy who is a lot older than I am?" I wasn't sure about the relationship, but he insisted. He sent flowers to my mother, chatted with my dad. I was with him from 17 to 23. It was six years.'

Then the relationship with Xuxa was over in 1986. The love that once set their souls aflame was gone from their relationship. The model married a motor-racing champion.

Pelé moved and met Selma Fonseca, a writer who was working with a reputed magazine. Pelé first met her in 1989 when she was twenty-three and he fifty. Selma said this about their relationship: 'We (met) in NYC.... After a long courtship we dated for nine months.... He wanted to get married but, because of various circumstances, I didn't. But he was loving, fun, a gentleman, always very grateful for his success and generous. He was happy to sign autographs, take photos and hug his fans, it was awesome to see how he took the time for everyone.'

In 1988, Queen Elizabeth II of England awarded him honorary knighthood at Buckingham Palace. He also became a commentator for the World Cup in France.

In 1991, Sandra Machado, a twenty-six-year-old woman, went to the civil court of São Paulo, claiming that the soccer superstar Pelé was her father but he refused to take responsibility for her. She prayed to the court to establish that Pelé was her father and get her all the benefits of being his daughter.

Sandra was Pelé's daughter from his relationship with his house help Anisia Machado. He had an affair with her in 1963. A year into the relationship, Anisia gave birth to Sandra in 1964. Anisia did not tell Sandra about her father or her name for some years, but later, she revealed to her that she was born out of her relationship with the legendary footballer. But Pelé did not recognize the girl as his daughter.

When Pelé came to know about the litigation, he rejected the young woman's claim as a tissue of lies. Sandra told him, 'Why don't you give your DNA sample to settle this issue forever?'

'What nonsense? Should I give a sample for a test for anyone claiming to be my blood?' said Pelé.

Sandra wanted to pressurize Pelé. She contested an election for city council in Santos, where Pelé's old team was located. She told the world that she was the daughter of the legend Pelé, but he refused to accept her. At that time, in 1994, the United Nations had appointed Pelé as UNESCO Goodwill Ambassador, and in 1995, he joined the government of Brazil as the minister for sports. Before that, in 1992, the United Nations appointed him ambassador for ecology and the environment.

The civil court, on Sandra's repeated requests, ordered a DNA test for paternity and directed Pelé to give his DNA sample. Pelé ran out of options and had to comply with the court's order in 1993. The forensic report on the DNA samples came after three years in 1996 and established that Sandra was his child. She could use the surname Nascimento.

Sandra continued to fight for her rights and for being recognized as Pelé's daughter. She wrote a book, *The Daughter the King Didn't Want*, in 1999. Pelé was known as the king of football. The book hurt the superstar.

In 2001, she filed a suit to the same civil court in Sao Paulo, saying that she did not enjoy the emotional and financial support his other children did. Therefore, Pelé must give her compensation. However, the court rejected her plea.

In 1994, Pelé married Assíria Lemos Seixas, who became his second wife.

Born in 1960 in Brazil, Assíria is a gospel singer, songwriter, and pastor. She studied music at the State

University of Londrina and started her career in the 1980s. Pelé met her in New York in 1985. She was then married. He spent time with her. By the late 1980s, her marriage broke up, and she started a relationship with Pelé. They got married in Las Vegas. Pelé loved her voice when she sang gospel songs.

She became pregnant with twins, Joshua and Celeste, and gave birth to them on 28 September 1996.

In 2000, the world football governing body, FIFA, named him and Diego Maradona player of the century. In 2005, Pelé suffered health problems. He underwent eye surgery, had a hip replacement, and was hospitalized for a urinary tract infection. On the other hand, Pelé's relationship with Assíria did not last long, and they parted ways in 2008.

More than seven years after divorce, Pelé married Marcia Aoki, a forty-two-year-old Japanese Brazilian entrepreneur, in 2016. Pelé was then seventy-three. The two had met in the 1980s at a party in New York City when she was a teenager. Thereafter, she reunited with him in 2008, and they started a relationship in 2010. They visited each other's places, exchanged gifts, and spent time together. Finally, they got married at a resort near Sao Paulo in 2016.

Marcia divorced her husband in 2008. She owned a business that imported and exported catering equipment. Pelé had no children from this marriage. He described her in an interview as 'the last great passion of my life'.

In September 2021, Pelé was diagnosed with cancer by the doctors of Hospital Israelita Albert Einstein at Sao Paulo, and he died there on 22 December 2022 at the age of 82. His coffin, draped in the Brazilian flag, was carried through the streets of Santos, and the body was buried in a cemetery in Santos.

17

Albert Einstein

In 1896, seventeen-year-old Albert Einstein (1879–1955), was enrolled for a four-year diploma course for teacher's training in the physics-mathematics section of the Polytechnic Institute (now ETH) at Zurich in Switzerland.

Mileva Maric, a twenty-one-year-old woman from Serbia, was also enrolled there for a course in teaching. Born in 1875, she was the daughter of a wealthy father who was an educationist and a member of parliament in Serbia. Her mother was an advocate of women's education, and she sent her daughter to Switzerland for higher studies against the existing convention.

Einstein and Mileva interacted closely, read physics books together, and wondered over the mysteries of nature. Both were bright students, and their interaction and friendship blossomed into a deep romantic relationship. They went to Lake Como in Italy in the spring of 1901 for an outing. They talked there about science, philosophy, and their dreams.

Einstein was born in Ulm, a town in Germany, on 14 March 1879. His father, Hermann Einstein, was a salesman and engineer, and his mother, Pauline Koch, was an educated woman with a love for the arts and the piano. She introduced Einstein to piano at the age of five.

By the end of 1900, Einstein got the diploma from the institute for a career as a teacher. After the course, three men of his class got the position of assistant at the institute, but Einstein did not get any job, and Mileva Maric failed the exam.

Perhaps the romantic affair affected Mileva's academic performance. She sat for the exam in 1899, one year later than the others in her group. Then she became pregnant after a short holiday at Lake Como in 1901, and her dream of a career in academics devolved into a nightmare.

She took her second and last attempt at the exam in July 1901. This time, also their teacher, Prof. Weber, failed her. After this disaster, she left the institute and went to Novi Sad, a city in Serbia, where she gave birth to her daughter, Lieserl, in January 1902.

Mileva Maric persuaded Einstein to marry her. Einstein said they should wait a bit as he did not have a job. Einstein's father also insisted that he should find a job before marriage.

Then a breakthrough came in Einstein's life. He got a job at the patent office in Bern in December 1901 with the intervention of his friend's father.

Einstein's father permitted him to marry Mileva, but his mother objected to the proposal. She thought Mileva Maric was 'too old' and 'physically defective'. Anyway, Einstein, twenty-three, tied the knot with Mileva at Bern on 6 January 1903. On 14 May 1904, their son, Hans Albert, was born.

In a letter to Mileva Maric, Einstein called her a 'creature who is my equal and who is as strong and independent as I am'.

Einstein completed his two famous essays, which later made him a global superstar of science and brought about major breakthroughs in the way we understood light, gravity, and the universe, in 1905 when he worked at the patent office. The papers included his 24-page doctoral dissertation on the photoelectric effect, Brownian motion, special theory of relativity, and the equivalence of mass and energy. The year 1905 is celebrated as an annus mirabilis, year of miracle, for the discipline of physics.

Some experts suggest that Mileva was Einstein's collaborator and equal in intelligence. After marriage, the couple lived in Bern, but Mileva was not happy with Einstein. He was busy with his work and spared no time for her. She said, 'He lives only for science. We are unimportant to him and take second place.'

While Mileva was pregnant with their second son, Eduard, in 1910, Einstein wrote to his earlier muse Marie Winteler: 'I think of you in heartfelt love every spare minute and am so unhappy as only a man can be.'

Marie Winteler, born in 1877, was Einstein's first love. In 1895, while he was studying at the Argovian Cantonal School at Aarau town in Switzerland, he stayed with the Winteler family. Marie was the daughter of the landlord and was two years older than him. Marie, with grey-blue eyes and short golden hair, fascinated him, and they started dating. They bantered and kissed, sitting on the banks of the Aare River.

However, in 1897, Einstein wrote a letter to her from Zürich and told her he could not carry the relationship any further as he needed to focus on his studies. That ended the relationship and left Marie heart broken. Later, in 1910, she married Paul Winteler, a teacher. However, Einstein did not forget beautiful Marie. He kept up correspondence with her, and in 1909, he wrote to her, 'I continue to live with the memory of the few hours in which miserly fortune brought you to me.'

Einstein lived with Mileva and his son, Hans Albert, in Bern until 1909. After a short stay in neighbouring countries, he returned to Zurich in 1912 and got the job of a professor at his alma mater. Their second son, Eduard, was born in Zurich on 28 July 1910.

In 1913, the physicist Max Planck called him to Germany's capital, Berlin, to promote Einstein's career and make him join the Kaiser Wilhelm Institute for Physics. It was a good offer, and Einstein agreed to report at the reputed academic institute. Mileva, however, did not like to leave Bern, and she was distressed by this development. Nevertheless, the whole family, including their two sons, shifted to Berlin. In those years, Einstein was also busy with the complexities of the general theory of relativity.

Then his marriage entered a turbulent phase after 1912 as Einstein encountered his cousin Elsa Löwenthal in the spring of 1912 and felt attracted to her.

Einstein's attraction to Elsa disturbed the introverted and insecure Mileva. She told Einstein that he would not live in peace if he dumped her. Einstein conveyed to her that he was doing nothing wrong, and she should not disturb his study of the secrets of science. He gave her a set of rules to follow if she wanted to live as his wife.

However, Mileva was not ready to accept his liaison with Elsa. She left Einstein in Berlin in the summer of 1914 and returned to Zurich with their sons. Einstein went to the railway station to say goodbye to his family. When the train was to depart, he cried.

Now Einstein was alone at home. This separation was to become a permanent one. He sent about half of his salary to his wife and sons for maintenance. In 1914, he requested a divorce from Marie, but she told him she would not divorce him at any cost. This complicated the situation.

The stress and strain continued in the relationship. Mileva realized that there was no point in dragging the relationship on when Einstein was seriously looking forward to ending it. Finally, the couple divorced on 14 February 1919. Mileva set a condition for the divorce that if Albert Einstein received the Nobel Prize, the prize money should come to her for the use of their sons. Einstein agreed to the proposal, and the relationship ended. After ten years of marriage, they were no longer wife and husband.

Elsa Löwenthal, whose relationship with Einstein had rattled Mileva, was a thirty-six-year-old, blue-eyed, fair cousin of the physicist's. Einstein's and Elsa's mothers were sisters. While in Berlin in April 1912 for official work, he had come to visit his uncle Rudolf, Elsa's father. He met the lady there after a long time. The two took a trip to the forested Wannsee Lake near Berlin. Thereafter, they started a secret correspondence. They were supposed to burn each other's letters after reading. At that time, Einstein taught at a university in Prague.

Then it became obvious to the world that the physicist was in a relationship with Elsa. Elsa's parents told Einstein that he should marry their daughter without a delay. However, Einstein was in no hurry to marry her. Perhaps, he wanted the woman as no more than a romantic partner.

Elsa had been married to Max Löwenthal, and she had three children from him. She divorced Max in May 1908 and moved with her two daughters, Ilse and Margot, to an apartment in Berlin. She was a regular part of the high society of Berlin and had artists, musicians, writers, and journalists as her friends.

In 1915, in a letter, Einstein regretted the pressure put on him for the marriage. He wrote: 'The attempts to force me into marriage comes from my cousin's parents and is mainly attributable to vanity, though moral prejudice … plays a part.' Finally, Einstein relented. He obtained a divorce from Mileva to marry Elsa Löwenthal.

They were married in 1919, the year he divorced Mileva. Einstein kept meeting his sons and remained concerned with their future. He took Hans sailing on Lake Constance at the foot of the Alps. His younger son, Eduard, had a nervous breakdown when he reached university for study and was diagnosed as schizophrenic. Einstein often played violin with Eduard.

While life was sailing smoothly with Elsa, Einstein looked for a private secretary in 1923. Earlier, his stepdaughter Ilse had worked as his secretary. But Ilse fell ill. A young woman of twenty-three, Betty Neumann, replaced her. She was a native of Austria and had come to Einstein's friend Hans Mühsam's home in Berlin for a holiday. Hans was her uncle.

Betty offered her services to the world-famous physicist. She was awed by his personality and fame. Einstein, on the other hand, was attracted by her beauty, youth, and grace. He became close to her after a few months.

Soon Elsa learnt about their relationship. In the beginning, it hurt her, but she became reconciled to the reality. She remained loyal and caring towards Einstein and was his pillar of strength. She realized that he was a genius and should be above ordinary standards. She accepted him as he was and gave her full care and respect.

Einstein's relationship with Betty became a tangled web. In a letter to Neumann, he fantasized about living with her and Elsa together in a big house. Neumann dismissed the idea. Then he said she had more appreciation 'for the difficulties of triangular geometry than he'.

Betty's uncle and her parents also came to know about her deep association with Einstein. She was engaged to be married to a middle-aged man in December 1923. However, her engagement was broken. Einstein could not bring himself to divorce Elsa. He was also aware of the age difference between them. Finally, they realized that they could not carry on with the relationship anymore. Einstein decided to break it off. By the end of 1924, they terminated their contact, and Betty returned from Berlin to her parent's place in Austria.

In 1933, Einstein migrated to the USA. Before that, he became friends with several women, including Austrian blonde Margarete Lebach, a rich businesswoman Estella Katzenellenbogen, and a wealthy Jewish widow Toni Mendel. He was also friends with a Berlin socialite, Ethel

Michanowski. The ladies socialized frequently with Einstein and went for sailing, read books, and attended concerts with him.

In a letter to his stepdaughter Margot in 1931, he complained that Ethel Michanowski followed him to England, and her pursuit of him was getting out of control. Ethel was a friend of Margot's. His wife, Elsa, came to know about his involvement with Ethel. Einstein became defensive and said, 'One should do what one enjoys, and not harm anyone else.' In another letter to his stepdaughter Margot, he wrote that out of all the women, he was attached to the Austrian blonde Margarete Lebach, who was harmless and decent.

During that period in 1924, he wrote to Mileva: 'You should enjoy what life has given you—like the wonderful children, the house, and that you are not married to me anymore.'

In 1933, Einstein and Elsa migrated from Berlin to New Jersey in the USA owing to the rise of the Nazi Party in Germany. Here, Elsa developed serious health problems and died in 1936. Her death made the days tough for Einstein, but he kept himself busy with his work.

Mileva Maric died in 1948 at the age of seventy-two in Zürich after suffering a stroke. She was buried there in a cemetery.

On 17 April 1955, Einstein experienced bleeding in his stomach. He refused surgery, saying, 'I want to go when I want. It is tasteless to prolong life artificially. I have done my share; it is time to go. I will do it elegantly.' He died the next day on 18 April 1955 at a hospital at Princeton, New Jersey, at the age of seventy-six. Until the last moment, he was busy working on the problems of science.

18

Fyodor Dostoyevsky

Fyodor Dostoyevsky, the famous 19th-century Russian writer, was released from a Siberian labour camp on 14 February 1854 after four years of hard labour. He was thrown there for being part of a group of radicals, socialist writers, and intellectuals during the reign of Emperor Nicholas I.

The emperor's men had sentenced him to be executed by a firing squad. However, just when the firing squad raised their rifles to fire at his breast, a message of reprieve arrived. As an alternative to death, Dostoyevsky was to perform forced labour for four years in a camp at Omsk in Siberia.

However, Dostoyevsky had no relief after the term ended. He was forced to serve in the Siberian army corps of the 7th Line Battalion in Semipalatinsk, a city in eastern Kazakhstan, as a soldier. There, he encountered Alexander Isaev and his wife, Marya Isaeva, while tutoring children.

Marya Isaeva was 'blond, pretty, highly intelligent'. They had a young son. Alexander had been a schoolteacher and a custom official. He spent his time drinking with urchins in the tavern of Semipalatinsk. He neglected his wife and son.

Marya's beauty and youth captured the author's heart. A romance blossomed between the two. However, their good days were cut short when Marya's husband was transferred to Kuznetsk, a town in the Siberian wilderness. She moved with her husband and left the novelist's heart wounded. Dostoyevsky eased his heart by writing letters to her.

In one letter, Dostoyevsky wrote: 'Is mere separation to alter us? I believe not; for the parting from you, my dear friends, lies so heavily upon me that alone I can judge how very much I cling to you.'

In another letter, he wrote, 'The simple fact that a woman held out her hand to me has constituted a new epoch in my life.... Even the best of men is nothing more than a blockhead. The heart of a woman, her compassion, her interest, the infinite goodness—these are irreplaceable. I found all that in you.'

She wrote to him about her loneliness, the misconduct of her alcoholic husband, the absence of love's sweet solace, and the extremity of the climate.

Marya's husband died in the summer of 1855. Now the lady was free, and Dostoyevsky could offer to marry her. He travelled 2000 km west on a train from Semipalatinsk to meet Marya at Kuznetsk. But to his disappointment, Marya had fallen in love with a young schoolteacher. Dostoyevsky still pursued her and told her to come to him.

He loved her dearly. His friends mediated between the two. Betrayed by Marya, he had an epileptic attack, and he told her that he would die if she did not marry him. Through persistent endeavour, Dostoyevsky at last won her heart and he, aged thirty-six, married her at a church in a Siberian village in Kuznetsk on 6 February 1857. An ex-lover of his bride, Vegunov, stood as a witness to their marriage. They went for a honeymoon to Semipalatinsk.

After marriage, he authored *The Insulted and Injured* in 1860. He depicted himself in this work as an author helplessly infatuated with a young girl who is in love with an aristocrat.

Troubles in their relationship started immediately after the marriage, and they could not enjoy matrimonial bliss. Dostoyevsky suffered from seizures and epileptic attacks. When Marya saw the shrieks, fainting fits, the convulsive movements of the limbs, and the foaming at the mouth, she was devastated. Their relationship came to a breaking point.

He wrote to a friend: 'If you wish to know what is up with me, what can I tell you? I have burdened myself with the cares of a family and I pull them along.'

Dostoyevsky had his first epileptic attack while he was serving the sentence in the Siberian prison. He spent time in confinement, his hands and feet shackled. He was stuffed in a cell with 200 convicts who had only one washroom to use. The first epileptic attack paralysed him there and had his hands trembling with fever every night.

Dostoyevsky changed himself and behaved like a friend to his wife to save their marriage. However, the strain continued building in their relationship. Marya died of tuberculosis in April 1864.

While married to Marya, Dostoyevsky, forty, met twenty-one-year-old Apollinaria Suslova during one of his public readings in St Petersburg in 1861. He was now a famous and established author in the country and was being ranked in the league of authors like Leo Tolstoy. Apollinaria was an aspiring writer and an attractive woman. 'She was a thin graceful 22-year-old beauty with blue eyes and a thick mass of gorgeous red hair.' She brought her writings to Dostoyevsky and took his advice on how to write well. She was also awed by his stature. She wrote a letter to him, revealing her feelings for him. Dostoyevsky also fell for her beauty and elegance in a few meetings. Then their relationship became intimate, and Apollinaria had her 'first and deepest amorous relation' with Dostoyevsky.

However, when Apollinaria was tangled with the author in love's sweet heat, she demanded that he should divorce his wife, Marya. Dostoyevsky could not immediately meet her request as his wife was sick with tuberculosis. This made the lady nasty and rambunctious.

Dostoyevsky and Apollinaria went on a secret tour to Europe from August 1862 to late 1863. They had a long period of romance, fights, and sightseeing. Dostoyevsky continued writing novels and threw himself into gambling. But while in Paris, in the spring of 1863, she was smitten by Salvador, a medical student from Spain. She roamed around with the new friend, sipped red wine, danced with him at the bar, and climbed snowy mountains. Dostoyevsky was broken. He also lost money in roulette and returned to Russia by the end of 1863 when he was penniless.

Back from Russia, Dostoyevsky exchanged letters with her and tried to win her back. He wrote to Apollinaria's sister, 'I still love her, I love her very much.' Soon, Apollinaria was forsaken by her Spanish admirer and was staring at a bleak future.

Dostoyevsky again met her in Europe, but her passion for Dostoyevsky had waned. She became friendly with the woman novelist Evgenia Tur and other luminaries. She travelled from cities to cities in France and Switzerland.

Finding Apollinaria whimsical, Dostoyevsky became friends with two women, Martha Brown and Anna Korvin-Krukovskaya, and exchanged letters with them.

Martha Brown was living with Peter Gorsky, a contributor to the *Epoch* magazine, which Dostoyevsky had founded. She wrote letters to Dostoyevsky during 1864–1865. She was a daughter of a landowning family and had toured most of western Europe in the company of various men. She had become friends with a man named Flemming, through whom she met Gorsky, a retired military officer. Gorsky had literary ambitions, and he published his work in *Epoch*. She met Dostoyevsky one day at the office of *Epoch* when she had come there with Gorsky. Martha was not happy with Gorsky as he was an alcoholic and had made her life miserable.

Dostoyevsky entrusted Martha with proofreading and translation work at the *Epoch* office. She finally left Gorsky because of his misbehaviour and suggested in a letter to Dostoyevsky that she wanted to be friends with him. Dostoyevsky published his book *Notes from Underground* during this period.

At the same time, Dostoyevsky, forty-five, met Anna Korvin-Krukovskaya, twenty-two. She wrote short stories, which were published in the journal he was editing. She was the daughter of a retired lieutenant general who lived at Palibino at the Polish–Russian border. On 22 February 1865, she wrote to Dostoyevsky that her father would like to receive him at her home in Petersburg. Dostoyevsky asked details about her and her family members in a letter.

Anna's family members travelled to Petersburg for a meeting with Dostoyevsky in 1865. Dostoyevsky came to their place. Anna's mother was also present there. The meeting did not go as per Dostoyevsky's expectations. Several ladies from Anna's family remained present all the time near the two. Dostoyevsky wanted free time to interact with the lady, but that did not happen. He left the place in disgust within half an hour. He visited Anna again, and this time, the two talked as if they were old friends. No one, except Anna's sister Sofya, was around. He talked about his past and a novel that he intended to write.

After the meeting, Anna told her sister that she liked Dostoyevsky, but she did not intend to marry him. She said the interaction with him showed that Dostoyevsky needed a woman who would be entirely submissive to his will. She would not fit the bill. Anna then, in the mid-1870s, married a French radical and revolutionary, Charles Victor.

Dostoyevsky's wife, Marya, died in 1864, and he was single. The same year, his brother Mikhail, who helped him in publication work, also died. Dostoyevsky still pursued Apollinaria Suslova and looked for a stable relationship with her. He requested her to marry him. However, she said, 'Sir, I no longer love you. Please look for someone else.' She wrote in her diary: 'Today Dostoyevsky was here, and we argued and contradicted each other all the time.' Both of them were in the Russian city of St Petersburg, and it was November 1865. Dostoyevsky now found Apollinaria more difficult to handle; she was a changed woman.

Dostoyevsky later said she was 'a sick selfish woman', whose 'selfishness and self-esteem were colossal'. That time, he was working on his masterpiece, *Crime and Punishment*, the first of his great novels. This work was to become one of the greatest novels of the 19th century. He secluded himself to concentrate on this book, while Apollinaria wanted him to spend time with her.

Finally, rejecting Dostoyevsky, she married a literary fan of Dostoyevsky's in 1880 after a courtship.

Dostoyevsky was always short of money and uncomfortable under the burden of credit. Gambling was an effort to get easy money to pay the creditors who were chasing him through court notices.

In 1866, he entered into a contract with a publisher named Feodor Stellovsky. As per the terms of the contract, Dostoyevsky was to give him a 160-page-long novel by 1 November 1866 for some amount of money. It was already the beginning of October 1866, and he had just a month to finish the work. If he failed, Stellovsky would get the right to publish whatever Dostoyevsky would write over the next nine years without paying him any royalty. Dostoyevsky was already busy writing *Crime and Punishment*, which was being published serially. His eyes were under strain because of constant reading and writing, and he required an assistant.

To meet the deadline, Dostoyevsky hired a stenographer, Anna Snitkina, twenty, through a professor of stenography who taught this lady. Dostoyevsky was then forty-five and was widowered.

Anna Snitkina came to Dostoyevsky on 4 October 1866 to take dictation for his book *The Gambler*. She was an attractive young lady from a well-to-do family. She had been well educated in the Jesuit School at Petersburg and had graduated from a secondary school in 1864. She was happy to get the job and thought that she would earn money by her own labour and become an independent woman.

She had heard of Dostoyevsky from her father, who had died recently. He interviewed the lady and started the dictation session.

Besides dictation, Dostoyevsky chatted with her like a friend and told her unhappy incidents from his past. She was touched by his story. Dostoyevsky also told her he liked her; she was a dream of his yearning heart. Anna noted in her diary about the interaction with the author: 'This man, to all appearances withdrawn and severe, was telling me of his past life in such detail, so openly and naturally, that I couldn't help feeling amazed.'.

One day, Dostoyevsky asked her why she had not married till then. She said two suitors were pursuing her, but she did not like them. She said she wanted to marry for love, not someone who pursued her or whom her parents told her to marry. Dostoyevsky agreed that love was all important. Slowly, meeting Dostoyevsky became the centre of Anna's life, and everything else became uninteresting and insipid. 'I rarely saw my friends and concentrated wholly on work and on those conversations we used to have.' She felt the talk of young men around her was trivial in comparison to Dostoyevsky's 'fresh and original' views. Anna was now under his spell. When she returned home, she thought about Dostoyevsky and waited for the next day to go to him again.

Dostoyevsky wrote books or read at night, slept through most of the morning, and rose in the early afternoon. The deadline for completion of the book, 1

November 1866, was arriving, and the two worried that they would be separated from each other after the completion of the work.

Dostoyevsky finished *The Gambler* on time in twenty-six days. He re-created 'the strained intensity of the love-hate bickering' among his three great loves: his unfulfilled love Apollinaria, his wife Maria, and his stenographer Anna Snitkina intersected. Apollinaria was the protagonist. In the plot of this work, he acquired what he failed to achieve in real life. The protagonist, a beautiful woman, loved the self-destructive gambler.

A few days later, Dostoyevsky visited Anna's house in the evening and kissed her hand. He proposed that she should work with him on his ongoing work *Crime and Punishment*. She agreed gladly.

Anna visited Dostoyevsky for work on his next book on 8 November. He was happy and excited to see her. Dostoyevsky asked her whether she liked him. She replied she had fallen in love with the hero of the tome *Insulted and Injured*. Soon they got engaged and kept their decision secret. Dostoyevsky required money for the marriage ceremony. The sale of his book was his only source of income, and his liabilities were huge.

Finally, Dostoyevsky married Anna on 15 February 1867 at the Trinity Izmailovsky cathedral in Petersburg in the presence of his family members. 'The cathedral was brilliantly lit, a splendid choir sang, many elegantly dressed guests were there.' His first wife, Marya, had died three years ago. Anna was happy: 'I drank more goblets of champagne during those ten days (after marriage) than I did all the rest of my life.' The groom was also elated. He told his friends: 'Look at that charming girl of mine! She is a marvellous person, that girl of mine! She has a heart of gold.'

The age difference between the two was twenty-five years. Anna looked like a girl. But she reassured him that she would age quickly. She says, 'And although this promise was meant as a joke, the circumstances of my life made it come true.... The difference in age between my husband and myself soon grew almost imperceptible.'

After the marriage, Dostoyevsky decided to go to Europe on honeymoon on 14 April 1867. They took a train from Petersburg to Berlin and then on to Dresden. They spent the evenings walking, drinking beer, and listening to brass bands. Anna was initially overwhelmed by Dostoyevsky's chaotic lifestyle. What Anna calls Dostoyevsky's 'irritable, volcanic nature' also led to continual disagreement between the two.

Dostoyevsky's obsession with gambling also caused strain in their marriage. It became an enemy of their marital happiness. From Dresden, Dostoyevsky decided to move to Hombourg in north-eastern France. He was afraid of being jailed in Russia for not paying his debts. Gambling, he thought, was an easy way to bounty. In Hombourg, though, his coffers ran dry, and he lost 'everything, down to the last kopeck'. Then the couple went to Baden-Baden, south-western Germany. He chased luck in the casinos there also.

Sonya, their daughter, was born a year after their marriage in Switzerland in 1968. Dostoyevsky's memory was weakened by epilepsy. He wrote, 'I don't recognize people anymore. I forget what I read the day before.' He moved from Geneva to Florence and started working on *The Idiot* in 1869. They spent four years in Europe outside Russia.

One of the biggest liabilities for Dostoyevsky was the huge debt that had accumulated over the years. Anna took charge of the situation, managed his life, and worked as his literary agent. She dealt with the publishers and negotiated good bargains for the author. Her ingenuity helped Dostoyevsky pay off large debts and bring happiness in his life.

Dostoyevsky wrote a philosophical novel, *The Brothers Karamazov*, which explored issues like faith and doubt, good and evil, moral responsibility, and the like. It was published in serial form from 1879 to 1880.

Dostoyevsky fell ill in January 1881. He told Anna that he loved her as much as he could, and he had never cheated on her. He died on 9 February 1881, and his body was interred in the Tikhvin Cemetery at the Alexander Nevsky Convent at Petersburg. Then Anna Snitkina was a young woman of thirty-five. The two remained married for fourteen years. She remained committed to him and did not remarry after his death.

19

Charles Sobhraj

Charles Sobhraj, twenty-five, proposed marriage to Chantal Compagnon, twenty-nine, in 1969 at a casino in Deauville, Paris. The lady said she wanted a little time to convince her father about the marriage. After the party, he drove a stolen sports car with Chantal next to him. The car moved at an insane speed, and he told her to agree to the marriage proposal.

The police were on the lookout for the car. They overtook Sobhraj on the highway and directed him to stop the vehicle. They arrested him with the car. Chantal was flabbergasted and had to hire another vehicle at night to go home.

Sobhraj spent eight months in a prison in Rouen for this case. He used his time in prison to do a course in French law. He wrote love letters to Chantal. In one letter, he wrote: 'What a joy you are, what a marvel, what a wonder.... Let's close our eyes and dream, dream, dream that we are lying next to one another.... God will protect our love.'

Chantal worked as a file clerk in Paris. When he came out of prison, he approached Chantal and sought apologies for the inconvenience he caused to her when the police had accosted him in her presence. He lavished gifts on her and took her to bars, nightclubs, and casinos. He came across as a suave, handsome, and sharp guy.

They got married at the mayor's office in Paris one October afternoon in 1970. Sobhraj's mother and Chantal's parents attended the marriage ceremony. They spent some time together at a flat in the outskirts of Paris.

By the end of 1970, Chantal became pregnant. Sobhraj learnt that he may have to perform mandatory military service for France for eighteen months. This was a difficult situation for Sobhraj. However, he joined the service and was soon discharged because of his disorderly and unbecoming conduct. After coming home, he rented a car and went on a tour of Europe with Chantal.

Then he planned a visit to Asia where he thought there were lots of opportunities. He loaded his borrowed car with water, cake, cash, and clothes. Along with his wife, Chantal Compagnon, he left France in October 1970, and their first destination was Greece. From there, he planned to move through Turkey, Iraq, Iran, Afghanistan, India and so on to Vietnam.

The journey of the couple was going to be interesting. In Greece, in September 1970, Sobhraj stayed at Hotel Plaza. However, he disappeared from the hotel without paying the bill. He also stole the passport, cash, and flight tickets of a British guest staying at the same hotel. He had raised bills by making several international calls from the hotel room. Chantal, ignorant of Sobhraj's conduct, wrote to her parents that they had a lovely holiday in Greece, and Sobhraj was working hard on business.

After dumping their car in Iran, they reached Delhi through India's western border by train. They rented a room in a hotel in south Delhi, and after a few days of roaming around Connaught Place, they left for Bombay (Mumbai).

They checked into a room in a hotel near the docks. Beautiful and presentable, Chantal was an asset for him to get acquainted with rich Indians. Sobhraj mixed with the people in pubs, casinos, and bars in the city and promised to deliver costly European cars, Dupont pens, and Rolex watches at throwaway prices. Sobhraj said he had contacts in the cities of Prague, Budapest, Kyiv, and the like. He could get people whatever they wanted.

He visited tourist places, beaches, and boulevards and lured people and cheated them. His lady delivered a baby girl named Usha in a hospital on 15 November 1971, and Sobhraj hired a flat for the family in the Malabar Hill locality, facing the sea.

Chantal was still not aware that Sobhraj was a criminal. He brought costly jewellery for her. She thought he was a practical joker, and his acts were pranks on unsuspecting people. She remained a good wife to him.

Then she came to know that he had an affair with a local girl in Bombay and vented her anger on the girl for seducing her innocent husband. She thought Sobhraj was a dashing, extraordinary, and gifted man and could be given leeway. She tried to behave as a normal wife and went to movie halls and dined at the Taj Mahal Hotel.

After some time, he took Chantal on a tour to Hong Kong in April 1972. Chantal spent time at luxury hotels, visiting tourist destinations, and shopping for dresses and jewellery. However, she still did not know what business Sobhraj was doing. She tried to learn about Sobhraj's business activities, his partners, and his office, but she could not elicit information despite her repeated requests. When she told Sobhraj that she also wanted to participate in the business, he told her he would think over it. He also complained of tiredness and showed no passion in the relationship. She became suspicious of his conduct and became sure that he was having extramarital affairs.

From Hong Kong, Sobhraj moved to Macau to give his wife and daughter all the luxuries. However, he lost a huge sum of money in gambling and sold his wife's jewels and his daughter's pearl necklace. This infuriated Chantal, and she decided to return to Paris. But she had no money. She also became aware that the police were looking for her and Sobhraj for not paying hotel bills.

In Macau, while facing difficulty in paying the hotel bill, Sobhraj got the idea of stealing jewellery. He took a flight to Delhi, leaving his wife and daughter in Macau. Chantal wrote to Sobhraj about the difficulties she and her daughter were facing in Macau. She asked him to return. 'All we want you is your presence around us. With you, even a hut in the forest would be a palace.'

While his family was in Macau, Sobhraj was on the prowl in India in June 1971, looking for his prey. He stayed with a friend at Hotel Oberoi-Intercontinental and planned to rob a jewellery store at Delhi's iconic hotel Chandragupta located in the diplomatic enclave. A jewellery store was located on the first floor of the hotel.

Sobhraj hired a few associates to perform this heist. He and his team went to the room of a cabaret dancer, Roma Jones, on the second floor, exactly above the shop. On the night of October 1971, Sobhraj started with a crude method for the robbery—he drilled the floor of a room to reach the jewellery store. However, he could not make a dent as the ceiling was made of impenetrable marble. Still, he attempted it for three nights, but the result came to naught.

Sobhraj tried another method. Roma called one of the store employees, Rakesh, and told him that she wanted to buy jewellery and to bring some samples of the items to her room. She introduced Sobhraj as the prince of Nepal. Rakesh came with a box of necklaces, rings, and bracelets of gold and rubies to her room. Roma also sat beside him and negotiated the price of the items. After a few moments of displaying the jewellery and negotiating the price, Sobhraj offered the jeweller a glass of cold coffee laced with drugs. Rakesh fell to his knees on the floor carpet within a few minutes.

Sobhraj pushed Rakesh behind the curtain and called the senior manager, Mohan Kumar. He drugged him too and got the keys of the store. He tied his hands with a plastic rope and shut him in the bathroom. He also drugged Roma Jones by lacing her coffee with a psychoactive substance.

Sobhraj collected a bag full of jewellery from the store and took a taxi to Delhi airport.

He bought a ticket to Tehran and reached the baggage examination gate. However, he saw a police team with the jeweller Mohan Kumar, looking for him. He thought it was not safe to stay there and escaped on the pretext of going to the toilet.

He left the airport and boarded a train for Bombay. The train ran overnight via Kota and Ratlam and reached Bombay Victoria Terminus the next day. He took a taxi and checked in to the Taj Mahal Palace hotel. His accomplices also reached the city.

They had planned to rob the Air India flight cash counter in Bombay. He visited a gambling den in the evening and played poker and lost money.

Charles required money as his wife and his daughter were still in Macau. He took up the business of selling old cars. He sold a Fiat car to a local at a low price. The police intercepted the vehicle, and during checking, they found that the documents of the vehicle were forged. The buyer told the police that he was not at fault and that he bought the vehicle from a foreigner named Sobhraj. Police further probed the buyer about Sobhraj's location and features.

The buyer led the police to Sobhraj. Police interrogated him about the origin of the vehicle and forged documents. Then they realized that Sobhraj was none other than the person whom the Delhi Police was looking for in the infamous heist at The Chandragupta. The police immediately arrested him on 11 November 1971 and handed him over to the Delhi Police.

A head constable from Delhi made a call to Chantal in Macau and said, 'Madam, your husband, Sobhraj, has been arrested.' Chantal became upset. She sat down and collected herself after the unnerving call. After two days, she and their daughter boarded a flight and landed in Delhi. Chantal thought her life and relationship with Sobhraj had come to an end.

During the arrest and police custody in Delhi, Sobhraj approached his father, Hatchand Sobhraj, for money. He had no money to pay the lawyers who would argue his case in the trial court.

Sobhraj spent about thirty days in prison, and he saw that he would not be released soon. He started to plan an escape from custody. He told the police officers on duty that his stomach was paining because of appendicitis. If he was not taken to a doctor immediately, he would die. The police got him admitted to Wellington Hospital. Chantal used to come to meet him during his custody. She brought a rose flower bouquet, a packet of dry fruits, and cookies for him. They talked in whispers and requested the police to give them more time to be together.

While he was in custody, during December 1971, Eastern Pakistan was fighting a liberation war with its western counterpart. Delhi city was under blackout. Chantal made queries to the police staff regarding the bail procedure. and Sobhraj escaped from the hospital taking advantage of the situation. He went to the railway station to buy a train ticket, where police, on alert and looking for him all over the city, identified him and brought him back to a police station in a jeep.

When Sobhraj was thrown in jail for the second time, Chantal decided to return to Paris. She sent a telegram to her parents with a request for money to buy an air ticket for the return journey. She was fed up with Sobhraj and did not want to see him. Help from her parents did not arrive, but she managed to send her daughter to France. Sobhraj, locked in a prison cell, wanted money to fight the legal battle and was confident that he would soon be free to travel to Hong Kong and Saigon. He told his wife to give him one more opportunity and that he would come out and hold her hand and place a rose bud in her hair.

Finally, he arranged money for the bail bond and came out of the prison on bail in January 1972.

After his release from police custody, he and Chantal drove from Delhi towards the north-west on the dusty, mountainous road to Paris.

When they reached Kabul, Afghanistan, he told Chantal that he would attend to 'business' for a short period and then they would move again. Chantal permitted him to halt there for a few days. They stayed at the famous five-star Intercontinental Hotel. He met smugglers and hippies and exchanged money, hashish, and gems with them and played baccarat for two months. Chantal enjoyed her stay in the hotel, shopping for jewellery and clothes, and the view of the snowy mountain in Kabul, but she told him to hurry up so that they could reach Paris.

In June 1972, Sobhraj said he was done with Kabul, and it was time to move. However, the hotel bill was huge, and he had no money to foot the bill. He had lost all the money in gambling. He stole a car from the hotel campus and drove towards the border to Iran on deserted roads.

The hotel management saw that Sobhraj had left without paying any money. They lodged a complaint with the police, who raised a nation-wide alert and looked for Sobhraj and Chantal.

Finally, the police intercepted them at the Afghanistan–Iran border and brought them to the police station. Sobhraj was put under arrest on 2 July 1972, and Chantal was released because she denied being his wife.

Charles realized Chantal must be distraught with his conduct. From prison, he sent her some money and a note: 'I am sorry darling for this small trouble. Everything will be fine soon. Your Love!'

Sobhraj realized it would be difficult to escape from prison at that place. He thought of tactics to escape the clutches of the law enforcement agency. He tried digging a tunnel with a kitchen spoon from the prison cell floor to come out. However, the prison authorities got an inkling of his intention, and his plan was foiled.

He made another attempt. He took out his blood through a syringe from his veins and collected it in a glass. Then he gulped the blood and vomited it. The guard on duty thought that Sobhraj was seriously ill. He took him to Wazir Akbar Khan hospital. There he added a sedative to the guard's tea. The guard lost consciousness after taking two sips, and Sobhraj scampered from there on 29 July 1972.

From Kabul, Sobhraj fled to Iran. He carried with him dozens of passports stolen from tourists. He sent money to Chantal in Kabul and called her to the Hotel Gibraltar in Tehran. They met there and were happy after the reunion like young lovers.

However, Chantal told him that she did not want that kind of life. They had a fight in the hotel room in the evening. She wanted to know what he was up to. 'If you put so much brain and energy into the legal profession, we would be millionaires. We would have a house in Rome and Paris. But you are wasting your genius in cheating and dodging the police.' Sobhraj slapped her and told her to shut up. She was enraged and threw used plates and forks on his face.

Then he mellowed down, held her hands, and sang a song, 'Oh Bird, oh please take me away; Let's go back to our imaginary land.' He told her to wait a few days. 'I am waiting for a friend to arrive here. We are working on an international trade business. Give me two days, honey!' Chantal was pacified and agreed to wait a little.

A few days later, the Tehran police arrested Sobhraj. They recovered several passports from his custody. Chantal was shocked. She told Sobhraj, 'I am not going to live this kind of life anymore.'

Sobhraj replied, 'I will always love you, baby.'

She thought she should divorce him, change her name, and never see his face again. She took a taxi to the Tehran airport and boarded a plane to Paris. She reached her mother's place in December 1972 and wept bitterly. She prayed to God that she might never see his face again.

Sobhraj requested his friends and relatives for money. He also decided to divorce Chantal, so he wrote to a friend that he would no longer live with Chantal.

In 1973, he telephoned his half-brother, André Darreau, twenty-one, and called him to Istanbul airport. Sobhraj was working there in the railway traffic office and spent time with girls in bars and cafes. André arrived there and Sobhraj took him to the Hilton Istanbul hotel. He wanted to make André a partner in crime. He had a long talk with his brother. He said, 'I have had many shocks in his life, but I learnt from each of them. Language is money. The more languages I know the more money I can earn. It comes very easily. You just have to concentrate.' He added, 'I use psychology the way fools use guns. It is my main weapon.'

Sobhraj started befriending the foreign women and men in Istanbul and cheated them. He promised them jewellery and gems, gave them hashish, played poker in casinos, and stole their money, credit cards, and passports. He brainwashed André and prepared him for being a partner in crime. He promised to send André to Hong Kong for a business studies course in a university there.

From Istanbul, Sobhraj and André flew to Athens and checked into a hotel. There they were to rest, make friends, and plan. Sobhraj read Nietzsche and Carl Jung. The study of psychology gave him more ways to manipulate the young and smart women he came across and take advantage of their weaknesses. He walked on the streets of Athens and visited bars and cafes, looking for gorgeous women and tourists with pockets full of money.

However, before they could go far, the Athens police arrested both Sobhraj and André based on intelligence about their offences in Istanbul.

André had a taste of police custody for the first time. In prison, Sobhraj had an idea and suggested to André that they swap their identities, but André did not agree. He did not want to take on himself Sobhraj's criminal record as André feared both of them would be handed over to the Turkey police.

Sobhraj then worked on a plan to escape from prison. He employed André and two others to dig a hole through the prison cell. However, the effort did not bear a result.

A year or so into his prison term, Sobhraj fell ill with diarrhoea and protested against the prison staff for bad food and ill-treatment. He went on a hunger strike and said he would not eat till the situation improved. Then the authorities took him to a hospital. A doctor checked his pulse and blood pressure and sent him back to the prison.

None of Sobhraj's tactics to escape police custody worked. Then he befriended a nurse and collected explosives through her. One day, when he was taken to court for a hearing during his trial, he set off an explosion in the vehicle and slipped away during the resulting smoke. He melted into the crowd and was gone within seconds.

Sobhraj reached Beirut. After escaping from prison, the first thing he did was to call a friend in Paris and ask him about Chantal. His friend told him that she had met a young American and had married him. She had gone to the USA with her new husband. The friend further told him she still missed him and loved him, but she could not live with him because of his misconduct. Sobhraj went into shock. This was a huge setback for him.

Later, the Greek police handed André over to the Turkish police, and he was to suffer eighteen years in a Turkish prison.

From Beirut, Sobhraj cruised to Thailand, where he started smuggling drugs. Then he came to Kashmir in India. There, he met a young woman, Marie-Andrée Leclerc, twenty-nine, a native of Quebec, Canada, at the Radisson Hotel in Srinagar in May 1975. Marie-Andrée worked as a medical receptionist in a hospital in Quebec and had come to India with her fiancé. Sobhraj introduced himself as Allen and told her that he was a photographer and a gem seller.

He pursued her, kissing her hand and calling her beautiful. He showed her his muscles and karate stances to impress her. His exotic looks and personality fascinated her. She fell in love with him, but she did not show him her feelings. They walked under the groves of chinar trees, drank red wine, and travelled to Gulmarg.

After some time, Marie-Andrée returned to Quebec. However, Sobhraj ran in her thoughts and imagination. She reminded him of his wife, Chantal, as both were French, beautiful, and quiet. Sobhraj also thought that Marie-Andrée could help him fool the authorities and his tourist victims. Sobhraj knew that his wit and confident demeanour had blinded her, and she was living under his influence. He wrote love letters to her and told her it would be great if she joined him in Thailand where he was planning to go next.

Marie-Andrée did not know Sobhraj's criminal background. Sobhraj wrote several letters to her, requesting her to come to him. In June 1975, he wrote to her: 'My darling … I love you more and more and desire strongly that you have my child…. I would love for you to be my wife and the mother of my children.' He again wrote to her in the same month: 'We would be able to have our baby by the end of 1976. What do you think, darling? Because by then, we will be stable. I have so many places and so many things to show. I desire your body and your caresses, my chérie adoreé.'

Marie-Andrée quit her job as a medical receptionist in Canada. She was fascinated by the offer. She dumped her fiancé, packed her rucksack, and took a flight to Bangkok in August 1975. She wrote in her journal: 'I am arriving in Bangkok. I feel like a just married girl coming for the first time to the bed of her husband, nervous but happy by the thought of a journey to be taken and possessed by the man she loves.'

She met Sobhraj at the Don Mueang Airport and felt happy. They stayed at luxury hotels and met tourists and businesspeople in the city. She posed as Sobhraj's secretary or wife. The couple looked impressive in stylish clothes and costly accessories. They freely interacted with foreign tourists. They went to the coastal town of Pataya and romanced there. She had a thirst for adventure and wanted to explore Sobhraj and the world.

At this place, Sobhraj's alias was Alain Gautier, and Marie-Andrée introduced herself to the world as Monique. She wrote in her journal: 'Life is going on … I have had two weeks of physical relations with Sobhraj that finally gave me a sense of communication both physical and spiritual … and some tenderness that is essential to me. I did, after all, give up my family and my country to be with my beloved.'

In Bangkok, Sobhraj and Marie-Andrée spent time with tourists and told them that they were traders in precious stones. They became friends with a tourist called Teresa Knowlton, a twenty-one-year-old American woman from Seattle. She had met Sobhraj while on her way to join a Buddhist monastery. She became one of his victims. He drugged and drowned her in a tidal pool at Pataya in October 1975.

He also killed several other tourists after sedating them. The investigation led the police to Sobhraj. In May 1976, the Thai police issued arrest warrants against Sobhraj and Marie-Andrée.

Before police could lay hands on them, they flew to Nepal. They used the passports of their victims to forge their identities and boarded a flight.

In Nepal, Charles Sobhraj and Marie-Andrée stayed in a luxury hotel, mixed with the tourists, gambled, and smoked hashish. He befriended twenty-nine-year-old American

Connie Jo Bronzich and twenty-six-year-old Canadian Laurent Carrière and killed them in December 1975.

After committing the crimes in Nepal, he and Marie-Andrée landed in Calcutta in January 1976. There, they met a tourist and scholar, Aaron Jacobsen, and accompanied him to Varanasi. A day later, the Varanasi police found Jacobsen's body in a hotel room. Sobhraj had drugged Jacobsen to death.

He used Alan's passport to create his new identity and boarded a flight with Marie-Andrée to travel to Singapore and then to Bangkok in March 1976.

After a short indulgence there, they returned to Goa in India and targeted another pair of tourists. He met a Dutch woman, Angelina Nunez, an eighteen-year-old backpacker, and told her about his gem work, love for photography, and connections in high society in Delhi. His words wove a spell over her heart and imagination. She began travelling with him. She says, 'He was very intense. I had a ring in my nose, and he pulled it out and there was blood everywhere. His eyes had no emotion. They were bad eyes. He had a killer stare.' He called the lady to Delhi.

He also met Barbara Smith, twenty-two, from Britain. She had fallen under Sobhraj's spell when she met him in Bombay at a cafe in June 1976. She was in financial difficulties, and her passport was ruined in the rain. Sobhraj introduced himself to her as a gem dealer and helped her. He called her to Delhi along with her friend Mary Eather, twenty-seven, a nurse from Sydney, Australia.

Sobhraj and Marie-Andrée took the Rajdhani Express from Bombay to New Delhi. They met Jean Luc Solomon, a French tourist in his mid-twenties, at Connaught Place at a shopping centre in June 1976 while buying clothes. Sobhraj told him he was from Paris, and he could give him gemstones at a discounted rate. He invited him to dinner at Shyam Hotel at Karol Bagh in Delhi.

He threw a dinner party and invited all his friends, including Solomon. During the party, Sobhraj mixed sedatives in Solomon's butter chicken. The next morning, police found Solomon's nude body on the balcony of the hotel room. His cash and travellers' cheques were gone.

After the game in Delhi, on 5 July 1976, the team of four went to Agra where tourists from all over the world flocked to see the Taj Mahal. They joined a group of twenty-two French student tourists. Charles Sobhraj told them about his French connection and had dinner with them at Minakshi Hotel, where they were staying. During dinner, Sobhraj distributed pills to counteract the effects of spicy Indian food and 'contaminated' water. However, the drugs took effect immediately, and the members of the group started collapsing at the dining table.

Sobhraj remembers, 'We bought capsules of antibiotics and in it, we put the drugs. As I almost reached the end of the 60 students, the first one started to fall down. The scene was like something in a horror movie. The police came, and I got arrested so they took me to a police station then they realised I was the second most wanted man in the world. The first one was Carlos the Jackal.'

Police investigated the case against them and put them on trial in the court. Sobhraj and Marie-Andrée were charged with the murder of Solomon.

In July 1978, a sessions court in Delhi convicted Sobhraj of culpable homicide 'not amounting to murder' of Solomon and robbery and sentenced them to twelve years in prison. Sobhraj acted as his own attorney as he had studied law. Marie-Andrée, however, was acquitted in this case.

Barbara Smith and Mary Ellen Eather were pardoned by the court, and they returned to their country in 1978 after a short stint in prison.

The court did not find sufficient evidence against Sobhraj and Marie-Andrée in the murder of Aaron Jacobsen.

While Sobhraj and Marie-Andrée were serving sentences in a jail in Delhi, the Thai government also wanted them to put them on trial for their crimes in that country. In 1985, India agreed to Thailand's request to extradite Sobhraj for the murders of a Turkish tourist and Teresa Knowlton. If Sobhraj was handed over to the Thai government, he risked a death penalty there. But the law of Thailand had a twenty-year statute of limitation. If the Thai government got them in its custody after twenty years of the commission of the crime, that is, after 1995, they could not put him on trial. Their prison term at the jail in India was going to end in 1988. So they had to leave the jail before they were handed over to the Thai government.

Sobhraj planned an escape from the high-security prison, and he, along with his associates, escaped the prison after drugging the jail guards in March 1986.

Marie-Andrée appealed to the court and the government that she may be allowed to go home as she was suffering from cancer. The superior court in Delhi heard her appeal and allowed her to return to Canada. Marie, thirty-eight, died in her hometown of Levis, near Quebec, on 20 April 1984.

After his escape from the jail in Delhi, Charles went to Goa. He mixed with foreign tourists, offered women gemstones, and roamed around on a green Rajdoot motorcycle. An inspector from the Mumbai Crime Branch was on duty looking for him. He saw him savouring seafood at the O'Coqueiro Restaurant on 6 April 1986. It was 10:30 p.m., and he was wearing a sun hat. The restaurant was a favourite of foreigners as it offered good food and international phone call facilities. The inspector of police and his team arrested him and brought him to Delhi. The police put him on trial, and the court sentenced him to 10 years imprisonment in the case of escape from prison.

Sobhraj did not try to escape this time. He served the full sentence and was released on 17 February 1997 from Tihar Jail in Delhi. He was fifty-two years old then.

He reached France in April 1997 without dallying on the route. He would not go to Thailand to face trial as his case was barred by a twenty-year limitation period.

After about seven years of leading a glamorous life and bragging about his achievements during his interactions with journalists, writers, television personalities, and filmmakers, he took a flight to Kathmandu, Nepal, in August 2003.

Decades earlier, in December 1975, Sobhraj and Marie-Andrée had travelled to Nepal using the passports of two Dutch backpackers. Now when he was in Nepal, journalists spotted him in the Yak and Yeti Hotel's casino in Kathmandu on 1 September 2003. They recognized the famous conman with a trail of criminal activities.

The journalists followed him for two weeks and wrote a news report: 'The Serpent Living Incognito in Thamel'. The Nepal police then raided the casino where Sobhraj was gambling. They arrested him and escorted him to the police station. They made a case of using forged documents for entering Nepal in 1975 against him.

Thereafter, the police reopened the double-murder case of two foreigners, namely, Connie Jo Bronzich and Laurent Carrière, who were killed on 21 December 1975. Connie Jo Bronzich was a backpacker from California. She travelled from Athens to Delhi and from there to Kathmandu. Laurent Carriere, a Canadian dropout from the University of Winnipeg, had joined her in Delhi. They had planned to spend Christmas at Mt Everest base camp in Nepal.

Police investigated and found evidence against Sobhraj. He had knifed Connie, set her on fire, and then dumped her body on the outskirts of Kathmandu in 1975. They filed a chargesheet against him in the Bhaktapur district court for the offence of murder. After a trial of about eight months, the Bhaktapur court found him guilty of the charges and sentenced him to life imprisonment on 20 August 2004 for Connie's murder.

Sobhraj filed an appeal to the Supreme court of Nepal against conviction and imprisonment. Nothing worked. In 2007, Sobhraj's lawyer appealed to the French president Nicolas Sarkozy for intervention in the case, citing his French nationality.

Sobhraj employed a lady lawyer named Satyakala Biswas to fight his case in Supreme court. She was a lawyer with a background in human rights.

The trial against him in the murder of his other victim, Laurent, continued, and the court convicted him in this case also in September 2014. The court awarded him a second life sentence.

While he was contesting his case in the Supreme Court, he required a French interpreter. Sobhraj issued an advertisement in a newspaper in 2008 that he was looking for a French translator for his legal battles. Satyakala's daughter Nina Biswas applied for the job. Within two weeks of their meeting, they were in love. Sobhraj said it was love at first sight for the two of them. She read the legal papers, the contents of first information reports, the chargesheets filed by the police, and the like and explained them to him. She brought chocolates and gifts for him during her visits. He told her that her eyes were beautiful, and her smiles gave him strength to fight the agony of life in prison. The understanding gave way to an engagement between the two in July 2008.

Nina Biswas, born in 1997 to a Bengali-origin businessman father and Satyakala Thapa, did her schooling at Kathmandu's St Martin's High School and got her law degree from Tribhuvan University, Kirtipur, Nepal.

She married Sobhraj on 10 October 2008, which was the day of Dashain, an auspicious occasion for weddings. She was twenty-two, and Sobhraj sixty-six. He came out of his prison cell for the ceremony, which was held in the prison courtyard. The bride wore a pink T-shirt and trousers, a nose pin, and a necklace, while Sobhraj wore a white shirt and his trademark cap. They exchanged vows and tikas (red vermilion marks on the forehead). The prison guards and inmates saw their marriage ceremony. There was no priest to preside over the function. Her mother Satyakala and her brother Sujoy Thapa participated in the ceremony.

Nina said if he was freed, they would get married in France according to French law. He was locked in Kathmandu's Central Jail when the wedding took place.

She met him regularly and talked to him on the phone when allowed by the jail authorities. After a few years of marriage, the relationship became strained, and she stopped calling him or visiting him. Her mother also stopped pursuing his case.

The Supreme Court of Nepal issued an order for his release on 21 December 2022. Twelve years of their marriage had passed. His family from France sent a new jacket, shoes, and other clothes for him. On 23 December 2022, Sobhraj took a taxi and went to Kathmandu airport for a flight to France. He was seventy-eight.

Nina reached the immigration counter. Sobhraj was there but was not interested in meeting her. He boarded the flight and took off for Paris.

20

Margaret Beaufort

Margaret Beaufort, thirteen, gave birth to a baby boy in a castle in Wales, England. The date was 28 January 1457, and bloody chaos and feuds raged in England. The mother named the boy Henry Tudor. This thirteen-year-old girl and her baby boy would change the history of England.

Margaret and her son were in a difficult situation and were fighting for survival. Margaret's husband, a nobleman named Edmund Tudor, had died of plague in November 1456, three months before Henry Tudor opened his eyes.

With her husband and protector gone, Margaret was helpless, and there was no one to provide food and resources. In the medieval world, men exercised power and control.

She looked towards her husband's brother, Jasper Tudor. Her dead husband and Jasper Tudor were connected to Henry VI, the emperor of England. They were his half-brothers, but they were connected to the king through their mother's side, not from his father's side. In medieval Europe, it was the male line that was reckoned for succession.

However, the connection to the king even through his mother's side was better than no connection. Margaret felt a bit safe with Henry VI on the throne. But, he was an incompetent ruler, and his crown was under constant attack. If the king was dislodged from the throne, it would be a disaster for Margaret too.

For stability and safety, Margaret looked for a husband. Before marrying Edmund Tudor in 1455, she had been married to John de la Pole in 1450, at the age of seven, but that marriage had been dissolved. Then, King Henry VI himself chose Margaret as a bride for his half-brother Edmund Tudor.

While she required a new husband to survive, as per the prevalent family and marriage code, she would have to leave her son with her relative if she married. She could not take him to her new husband's home.

She decided that she would lodge her son with her brother-in-law Jasper Tudor when she got married. Now, she intensified her search for a husband. She visited different places looking for a suitable man. Then England was plague-ridden and politically unstable. There was no certainty of life and safety of property, and everything was in a state of flux. Finding a husband was the responsibility of her guardians, but at fourteen, Margaret was doing that job for herself. She wanted power, safety, and influence for herself and her minor son.

In 1458, about a year after her husband's death, Margaret married Henry Stafford, thirty-three. Stafford came from an important noble family and wielded power. Margaret was happy. She had a husband who respected and cared for her. Her future and her son's future appeared to be secure. Her estates now flourished, and life was stable.

However, just three years into the marriage, in March 1461, her world turned upside down. Henry VI was deposed as the king of England, and his army was annihilated. The new claimant to the throne was Edward IV.

The new dispensation would look at Margaret and her son with suspicion as they were relatives of Henry VI and beneficiaries of his largesse. What was worse was that her husband, Stafford, had fought against Edward IV while the latter was trying to depose Henry VI.

Henry Stafford was able to escape the charge of treason and death. But Edward IV's men stormed into the castle where Margaret's son and her brother-in-law Jasper Tudor lived. The castle was captured. Jasper escaped, but her son Henry Tudor was picked up by Edward IV's men and taken into custody. But Edward IV stripped Henry Tudor of all his land and estate. Without landed property, Henry was nobody.

Margaret was back to square one. She had to get her son released and his land back. She had no child from her marriage with Stafford. Her first pregnancy at the age of thirteen was so traumatic that she was not going to have another child.

She could get a respite if she moved closer to the new king and expressed her loyalty to him. But it was a difficult task for her. She was emotionally attached to the deposed king, Henry VI, who was her relative and was now in exile in Scotland.

Nonetheless, she worked to become closer to Edward IV as she had no other option. Her husband Henry Stafford also came to the king, swore allegiance to him, and got a pardon in return. Slowly, the relationship with the king deepened. The king visited Margaret's house, accepted her invitation for hunting, and restored her estates. With the passage of time, she convinced the king that her family was loyal and reliable and that the estate of her son Henry Tudor could also be returned.

When everything appeared to be on the right track for Margaret, her world crumbled again. Edward IV's powerful ally, the Earl of Warwick, revolted against him, dislodged him from the throne, and made him a prisoner in 1469. Later, Edward IV escaped from the prison to Flanders. The Earl of Warwick further released Henry VI from the Tower of London and reinstalled him on the throne of England.

This abrupt change in the situation put Margaret in an embarrassing situation as she had become close to Edward IV, an enemy of Henry VI. However, Margaret knew how to walk through the volatile terrain. She immediately worked to prove her loyalty to Henry VI. She marched to the palace of Westminster, London, to petition the king and get back her son's estate. She told Henry VI that she was so happy to see him back on the throne. He was the rightful king of England and England would prosper and would be ruled with justice under him.

She had brought her son also with her to the palace. She told the king that she had named her son 'Henry' after the king. Henry VI was delighted to see the fourteen-year-old boy and called him close and blessed him. Henry VI also said something that shocked and surprised both the mother and the son. He said the young Henry would assume the helm of the state one day. This meant that young Henry Tudor would be king of England.

Then Margaret was in a tight spot again. By March 1471, Edward IV came from Flanders to England to fight and reclaim his crown. Margaret's husband Henry Stafford went to war in support of Edward IV. This was a difficult situation and could have annoyed Henry VI. She was caught between her loyalty to Henry VI and her husband's pledge to Edward IV. She kept track of the battle to know the direction in which the war was moving. However, Edward IV marched to London at a rapid pace, and neither Henry VI nor Margaret got much time to prepare or defend. Edward IV wore the crown again in April 1471 and ordered his generals to kill Henry VI.

This time, when Edward IV held the reins of the state, he was not in a conciliatory mood. His own son, his heir apparent, had been killed in the war. He started a purge of Henry VI's allies and nobles. He put to death two of Margaret's closest relatives. Margaret's son was the nephew of Henry VI, a close family member, thus meeting the requirement of execution. Margaret was earlier fighting for her son's land and property. Now, she had to see that her son escaped death. Henry Tudor was under the protection of his uncle Jasper Tudor. Edward IV's men would come soon for him.

Margaret, knowing what lay ahead, sent a servant to her son with a message directing him to flee and leave England. Henry Tudor, fourteen, sensed the danger and left England immediately for Brittany in France. Margaret heaved a sigh of relief. Her son would be alive at least, though she was not sure when and whether she would be able to see him again. Then came another tragedy. Her husband, Henry Stafford, who had fought for Edward IV, died of battle wounds in October 1471. Margaret was again alone and helpless.

Margaret, twenty-eight, was a widow again, and she had no safety and security. She stood where she had been fifteen years ago, at a crossroads, her property and privileges gone and her very life in danger.

Margaret looked for another husband for, without a male partner, a woman had no security or access to the king's court. Finally, in 1472, she married Thomas Stanley, a powerful noble. Margaret was his second wife, the first having died the same year. Stanley was very influential and was steward of the royal household. He was like a cabinet minister in Edward IV's court. This marriage was going to be decisive for the fate of England.

With the marriage, Margaret was back in the reckoning. She had direct access to the court. She could influence the course of politics in the country. Margaret also developed a good relationship with the queen, Elizabeth Woodville.

Things moved as planned, and Margaret was happy. She used every moment to reach closer to the centre of power. She again convinced Edward IV to give back all that was due to her son Henry. The king agreed, and the property and estate was restored. Henry Tudor became the Earl of Richmond and received a settlement of land. Now Henry would return to the court and be a nobleman.

Then everything fell apart. Edward IV's health failed, and he died on 9 April 1483. Edward IV's twelve-year-old son Edward V could succeed his father, but that did not happen. England had a new king, Richard III, the younger brother of Edward IV.

Margaret was again in trouble. Things that were taken for granted had become unsettled.

Richard III locked the two sons of Edward IV in the Tower of London and took the reins of government in his hands. On 6 July 1483, Richard III was crowned as king. Margaret and her husband Stanley showed loyalty to the new king; they attended the coronation ceremony. However, Margaret could not make herself loyal to the new king. She considered him a usurper of the throne. Then Richard III made a blunder. He murdered the two princes of Edward IV at the Tower of London. That made Richard III a hated figure. Margaret was also not sure how Richard III would deal with her and felt threatened by him.

She decided that Richard III, the monarch of England, should go. And who should replace him? Her son Henry Tudor.

However, there was a problem. One could become king only when one was male and descended from the male line of the king's family. Henry Tudor had a weak claim to the throne as his connection to the court was through the female line of succession.

Margaret planned something that would strengthen his claim and make his connection through women to the royalty irrelevant. What if her son married the daughter of Edward IV? That would throw Henry Tudor in the centre of the power struggle.

Elizabeth Woodville was grieving her husband's death. After her husband's death, her father had been executed, and her two young sons had been murdered by Richard III. She was herself trapped at Westminster Abbey, which was surrounded by soldiers.

There was one line of contact that Margaret could use to approach the wronged Elizabeth—a physician who visited both the ladies when required. Margaret approached Elizabeth Woodville and proposed her son's marriage with her daughter. Elizabeth Woodville accepted.

Then in September 1483, Margaret sent money to Henry Tudor, who was in exile in France, to come and invade England and end Richard III's rule. Henry assembled men, arms, and ships and sailed from France. She waited for him at the shore of England, but a storm in the English Channel threw the whole plan into disarray. Henry Tudor turned back and reached France.

Henry's attempt to invade England left Margaret red-faced. Richard III knew about the brain behind this rebellion and threat. An enquiry established her role as a conspirator and chief abettor. She had committed high treason. Richard III stripped Margaret of all her land, resources, and property. He directed Stanley to keep an eye on the activities of his wife. She should not have any servants or any means of communication, and her movements were to be strictly restricted. She was a dangerous entity.

Margaret was able to survive Richard's wrath only because of her husband. People who committed much smaller crimes were imprisoned, tortured, and executed. Stanley's high standing in the court gave her a chance where none existed.

Richard was wary of Henry Tudor, but dissatisfied men and disgruntled nobles flocked to or established contact with Henry Tudor. There were many nobles and powerful cliques in England who wanted Richard III to go. Then she sent a message to Henry to take a second attempt and land in Wales; he would have men and money waiting for him.

Henry Tudor got ready again, and on 7 August 1485, he landed in England with a large army. As promised, his mother sent him a huge amount of money to finance his march towards London. Margaret's role was again clear to Richard III, but this time he thought to tackle the risk posed by Henry Tudor first and then sort issues with Margaret. The lady knew that soon she would be either the mother of the king of England or both she and her son would be executed.

On 22 August 1485, the armies of Henry Tudor and Richard III, led respectively by them, met at Bosworth Field. In the ensuing battle, Richard III, with a larger army strength, was on the verge of vanquishing Henry Tudor.

Stanley stood outside the battle with a small force. Then Margaret sent him a message to join the war in support of her son. Before Richard III could defeat Henry Tudor decisively, Stanley's forces joined the battle from Henry's side and changed the course of the battle.

Richard III's army was defeated, and he was killed by the sword of Henry Tudor. Stanley picked up the fallen crown from Richard III's head and placed it on the head of Henry Tudor, twenty-eight. Margaret's son was the king of England. Henry Tudor, with the guidance and support of his mother Margaret Beaufort, forty-two, founded a new dynasty that would rule England for 120 years.

21

Nelson Mandela

Nelson Mandela (1918–2013) was South Africa's national leader, its first Black President, and a Nobel laureate.

In 1944, Mandela, twenty-six, while pursuing a law degree at the University of the Witwatersrand, Johannesburg, met twenty-year-old beauty Evelyn Mase. Evelyn was a cousin of Mandela's political mentor and anti-apartheid activist Walter Sisulu. Her father had died when she was a child, and her mother passed away when she was twelve. She lived with her brother Sam Mase.

Mandela stayed in Walter Sisulu's house and was studying law at the university at Johannesburg in 1943. Evelyn worked as a nurse at the Johannesburg General Hospital in Hillbrow. Sisulu, apart from being a relative, was a close friend of Evelyn's and her brother Sam's. Evelyn and her brother visited Walter Sisulu on social occasions. On one such occasion, she met Nelson for the first time in 1944.

Mandela, dressed in a white shirt with tie and coat, introduced himself to her. Evelyn, who was wearing a skirt and blouse scented with jasmine perfume, was impressed by Mandela's wit and physique. Evelyn remembers, 'I think I loved him the first time I saw him.... Within days of our first meeting, we were going steady and within months he proposed.'

When Mandela offered his hand to Evelyn in marriage, she readily accepted. Mandela tied the knot in a ceremony on 5 October 1944 at a court in Johannesburg. Relatives from both sides attended the function and feasted on rice, chicken, butternut, and salad. As Mandela was still a student and kept himself busy in political activities, Evelyn's salary as a nurse supported the family. They had no house to live in and moved to Evelyn's relatives seeking accommodation. Later, they rented a house in Orlando in 1946.

Mandela soon graduated into a serious political activist and a leader. He organized demonstrations and attended political meetings till late night. Young Evelyn, however, had no interest in politics. She was deeply religious and was a Jehovah's Witness. She did not like her husband to be away from her busy in political meetings and tours.

She told him, 'Nelson, you have no time for me. All the time you are busy with political activities. Why did you marry me if you had no time for family?' Mandela did not care much for her shouts and protests. Gradually, their relationship became strained. She also doubted his marital fidelity.

Mandela says, 'I could not give up my life in the struggle, and she could not live with my devotion to something other than herself and her family.'

After about twelve years of marriage, in 1956, Evelyn filed a divorce petition in a local court in Johannesburg, citing physical abuse and infidelity as reasons. Mandela filed a counter-report on the divorce petition, rebutting his wife's allegations.

While divorce was yet to be finalized, Evelyn separated from Mandela and moved to her brother's house. She had second thoughts about the divorce and withdrew her petition. Mandela was also not very keen on divorce as it could damage his reputation in the party, the African National Congress.

However, things did not normalize. Mandela thought it was time to say goodbye to Evelyn, as he needed the support of a companion. He filed for divorce from Evelyn Mase at a native district court. The court finalized his petition and granted divorce on 18 March 1958. The court gave Evelyn custody of all three children.

Mandela later wrote: Evelyn 'was a very good woman, charming, strong and faithful, and a fine mother. I never lost my respect for her, but in the end we could not make our marriage work.'

While he was separated from his wife and divorce was coming, Nelson Mandela met twenty-one-year-old Winnie Madikizela in 1957. Winnie worked as a social worker at Baragwanath Hospital in the Soweto area of Johannesburg. She looked pretty in a short-sleeved sheath dress with a bateau neckline. The thick layers of her shining, petal-soft hair and salt on her skin made her look attractive. She was South Africa's first Black female social worker. Her parents were teachers. She had earned a degree in social work from Jan Hofmeyr School of Social Work in Johannesburg in 1956.

Mandela was arrested from his home in December 1956 and was charged with treason. He was put on trial in Pretoria. His romance with Winnie blossomed during his trial in 1957. Winnie was eighteen years younger than him. Mandela says, 'I was both courting her and politicizing her.'

Mandela remembers: 'I cannot say for certain if there is such a thing as love at first sight. But I do know that the moment I first glimpsed Winnie Madikizela, I knew that I wanted to have her as my wife.' Mandela requested her for a lunch date. They got butter chicken, paneer tikka, and butter naan at a restaurant. He was amused by her reaction to the spicy curry. Mandela was a fitness freak who ate fat-free chicken and worked out at the gym. Winnie would go to the gym to meet him.

Nelson decided to marry Winnie. Winnie says, 'One day Nelson just pulled up on the side of the road and said: "You know, there is a woman who is a dressmaker, you must go and see her, she is going to make your wedding gown".... That's how I was told I was getting married to him!'

They got married on 14 June 1958, three months after Mandela's divorce from Evelyn. She wore the traditional attire of a bride. The marriage ceremony was held at Mandela's lawyer's office in the presence of relatives. Mandela had to take permission from the court to get married as he was a prisoner and had to travel from Pretoria to Johannesburg for the marriage ceremony. The court had given him four days to finish his obligations.

After the marriage ceremony, the couple had no opportunity to spend time as wife and husband. Boating on the Orange River or hiking to Table Mountain could wait. He sat on a train rumbling through the darkness of the night and returned to a prison cell in Johannesburg.

In 1961, three years after their wedding, Mandela was acquitted of the charge of treason, but he went underground as he was apprehensive that the government would arrest him on some other charge. In 1962, he was again arrested and imprisoned for five years after returning to South Africa from a trip abroad. He was convicted of leaving the country illegally and incitement to strike.

Mandela's political activities against White rule continued, and he committed more rebellious acts against the apartheid regime. In 1964, he was sentenced to life for the offences of sabotage, attempts to overthrow the apartheid regime, and other related crimes. He spent eighteen years in the prisons of Robben Island and Pollsmoor. He was released from jail in 1990 and was elected the first Black president of South Africa in 1994.

Winnie spent three decades fighting for her husband's release. She went to see him during prison visiting hours. She stood for hours under the sharp sun in a queue to meet her husband. She herself suffered torture, house arrest, and imprisonment for political activities. In 1969, she spent eighteen months in solitary confinement. She described the experience thus: 'My whole body was badly swollen, I was passing blood.... The whole experience was so terrible.... I had left little children at home in bed and I had no idea what would happen to them.' The couple had two children.

When Mandela walked out of prison in February 1990, Winnie stood at the gate to receive him and escort him to a vehicle.

Soon, however, the relationship between the two turned ugly. Within two years, in 1992, they separated. Political and personal differences grew between them, and Mandela suspected Winnie of having an affair with a lawyer, Dali Mpofu.

A letter allegedly in Winnie's handwriting written to Mpofu, complaining that he was not giving her time, was recovered and produced before the court for seeking divorce. Mpofu was twenty-six years younger than her. The court granted Mandela and Winnie divorce in 1996 considering the grounds. They had been married for thirty-eight years. Winnie remembered Mandela in 2010: 'He was loving, fond of children, a people's person and a very hard worker.'

Cleve Wootson, a journalist, commented on their divorce: 'In the end, it was a marriage that survived prison but not freedom.'

After divorcing Winnie, Mandela, on his eightieth birthday, married Graca Machel, fifty-two, in 1998. Mandela was nearing the end of his presidency in 1999.

Graca was the widow of the first president of Mozambique, Samora Machel. She married Machel in 1975, but he died in a plane crash in 1986.

Born in 1945, Graca was trained as a soldier in the liberation movement of Mozambique. She studied language and literature at the University of Lisbon, Portugal, and graduated in 1968. She served as a minister for education in the government headed by her husband Machel. She had an illustrious political and academic career and public life. She won several awards like the Africa Prize. She was made an honorary Dame of the British Empire by Queen Elizabeth II in 1997 for her humanitarian work.

Graca had known Mandela when her husband was alive. Mandela met her in Mozambique in July 1990 after his release from prison and was struck by her grace and personality. She again impressed him when she came to South Africa to receive an honorary doctorate from the University of Cape Town in 1992. An interaction with her led to a deep bonding between the two.

She says, 'It was just wonderful that finally we have found each other and can share a life together.'

Graca was twenty-seven years younger than him. She was reluctant to marry him because of her sense of obligation to the people of Mozambique. Her first husband, Samora Machel, had been a freedom fighter of his country and had led the struggle of his people against Portuguese colonialism since 1962. The country had won independence in 1975. She had two children with Samora Machel.

She came close to Mandela after the latter's divorce from Winnie in 1996. Mandela and Graca were seen together on overseas trips during a state function in Zimbabwe in 1997.

After her marriage to Mandela in 1998, she agreed to spend two weeks in a month with him in South Africa.

In a TV interview, Mandela said, 'I'm in love with a lovely lady. I don't regret the reverses and setbacks because late in my life I'm blooming like a flower because of the love and support she's given me.'

They bought a house with a large garden in Houghton, Johannesburg, in 1998. Their marriage ceremony was conducted at Mandela's presidential residence in Johannesburg on the afternoon of 18 July 1998. She wore a white shirt and a traditional Mozambican skirt called capulana at her wedding. They exchanged rings. When asked by the priest to kiss, they kissed.

Amina Cachalia, the widow of the African National Congress (ANC) leader Yusuf Cachalia, in her autobiography *When Hope and History Rhyme* (2013), said in 1996 that Mandela had visited her residence as a family friend.

According to her account, Mandela came to her house and sat with her on the sofa in the living room. He asked her: 'Do you know that you are an exceptionally beautiful, vivacious and young lady?'

Amina replied gently: 'I'm not a young lady; I am a middle-aged woman.'

Amina's husband, Yusuf Cachalia, had died in 1995.

She adds, 'He looked relieved and said: "Okay let's begin again." He repeated the sentence, substituting "old" for "young" lady. I screamed again and said that I was not an old lady either.'

She adds, 'Nelson was not a great romantic figure.... He would express his feelings in a rather matter-of-fact fashion.... But I could not return his gestures.'

Winnie continued to visit Mandela even after the divorce. She got on beautifully with Graça Machel. She attended Mandela's birthday party. She also visited him while he was hospitalized in Pretoria in 2013.

Mandela's first wife, Evelyn, died in April 2004 due to respiratory problems. She was buried in a cemetery in

Johannesburg. Mandela attended the funeral along with Winnie and Graça Machel.

Mandela passed away on 5 December 2013 at the age of ninety-five after suffering from respiratory infection at his home, Houghton Estate, in Johannesburg. He was buried on 15 December 2013 at his ancestral home, Qunu, in the Eastern Cape Province of South Africa.

22

Bertrand Russell

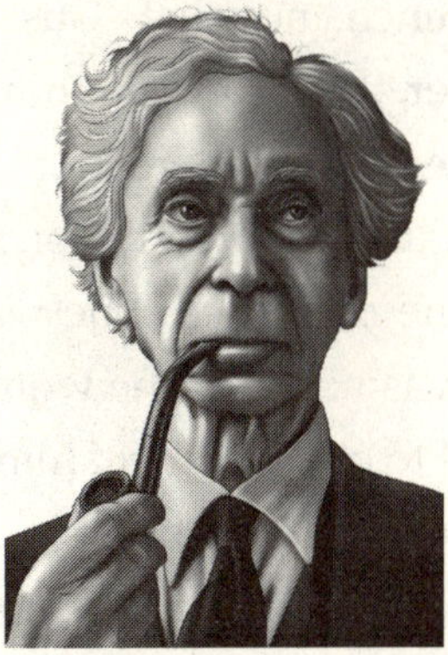

Bertrand Russell, seventeen, met Alys Pearsall Smith and her family members at her uncle's house in Surrey, UK, in the summer of 1889. Alys was five years elder to him and was a graduate from Bryn Mawr College, Pennsylvania, USA. Alys's family lived in the USA, and they visited London off and on.

In 1889, Russell's uncle Rollo called him to his house in Surrey, where Pearsall Smith's family had come from the USA to spend the summer. At his uncle's house, Russell saw Alys Smith, Pearsall Smith's daughter. She fascinated the young philosopher and mathematician at first glance. Russell says, 'She was at that time one of the most beautiful women it is possible to imagine, and gifted with a sort of imperial state.' She was studying at Bryn Mawr

College and was a friend of Walt Whitman, an influential American poet and journalist.

Russell joined Trinity College in 1890 and studied mathematics and philosophy. Here, he had the company of the bright minds of his time like John Maynard Keynes, Lytton Strachey, and Alfred Whitehead.

After this first meeting, Russell met the Smith family more frequently. Alys's brother Logour Smith familiarized him with the French novelist Gustave Flaubert, the essayist Walter Peter, the American thinker William James, and others like them. His interaction with Alys became intense, and he became devoted to her. She represented all the kindness that he cherished. She was five years older than him, and he was not sure she would wait for him for marriage. She used to come to meet him at Trinity College, and the two sat and talked for hours.

Russell said that one day in September 1893, he went for a walk with her before breakfast: 'We went and sat in a certain beech-wood on a hill ... and a place of extraordinary beauty looking like an early Gothic Cathedral... The morning was fresh and dewy, and I began to think that perhaps, there might be happiness in human life.'

That morning, Russell proposed marriage to Alys. 'I was neither accepted nor rejected. It did not occur to me to attempt to kiss her, or even take her hand. We agreed to go on seeing each other and corresponding, and to let time decide one way or the other.'

He adds, 'Although I was deeply in love, I felt no conscious desire for any physical relations.... Gradually, however, nature took charge of this matter.'

Russell graduated from the university with distinction in 1893.

In January 1894, Russell came to the house of Alys's parents who were now settled in London. That day, snowfall had completely covered London, and it was noiseless like a lonely hilltop. Russell kissed Alys for the first time. Alys still said she had not made up her mind whether to marry him or not. They spent the whole day together, kissing each other. Russell returned home late at night. Sometimes she seemed eager to marry him and other times not.

Russell's relatives, especially his grandmother, opposed his engagement and marriage to Alys. His grandmother arranged to send him to Paris as an honorary attaché of Lord Dufferin to distance him from Alys and prevent him from marrying her. He went to Paris in 1894. Alys joined him there. They went dancing and boating on the Seine at night. There, Alys agreed to get engaged to him in the fall of 1894. Russell soon returned from Paris as his heart was not there.

Russell had lost his mother when he was two, and his father when he was three. His paternal grandmother, Countess Russell, and his aunt Agatha Lyttelton brought him up at Pembroke Lodge in Richmond Park. This house was granted to his grandfather Lord John Russell by Queen Victoria. His paternal grandfather had been prime minister twice and had passed the Reform Bill of 1832, which expanded the scope of people who could be elected to the House of Commons. Remembering Queen Victoria's visit to the house of his grandfather Lord John, Russell's aunt has said, 'He was much subdued and did not treat her Majesty with the utter disrespect I expected.'

Finally, Russell married Alys on 13 December 1894 in St Martin's Lane, London. After their marriage, the couple went to Holland and Germany for their honeymoon and returned to Fridays' Hill in the spring of 1895. They rented a house and started their life.

Bertrand Russell wrote about the marriage: 'With my first marriage, I entered upon a period of great happiness and fruitful work. Having no emotional troubles, all my energy went in intellectual directions.... After dinner my wife and I used to read aloud in turns and in this way we ploughed through large numbers of standard histories in many volumes.'

In July 1900, Russell attended an International Congress of Philosophy and Mathematics in Paris and met the Italian mathematician Giuseppe Peano, an originator of symbolic logic. Russell says this Congress was a turning point in his life. He was impressed by Peano and started studying his works. In October 1900, he sat down to write *The Principles of Mathematics* and wrote 200,000 words in three months. In this book, he delved upon the contributions of top mathematicians and argued that mathematics and logic are identical. It became a classic reference.

By 1901, Bertrand Russell and Alys Pearsall Smith had been married seven years. Russell had just finished delivering lectures at Cambridge for two terms. That year, one summer afternoon, while Russell was bicycling on a country road, he realized that he no longer loved his wife. He thought that his change of heart wasn't really his fault, and it was Alys's flaws that were responsible for this disaster.

Alys was then staying at the residence of a common friend as she was ill and needed a change in environment. On the other hand, Russell was in Whitehead, working on a book. He used to write letters to Alys. Suddenly, his letters became cold and formal. She could not understand the reason for the change in his approach and felt worried. She thought he suspected her loyalty and faithfulness to him. She returned to Fridays' Hill and found him a stranger.

Russell told her he no longer loved her and would not share a room with her. His love for her was dead. 'The shock of this statement was so terrible that I almost died but I managed to keep up my outward appearance and went to Switzerland with Beatrice Webb (a feminist scholar and friend of Russell) for three weeks,' she wrote.

She did not confide her troubles to anyone as she felt it was too strange and would have injured Russell's reputation.

Alys did not find any woman responsible for turning her world into a tempestuous whirl! Russell's disenchantment with her was not a slow process but a sudden knockdown. She thought he would return to her and be fine after some time. She requested Russell not to break up their normal life and to carry on a life of mutual interest. She was sure she would win back her man. Alys even threatened suicide. He agreed to her request. Russell says he agreed because 'there was no other woman to whom I wished to go, and there seemed therefore no good reason for not doing as she wished'.

They carried on for nine years like that, though it was a grim time for both. He was busy writing books, and she was busy as an activist for social and political causes. They did not let their friends and relatives know that their world had fallen apart.

Russell came across Lady Ottoline Morrell, wife of Philip Morrell, in March 1911. Morrell was an English aristocrat, and her circle included towering intellectuals like Aldous

Huxley, T.S. Eliot, and D.H. Lawrence. She married the British member of parliament Philip Morrell in 1902.

One year younger than Russell, Ottoline was six feet tall with flaming red hair. She dressed flamboyantly. She had houses in London and Garsington and a mansion in Oxfordshire. Her friends visited her house and discussed literature, paintings, and philosophy.

Russell was one of her close friends. They exchanged around 3500 letters. Their relationship was a 'passionate alternation of ecstasy and discord'. Russell wrote of their first encounter: 'For external and accidental reasons I did not have full relations with Ottoline that evening, but we agreed to become lovers as soon as possible.'

Alys came to know about his intimacy with Ottoline. She was already bearing the separation and estrangement; now she had a new challenge and did not know what to do. She says, 'I was utterly distraught by that and felt I could not possibly carry on my life without him. I cried and cried for many days, and was sunk in an abyss of agony unutterable and unbelievable.'

She shifted from their house in 1911 to her brother's house. This was a separation from Russell. The divorce was yet to come. She never spoke to Russell again. The wound and the suffering were too great. She saw him a few times in the street or at lectures. When Russell lived in Chelsea, she sometimes stood outside his uncurtained window and watched him playing with children.

She told Bertrand Russell that she would apply for divorce and give the reason that he was in a relationship with Ottoline. Russell was in a fix as this would have caused a scandal, Ottoline's husband was a public figure. Russell told Alys that if she made an issue out of his relationship with Ottoline, he would commit suicide. This checked Alys.

In Ottoline, Russell believed that he had found a collaborator who might act either as joint author or as a muse in the production of his books.

Ottoline tried to encourage Russell, saying: 'It is extraordinary how different you are from most of the scholars…. It makes it possible for you to do things they could not even dream of.'

He wanted to write fiction, a work of imagination and beauty, to win her esteem. She was more impressed by literary work, a piece of art, a painting, or a sculpture than by a book of philosophy, logical analysis, mathematics, or an essay on sociopolitical issues—areas over which he had mastery and was gifted in. He was not able to produce things to her liking. He wrote to her: 'Three things I want but can't have—children, daily companionship and imaginative writing.'

He told Lady Ottoline, 'You need never have one moment's doubt of your power to help me … you can help me more than you will ever realize, because you will think it all comes from me, when it is you reflected in me…. I see a wonderful future for us stretching through the years, in which we shall help each other to bring good things to the world and have the bond of mutual strength and a great work in common (19 May 1911).'

Lady Ottoline accepted her role as a facilitator for the achievement of this harmony: 'I suppose in some mysterious manner I do help you to free the gods and goddesses within you—and to help them all sing together well in tune' (24 February 1912).

The two exchanged books, often with passages marked. Among their best loved authors were Shelley, Blake, Shakespeare, Dante, Milton, Leopardi, and Vaughan.

However, over a period of time, their affair gradually mellowed into a friendship.

In 1910, Russell was appointed a faculty member at Trinity College. The same year, he wrote *Philosophical Essays*, which dealt with ethics and theories of truth. Then, he, along with Alfred North Whitehead, took up the task of elucidating the logical deduction of mathematics. This resulted in a three-volume co-authored book, *Principia Mathematica*, during 1910–1913. His eminence increased, and Harvard University, USA, sought to make him part of its regular faculty.

Russell published *The Problems of Philosophy* in 1912. He argued that philosophy was repeating failed attempts to answer questions like whether we can prove that there is an external world. Can we prove cause and effect? Russell said philosophy cannot answer any of these questions. Philosophy's value must lie elsewhere. The book became popular reading and a textbook for philosophy students.

In 1914, he went to lecture at Boston University, USA. Now he was an international luminary. He published a collection of lectures, *Our Knowledge of the External World*. There, he came across T.S. Eliot, then a student at Harvard, which was located a few kilometres from Boston University. Later, Russell became romantically involved with Vivienne Haigh-Wood, Eliot's wife, for a short period.

Love blossomed between Russell and Lady Constance Malleson in 1916, and their relationship continued till 1920. The lady was an actor and was known professionally as Collette O'Niel. She was in an 'open marriage' to the actor Miles Malleson. Russell was then a well-established philosopher and a social activist.

During the First World War, Bertrand Russell passionately campaigned for peace, wrote articles, and took part in the 'No Conscription Fellowship'. His activism and views against war alienated many of his friends, and Russell stood alone. He was dismissed from the post of lecturer from Trinity College in 1916. Harvard University offered him a post as lecturer, but the British government did not give him a passport to travel to the US.

It was during this turmoil that he came across Collette O'Niel. She attended the trial of the pacifist Clifford Allen, who argued that citizens should not be conscripted for war. Russell also appeared in court in favour of Allen.

After the initial interaction, Russell began an intense love affair with Collette. Both loved walking and often went for tours to the countryside. They talked about novelists, philosophers, politics, and the danger to the world from violence. During these tours, they occasionally stayed at inns on the banks of the Thames, pubs, and hotels. In October 1916, she wrote to Russell: 'The thought that we may be able to get away to the country together sends me quite wild with delight. If we do manage it, the place to go is the Cat and Fiddle.... It's a small rough stone pub with five windows and a door. It stands higher than any other pub except the Snake. There's nothing but empty moorland. I think it must be a bit like Wuthering Heights. I'm going to find out more about it.'

Russell remembered his time spent there: 'A three days' honeymoon.... It was bitterly cold and the water in my jug was frozen in the morning. But the bleak moors suited our mood. They were stark, but gave a sense of vast freedom. We spent our days in long walks and our nights in an emotion that held all the pain of the world in solution, but distilled from it an ecstasy that seemed almost more than human.'

However, the relationship with Collette O'Niel was not easy. She took her career seriously, and did not want children. Russell was uncomfortable. Their paths finally diverged in 1920. However, they remained friends until Russell's death.

After the divorce, Russell, forty-nine, married Dora Black, twenty-seven, on 25 September 1921 at Battersea Town Hall, south London. They were already in a relationship, and Dora carried their seven-month-old baby. Russell named their first child John Conrad after the Polish British novelist Joseph Conrad.

Dora studied languages at Girton College, University of Cambridge. In 1915, she came to London and enrolled at the University College London to study French thought. Her father, Sir Frederick Black, was a distinguished civil servant in the British government. Over the years, she graduated into a well-known feminist, author, and peace activist. She met Bertrand Russell first through her friend and Russell's student, Dorothy, in 1916. They went on walking tours of the open country tract and hilly areas in the summer of 1916. They met for tea, in bookshops, and at demonstrations against war. Their relationship further deepened. Russell invited her to join him during his summer holidays in 1919, and then they became romantic partners. They visited Soviet Russia in 1920 after the Bolshevik Revolution to see how communism worked in reality. She rejected Russell's offer of marriage in the beginning. However, Bertrand

Russell insisted that they should get married as she became pregnant during their relationship. Russell wanted his child to be 'legitimate'. After marriage, they lived in Lavender Hills in south London.

Their second child, Kate, was born in 1923. Dora authored a book in 1925 on the inadequate education of women and inequality, *Hypatia or Woman and Knowledge*. She felt the laws regulating marriage contributed to women's subjugation. She believed that men and women were polygamous by nature and should, therefore, be free to engage in sexual relationships beyond the restriction of marriage.

The year after 1921 was a period of intense writing activity for Russell. He wrote *The Analysis of Mind* in 1921 where he discussed mind and matter. He wrote a popular book in 1927, *Why I Am Not a Christian,* based on the talks he gave that year organized by the National Secular Society. He questioned the morality of religion, which he said was based on fear. Russell also wrote the bestselling book *Marriage and Morals* in 1929, questioning the Victorian notions of morality. Then he wrote another bestselling work, *The Conquest of Happiness,* in 1930.

The couple opened a boarding school called Beacon Hill School, which was run according their principle and theory of education for their children and their friends' wards.

During the late 1920s, Dora told Russell that her third child had been sired by American journalist Griffin Barry. Russell could not bear the news that Dora gave to him. Dora had met Barry in the US in 1928, and they had two children together—Harriet, born in 1930, and Roderick in 1932.

Dora wanted to raise the children fathered by Griffin Barry with the children she had with Russell.

At this juncture, Russell came in contact with Patricia Spence and became friends with her. He left Dora in 1932. Dora did not want to leave him, but Russell wanted to end the relationship. The legal fight for divorce started and continued for three years, and the court granted them divorce in 1935.

Dora Black had employed Patricia Spence in 1930 as a governess for their children. She was a twenty-year-old undergraduate at the University of Oxford, and they were married at the Midhurst register office on 18 January 1936. They had one son, Conrad Sebastian, born in 1937. She assisted him in writing *Freedom and Organisation 1814-1914*, a political history.

In 1949, Russell and Alys renewed their acquaintance and began a correspondence that continued for two years. In April 1950, aged eighty-two, Alys sent him a letter: 'I have so enjoyed our two meetings and you have been so friendly, that I feel I must be honest and just say once that I am utterly devoted to thee, and have been for over 50 years. My friends have always known that I loved thee more than anyone else in the world.... I shall still hope thee can spare time to come to lunch or dinner before very long.... Thine ever, Alys.'

Meantime, in 1938, Russell began an extended visit with Patricia to the United States, teaching first at the University of Chicago and then at the University of California at Los Angeles. He also lectured at Harvard University, and in 1940, he received an appointment to teach at City College, New York. However, right-wing activists opposed his lecture and appointment because of his views on marriage and morality. The Supreme Court cancelled his appointment on the ground that he was an alien and an advocate of immorality. Patricia stood by him and defended him.

A millionaire, Dr Albert Barnes, rescued him and gave him an appointment to lecture on philosophy at his foundation in Philadelphia, USA. These lectures later made up his book *History of Western Philosophy*, a bestselling book published in 1945. He returned to Britain in 1944 and continued to write and lecture there. He was re-elected a fellow of Trinity College, Cambridge, in 1944.

In 1948, he published *Human Knowledge: Its Scope and Limits*, which was the last of his major philosophical works.

After twelve years of marriage, Russell and Patricia had an acrimonious separation in 1949. She was not happy with him and sued for divorce on the grounds of desertion. The divorce was finalized in 1952.

Russell was lecturing at Princeton in 1950 when he came to know that he had been awarded the Nobel Prize in literature 'in recognition of his many-sided and significant writings, in which he appeared as the champion of humanity and freedom of thought'. He went to Stockholm to receive the prize; there, he delivered a prize-receiving lecture that was later published as a part of his book *Human Society in Ethics and Politics* (1954).

After the divorce with Patricia in 1952, Bertrand Russell, eighty, married Edith Finch, fifty-two, in 1952. He first met the lady in the early 1930s through his first wife, Alys. She was a graduate of St Hilda's College, University of Oxford, and taught English literature at Bryn Mawr College, Pennsylvania. She also worked as an editor for the *New York* magazine.

He met Edith again in 1950 when he went to New York to deliver the Matchette Foundation lectures. Their relationship developed quickly, and they married two years later. They lived at their house at Richmond with Russell's eldest son.

Russell continued his writings, lectures, public speeches, and peace activism. He was disturbed by the Cold War between the USA and Soviet Russia. In 1961, he wrote to the US President Kennedy and Soviet Union Premier Khrushchev, telling them how to manage the Cuban missile crisis.

His first volume of *The Autobiography of Bertrand Russell* was published in 1967.

Russell's marriage to Edith, unlike his previous ones, brought him happiness. The couple worked together, campaigned together, and lived together in what seemed to be absolute harmony.

They moved to north Wales, where they lived out their final years together, overlooking the great wild fells of the British countryside.

He dedicated his autobiography to Edith, a woman for whom he had spent eighty years searching:

Through the long years
I sought peace,
I found ecstasy, I found anguish,
I found madness,
I found loneliness,
I found the solitary pain that gnaws the heart,
But peace I did not find.

Now, old & near my end,
I have known you,

And, knowing you,
I have found both ecstasy & peace,
I know rest,
After so many lonely years.
I know what life & love may be,
Now, if I sleep,
I shall sleep fulfilled.

Russell died at 8 p.m. on 2 February 1970 at the age of ninety-seven after a brief spell of influenza. His body was cremated in Colwyn Bay, and his ashes were scattered over the Welsh mountains.

23

Alfred Nobel

In 1876, Alfred Nobel, forty-three, gave an advertisement in a newspaper in Vienna: 'Wealthy, highly educated elderly gentleman seeks a lady of mature age, versed in languages, as secretary and supervisor of household.'

Bertha Kinsky, thirty-four, the daughter of an Austrian army officer, had fallen on hard times and applied for the job after she saw the advertisement. She reported to Nobel in Paris. He lived there for most of his later life from 1873 to 1891 and set up a laboratory in the Sevran commune of Paris. Sevran was then the French capital of gunpowder and explosives.

Earlier, Bertha was in the service of the aristocratic, wealthy Viennese industrialist Baron Karl von Suttner. While she taught the children of the family, she fell in love with young Arthur von Suttner, who was seven years younger than her. Arthur's parents came to know about the affair between them. Bertha, in their opinion, was no match for their aristocratic son. They sacked Bertha from the job and told their son to distance himself from her.

Thus, Bertha's job was lost, and she had to find a new means of livelihood. Then she came across the job advertisement from Alfred Nobel.

She worked for Nobel for a few weeks. He was a reputed man, a rich entrepreneur and scientist who had invented a new explosive called dynamite in 1867. Bertha was beautiful with golden hair and a long neck. Nobel was immediately smitten by her elegance and luminous presence. She drafted letters and reports for him. After a few days, Nobel told her, 'You are stunning. I am in love with you. Would you marry me?' But Bertha had already given her heart to Arthur Suttner. She said she was not available. She had already pledged her love for a gentleman.

Nobel was disappointed. In 1876, Bertha eloped with Arthur to western Georgia. They got secretly married there in 1883 and lived a simple life. Nobel saw her only two more times, but he corresponded with her all his life, and they remained friends for more than twenty years.

Much before the encounter with Bertha Kinsky, Alfred Nobel had suffered acute heartache. The cruel hand of fate had snatched his love, a Swedish girl working as a druggist's assistant in Paris. In 1851, when eighteen, Nobel wrote a poem showing his feelings for the girl whom he had met in the city. He gave the context of the poem:

> I came to Paris—an ocean where passion creates stormy weather
> and causes more wrecks than ever the salty waves did...

> My life, before then a desolate desert, came alive in felicity and hope. I had a goal, a heavenly goal: to win this lovely girl and to be worthy of her. I felt infinite happiness and we met again, and again and again, until we had become each other's heaven; and I became acquainted with the sweet compassion in her love and sealed it with a kiss, a chaste and holy kiss, of purest affection, even if no eye was there, except that of the Almighty, to watch over us.
>
> This could have ended in the usual way and provided joy and worry, but it was not meant to be; another bridegroom (death) had a stronger claim over her—she married to the grave.

The young girl died of tuberculosis while Nobel was still in the French capital. Her death, he claims, turned him into 'a forsaken termite in the world of the living'.

As soon as Bertha disappeared in 1876, Sylvie Hasson walked into Alfred Nobel's life. Though immensely wealthy, Nobel was not married and was a lonely man with few friends. He had poor health, and depression weighed on his spirit. He had educated himself through private tutoring and never attended an institution of higher learning. He experimented tirelessly in his lab and believed, 'If I have a thousand ideas and only one turns out to be good, I am satisfied.'

Sylvie came from a modest, middle-class family in Vienna. Her father, Hartmut Hasson, moved with his family from Vienna to Celje, Slovenia, in 1873 and started a wood trade there. Soon, he established himself in the local bourgeois society and became a prominent wood merchant.

In 1876, Sylvie, aged twenty-five, left her father's place and came to Vienna. She joined a stationery shop selling stationery and worked as a flower seller. Alfred Nobel, forty-three, then a scientist and one of the richest men in Europe, came to buy a bouquet of flowers at the shop. Sylvie's soft voice fascinated Nobel, so he invited her to a meal at a restaurant.

When Sylvie met him the second time, she told him that her life was difficult, and she had been unhappy in her youth. She had a father who did not understand her needs and did not care about her. Her stepmother was evil incarnate. She had to leave Celje because of them, and she came to Baden, 26 km from Vienna, to earn her daily bread.

Nobel had established himself as an inventor, scientist, and entrepreneur with factories and labs across the major cities of Europe. He was touched by Sylvie's painful story. After that evening, they started meeting more regularly at Baden. When away, he wrote letters to her, telling her he missed her voice, her smiles, and her company. Sylvie replied to his letters. He called her 'my love, sweet child'. Letter writing between the two continued for almost two decades (1877–1886).

Nobel was cautious in his relationship with the young girl Sylvie Hasson. He was afraid that if their relationship became public, his name and reputation would suffer a blow.

Nobel arranged all the comforts and facilities for Sylvie, as a lover would do for his beloved. He rented an apartment for her in Vienna, and in 1878, he invited her to live with him in Paris. There he bought a luxurious apartment for her.

Alfred Nobel continued to write regularly to Sylvie when he was away on business or she went to another city. He referred to her in his letters as 'Madame Sylvie Nobel'.

In the course of time, Nobel felt that Sylvie should be educated and should possess charm and poise. She should show class and finesse and be able to navigate high society. He wanted to be able to talk about his problems and issues with her. He wanted her to study, take a degree, and enrich her mind. He introduced her to reading books, appreciating art, and writing poetry. Nobel himself was fluent in Swedish, Russian, German, English, and French. He wrote novels, poetry, drama, and letters apart from working on technological inventions. He believed, 'A recluse without books and ink is already in life a dead man.'

However, Sylvie did not show any interest in learning. Nobel felt disappointed. In one letter, he wrote, 'I've been telling you since the first day, get the necessary education. But you didn't think it was necessary, and you were far from wanting to at least partially correct the sad state of affairs. A person can be head over heels in love, but a letter like the one you write can only act as a blow to the heart.'

Sylvie wanted to get married and have a husband rather than live as Alfred Nobel's friend. Nobel did not agree to that as he wanted a partner whose intellectual level was above average. He told Sylvie, 'You neither work, nor write, nor read, nor think.

Slowly, the relationship between the two became strained. Nobel said she was the cause of his intellectual decline. Sylvie realized that she could neither leave Nobel nor find a good husband.

After 1879, their relationship became more strained. Nobel suspected that Sofie had had an affair with his nephew. Once, he complained to Sofie's relative that she had cheated him and had an affair with an engineer. By

1884, their relationship began to unravel. He did not want Sofie to use his name. Still, Nobel gave her all the comforts of life. He bought her a villa in Baden in 1884.

In 1886, Sofie moved back to Vienna from Paris. For her, life in Paris meant being mostly confined to the four walls of the home, a life without meeting anyone. She loved Vienna, its roads, its theatres, and its shopping centres and felt homesick at the new place. She returned to Vienna and felt better. She realized that she was ill and depressed when she was not in Vienna, and as soon as she reached Vienna, all her woes and sickness were gone. This worried Nobel.

Away from Sylvie, Nobel felt forsaken and lonely, and he travelled from Paris and visited her regularly in Vienna and paid her bills. However, Sylvie lived a carefree and spendthrift life and did not reciprocate his affection and warmth.

In 1887, Nobel developed ballistite, a smokeless propellant used for rifle grenades. It was referred to as the 'crowning glory' of his research career.

At the end of 1890, Nobel learnt that Sylvie was pregnant. This news shocked him, and he asked her for the truth. Sylvie told him that his information was correct and he was the father of the baby she was expecting. She said, 'Now, we should get married.' Nobel told her she was being untruthful.

Finally, Sylvie agreed that the child was not his but one born as a result of a relationship with a young Hungarian cavalry officer, Nikolaus Kovar. She gave birth to a girl child, Magdalene, in 1891. Nikolaus had to leave military service and work at a champagne factory. He married Sylvie Hasson in September 1895 but their time as husband and wife was brief.

Nikolaus showed proficiency in mathematics and is regarded as a mathematician as well. Some experts believe that Nobel did not like Nikolaus and did not apportion his wealth for the Nobel Prize in the field of mathematics because of Nikolaus.

After her marriage with Nikolaus, Nobel declared that his tie with Sylvie was over. However, Sylvie did not want Nobel to leave her life; he was her only source of emotional and economic security. She requested Nobel to approve her marriage to Nikolaus. 'I have always showered unconditional love on you. Please do not leave me, for God's sake.'

After the initial shock at Sofie's conduct, Alfred Nobel gave in to her entreaties. He sent her a monthly sum and apportioned for her a life annuity of six thousand guilders in his will.

Alfred Nobel had a conflict with the French government, which accused him of treason for selling ballistite to Italy. Because of the tension, he left Paris in 1891 and moved to San Remo, Italy. He worked there for some time and established a laboratory. In 1894, Nobel acquired the firm AB Bofors in Karlskoga, Sweden, one of the largest arms manufacturers in the world.

Nobel donated 94 per cent of his fortune (about US$234 million out of US$250 million) to be used for the Nobel Prize. He came up with the idea of using his money as a prize after his brother, Ludvig Nobel, died in 1888. Then a French newspaper mistakenly thought Alfred Nobel had passed away. The newspaper published the news with the headline 'The Merchant of Death is Dead'. The newspaper further said, 'Dr Alfred Nobel, who became rich by finding ways to kill more people faster than ever before, died yesterday.'

This was a shocking headline and news story for Alfred Nobel. He had invented dynamite and other types of explosives, which made weapons more destructive. He gauged the public opinion about him and felt he had to work to change his image. He came up with the idea of Nobel Prizes. He set up the Nobel Prizes in his will for honouring outstanding contributors from the streams of physics, chemistry, medicine, and literature with a prize.

In Georgia, Bertha Kinsky took up writing books and contributing to newspapers. She wrote *Inventory of the Soul* in 1883 and took a pro-disarmament stand in this work. She argued for the inevitability of world peace due to technological advancement. She then returned to her husband Arthur Suttner's family in Austria. There, she engaged in peace activities and wrote the book *Lay Down Your Arms* in 1889.

After reading her book, Nobel wrote to her, 'I have just finished reading your masterpiece.' He also called her 'an Amazon who so valiantly wages war on war.'

In 1892, Bertha invited Nobel to join a peace conference that she had organized at Bern, Switzerland. That year Nobel had got a patent for ballistite, an improved version of dynamite, and extra-dynamite. Nobel contributed money for Bertha's activities. He attended the peace conference incognito. He said, 'Fear can never end war. Fear is the stuff from which war is manufactured. The answer is not fear but love.'

Nobel insisted the best way to end war was to create a destructive weapon that would make war unthinkable.

He kept making munitions and supporting Bertha's peace efforts.

Bertha inspired and convinced him that he should also award prizes to people who contribute to peace in this world. The two argued in their letters about who was eligible and what kind of contribution in the area of peace should make one eligible for the Peace Prize. He thought the effort for arbitration and working against prejudices that caused war should get a prize. They could not settle the argument while Nobel was alive.

At San Remo, Italy, Alfred lived alone with servants, none of whom spoke Swedish. Earlier, he had suffered a stroke and had lost the ability to speak except in Swedish. He wrote, 'How sad it is to be without a friend who could whisper a consoling word, and would one day gently close one's eyes.'

He died there of cerebral haemorrhage at the age of sixty-three on 10 December 1896. His ashes were buried in Stockholm. A year before his death, on 27 November 1895, he deposited his will in Stockholm.

After Nobel's death, experts debated over who should get the Nobel Peace Prize. In 1905, the Nobel committee awarded Bertha Kinsky the Peace Prize for her effort for peace and for writing the book *Lay Down Your Arms*. She became the first person to get a Nobel Prize in this domain. She became the second woman to win the Nobel Prize after Madam Curie.

24

Rabindranath Tagore

Rabindranath Tagore met twenty-year-old Anna at the latter's residence in Bombay in 1878, when he planned to go to the United Kingdom for higher studies. Anna was to teach the future Nobel laureate English before he set sail for England. Rabindranath was then a lean youth of seventeen with shining eyes.

Anna, whose complete name was Annapurna Turkhad, belonged to an anglicized family and wore a shirt and trousers. Her father, Dr Atmaram Turkhad, a renowned social reformer based in Bombay, was a friend of Satyendranath, the first Indian Civil Services (ICS) officer and Tagore's elder brother. Anna had recently come to India from Britain and spoke English, French, and German with ease.

During this period, while Anna taught Tagore English, Tagore recited his lyrical verses and romantic poetry and enthralled the tender soul.

After a brief stay in Bombay, it was time for Tagore to depart. Tagore boarded the ship *SS Poona* and sailed the Arabian Sea for a long journey. In England, he enrolled at a public school in Brighton, a town in the south of England, and later attended lectures at London University.

However, the lingering memory of their meeting in Bombay assailed the two souls. Anna wrote to Rabindra, 'Poet, I think that even if I were on my deathbed, your songs would call me back to life.'

Tagore was no less seared by the scars of separation. He wrote to her in Bengali, 'The dense forest, that is the human heart, is filled with endless blossoms. The flowers wither but they leave an enduring fragrance.'

Tagore addressed Anna as 'Nalini', meaning lotus, and wrote poems in her memory. Anna's father went to Kolkata with a proposal of marriage of his daughter with Gurudev, but Tagore's father rejected the offer. Tagore was younger than the lady. She would not make a suitable wife.

Then Anna lost hope of marrying the poet and married a Scottish national. Thereafter, she shifted to Edinburgh.

In England, the handsome Tagore lived in the house of Mr Scott as a paying guest. Scott had two young, pretty daughters. One of them developed a deep attachment to the young poet. Tagore kept himself restrained. He later wrote he believed the girl was his lover in his previous life. He wrote a book, *Two Days*, on his attachment with Anna and Dr Scott's daughter.

In 1880, Tagore returned to Bengal after two years in England. He continued writing stirring poems and stories, attracting the best minds.

His elder brother Jyotirindranath was married to nine-year-old Kadambari Devi in Kolkata on 5 July 1868. Jyotirindranath was then nineteen. The girl's father was an employee at the Tagore residence at Kolkata. Kadambari was tasked with learning and educating herself at Tagore's home.

When Tagore came from England in 1880, Kadambari became his literary companion. While Jyotirindranath ran the family estates, Tagore would read his poetry out loud to the lady. She was two years older than Tagore, and the two became friends. She read his lines about floating clouds, the sorrow of separation, love and desire, and leaves rustling in rainy darkness and shared her feedback with him. He nicknamed her Hecate, the Greek goddess of the night, the moon, and magic. Tagore wrote a song dedicated to her: 'Thou art the guiding beacon of my life.'

Tagore was then nineteen. The elders of the family decided that now it was time for Tagore to get married.

In 1883, twenty-two-year-old Rabindranath tied the knot with eleven-year-old girl Bhavatarini Devi as per the rituals of the Brahmo Samaj. Bhavatarini's father worked at the Tagore estate.

Kadambari kept herself busy with poetry and the images of blue sky, sparkling days, and monsoon evenings. But she felt lonely.

Four months after Rabindranath's wedding, the morning of 19 April 1884, she took an overdose of opium and closed her eyes for eternity.

We have played alongside millions of lovers,
Shared in the same shy sweetness of meeting,
the distressful tears of farewell,
Old love but in shapes that renew and renew forever.

The death of Kadambari, a close friend and companion, broke Tagore's spirit. He wrote, 'With her death it felt as though the earth had moved away from under my feet and the light had gone out from the sky. My world felt empty and my life dull. I never imagined I would ever get over the delusion of this void.'

The poet shared his pain with his friend and freedom fighter, C.F. Andrews: 'But where is the sweetheart of mine who was almost the only companion of my boyhood and with whom I spent my idle days of youth exploring the mysteries of dreamland?'

Kadambari did not cease to dominate the young poet's thoughts even after her death. Rabindranath penned the lyrics 'Pray, Love, Remember', a popular Rabindra Sangeet (Tagore Song), in her memory. He composed the song 'The one who went out of my life' in her memory. The song evoked pangs of separation.

Tagore's wife, Bhavatarini, was enrolled at a local school so that she could educate herself and appreciate literature, painting, and music. The young girl learnt things quickly and read English tomes of the masters after some time. She came to love the works of American author Mark Twain.

Rabindranath gave his wife Bhavatarini the name 'Mrinalini'. This rhymed with 'Nalini', the name he had given to Anna, who once stole the peace of his heart.

Tagore grew to love his wife, though the memory of Kadambari did not fade. Mrinalini read books, learnt to appreciate his elegant prose and magical poetry, and picked up different languages. She bore him children.

In 1902, Mrinalini Devi became ill and passed away the same year at the age of twenty-nine, leaving Gurudev desolate.

Tagore was then forty-one and chose not to remarry. Mrinalini's memory disturbed him. He published a volume of twenty-seven poems titled *Remembrance* and dedicated the work to her. The sweet and tense relationship between the two is summed up by a line Tagore once wrote to her, 'If you and I could be comrades in all our work and in all our thoughts it would be splendid, but we cannot attain all that we desire.'

Tagore won the Nobel Prize in literature in 1913. This changed the track of his life and made him famous. His writing created excitement in Europe and America. His sweet, lyrical, and enchanting lines from his award-winning *Gitanjali* earned him the reputation of 'the great mystic from the East'. He went on a tour of the world. He also visited South American countries during 1924–1925.

In 1924, the Nobel laureate landed in Argentina. He met thirty-four-year-old Victoria, a bibliophile and the publisher of literary magazine *Sur*. Tagore had fallen ill on the tour and was in poor health when he reached Argentina.

Victoria was enamoured with Tagore after reading Andre Gide's French translation of *Gitanjali*. Tagore was an icon for her. She received Gurudev and took him to her family estate at San Isidro near Buenos Aires.

The bearded poet spent two months at her villa at San Isidro. During this period, Tagore touched the inner chord of Victoria's soul. She gave him all the care and love possible. Tagore was also touched by the beauty and grace of the gentle lady. She inspired him to take up a brush, and he began painting again. Tagore composed thirty poems on romance, loneliness, separation, darkness of time, love, and longing. One of the poems ran as follows:

> While walking on my solitary way
> I met you at the dusk of nightfall
> I was about to ask you take my hand
> When I gazed at your face and was afraid.
> For I saw there the glow of the fire that lay asleep
> In the deep of your heart's dark silence

The mystic poet left Argentina, but the two remained in touch through letters. Tagore sent his poems to her, conveying sacred love, the meaning of life, the hope of meeting again, the beauty of the sky, the fragrance of blooming jasmine, and silent worship at temple at midnight. In 1930, Victoria organized an art exhibition for the poet in Paris. There, Tagore met Victoria for the second and last time.

The first Nobel laureate of India, Rabindranath Tagore, passed away at his childhood home, Jorasanko Thakurbari, in Kolkata in 1941 at the age of eighty.

25

Muhammad Ali

One October afternoon in 1953, twelve-year-old Cassius Clay (1942–2016) had gone to Louisville's Columbia Auditorium to see a sale-cum-exhibition by Black merchants. When he came out of the auditorium, he found that his new red-and-white cycle was gone. He walked to Louisville police station to report the theft. The police station had a gym, and some police officers were sparring in a boxing arena.

While Clay waited for the redressal of his grievance, police gym trainer Joe Martin invited him to the boxing gym. He saw the men practising boxing moves and was instantly enthralled. He went into the arena, traded fists, and impressed the police officer with his speed and strength. He came the next day and again joined the men at the gym. When he was hit hard, he neither panicked nor got angry.

Soon boxing became his passion. When not at the gym, Clay exchanged punches with his brother Rudy and his friends. In the mornings, he jogged the streets of Louisville, wearing heavy steel-toed work boots. 'All he wanted to do was to run, train and spar.'

Clay's father, Cassius Clay Sr, was a sign painter, and his mother, moon-faced Odessa Clay, worked as a housemaid at the houses of upper-class White people at Louisville. Their house was like a cottage in an all-Black neighbourhood. Clay joined a private gym and honed his skills. Boxing then was an easy way for a Black boy to soar and shine in the USA. He worked hard and mastered the techniques. In August 1960, he won the gold medal in the light heavyweight category at the Rome Summer Olympics.

After this win, Clay turned to becoming a professional boxer. A consortium of Kentucky millionaires backed him and offered him lucrative contracts in boxing. They saw opportunity and potential in Clay. He took his first professional match on 29 October 1960. He won the match and earned US$2,000.

Clay required a boxing trainer. A good trainer would make a lot of difference in his career. He approached Angelo Dundee, a reputed boxing trainer, and made an agreement to work under his guidance. Dundee ran Fifth Street Gym at Miami Beach, Florida. Clay shifted to this place and started taking training. Angelo Dundee was of Italian origin and had trained top boxers of the USA. He would work with Clay for his entire professional career.

While Clay was taking baby steps in the boxing profession, Sonny Liston was at the top of the boxing world. He won the heavyweight boxing championship in 1962, defeating Floyd Patterson. He was an ex-convict, a former mob enforcer, and had destroyed several heavyweight boxers. He thumped the popular two-time champion Floyd Patterson into unconsciousness in a minute on two separate occasions. The press considered Liston among the sport's all-time punchers, the 'invincible one'. 'Liston was the biggest baddest fighter in the world and to those who understood the sport, he seemed invincible.'

Clay wanted to fight no one other than Liston. Apparently, this was a foolish idea. Clay was talented and strong and had won an Olympic medal at Rome in the light heavyweight category. But he was nobody in the world of heavyweight professionals. Yet Clay wanted a match with Liston. He created lots of light and thunder, openly challenging Liston in the media and in public forums. Liston was curious about this boy challenging him. Clay said he would knock Liston out in eight rounds. He tried to unnerve Liston, making irresponsible statements. His mantra was 'Float like a butterfly, sting like a bee. The hands can't hit what the eyes can't see.'

Nevertheless, a match was organized on 25 February 1964. On the morning of the fight, the columnist Jackie Gleason wrote, 'Sonny Liston will win in eighteen seconds of the first round, and my estimate includes the three seconds Blabber Mouth will bring into the ring with him.'

Clay dominated the fight. He punched a cut on Liston's face. In the fourth round, he had a burning sensation in the eyes, suspected to be caused by oil. He feared some foul play by the opponents and thought to quit. His trainer Angelo Dundee told him to continue. He pushed him back, shouting, 'Keep dancing! Hit and run!' Liston was flat on the ground after six rounds. Clay screamed, 'I am the king!' This victory became the iconic image of Clay.

Martin Luther King Jr congratulated Clay by sending him a telegram. Clay had some time back come into contact with Malcolm X, a civil rights activist and spokesperson of the Nation of Islam. He was convinced by Malcolm's talk of Black empowerment and the promotion of Islam within the Black community. Two days after his win over Liston, he joined the Nation of Islam and changed his name from Cassius Clay to Muhammad Ali. He considered Cassius Clay a slave name.

Ali, twenty-two, came in contact with Sonji Roi, twenty-three, a girl from a humble family, in 1964. Her parents died when she was young. With no means to support herself, she took up a job as a waiter in nightclubs. Ali met her at a Miami nightclub where she was working as a cocktail waiter. He told her she was the prettiest girl he ever saw.

Ali had just won his first heavyweight championship, defeating Sonny Liston. Ali proposed marriage to her the night he met her. She looked alluring, and her eyes seemed to hold secrets. They dated for just a month, visiting the riverside, cafes, and a rose garden. He asked for a kiss, but he did not know how to kiss. Sonji says he fainted when she held him in her hands and taught him how to kiss. The couple married at the office of a justice of the peace in Gary, Indiana, on 14 August 1964 as per the Christian tradition. The bride wore an ordinary summer dress, while Ali was in a business suit.

However, the couple separated after less than two years, and their divorce was finalized in January 1966. They had no issue out of the wedlock. One of the causes of divorce was Ali's association with the Nation of Islam and his change in perspective on life. He wanted Roi to dress like a Muslim woman, but she did not like Ali's suggestion. Their differences intensified, and finally, the two decided to separate. Ali filed for divorce in a Miami courtroom. He complained that her clothes were too revealing, and he did not want his wife to wear such clothes.

After the divorce, Roi moved to Chicago and took up modelling and singing. She married a corporate lawyer, Reynaldo Glover, and the couple was blessed with two children.

For the next three years, Ali dominated the boxing arena. In a rematch against Sonny Liston on 25 May 1965, he knocked him out in the first round.

Ali met Belinda Boyd (Khalilah Camacho) for the first time in the spring of 1964 when she was selling grocery items at a Nation of Islam store in Chicago. When Ali left the store, Belinda imitated his manners, his accent, and his gestures before her friends. Ali liked the girl and told his friends to find out details about her parents. Belinda was then fourteen and as tall as Ali. Her ancestors had come to the USA from Pakistan.

Ali followed the girl. Her body, carved with perfect lines, and her captivating charm stirred passion in his heart. He waited for her to finish her duty so that he could drive her home. Belinda was also fascinated by Ali. She prayed to God to give her Ali as husband. The odds were high. He was an Olympic gold medal winner, a world heavyweight champion, and married. She was a minor.

After a year or two of interaction, Ali went to her house and talked to her father, seeking her hand in marriage. Belinda was now sixteen and in high school.

Ali was in trouble with the government. In 1966, he refused to be drafted into the military for fighting in the Vietnam War. He asked the authorities, 'You want me to do what the white man says and go fight a war against some people I don't know nothing about?' The media called him an unpatriotic coward. He was sentenced to five years imprisonment for refusing induction into the US armed forces, but his appeal at the Supreme Court kept him out of the prison.

Belinda's father asked him how he was going to run his family as he had lost his licence to box and his world title. Ali said everything was going to be normal very soon. He would get his job and his title back. Belinda's father was satisfied with his answer. Ali had finalized his divorce with Sonji Roi in January 1966.

Belinda, seventeen, married Ali on 18 August 1967 at a ceremony held in Ali's two-bedroom house. A Baptist minister presided over the ceremony. After marriage, Belinda changed her name to Khalilah Ali.

Belinda was serious about her husband's career. She started doing her bit to restore his title. She worked as Ali's publicist and planner. She campaigned to make him a people's man, so that people came forward in his support and an opinion was built in his favour and he could get his boxing licence back. She booked speaking engagements for Ali at colleges around the country. She took action to influence reporters and sports casters. She approached them and requested them to help with Ali's image make-over.

Through this period, Ali was worried that his career was ruined, and he was going to jail for his stand against the war. His appeal against conviction was still pending at the Supreme Court. He would tell his acquaintances that the government was sending him to prison in a short time. Belinda told him to think positive and believe everything would be back on track.

Belinda says, 'I started the campaign to make him the people's champion.... I had buttons and stickers with his name and picture on it. I would hand them out to everybody.' She booked speaking engagements at colleges around the country, which would pay him US$1,500 to US$2,000 per visit. To influence sports reporters, she would send them birthday cards and postcards from places Ali visited. In 1969, the couple had their first daughter, Maryum, and shifted to a house in Winwood, a neighbourhood in Philadelphia.

Finally, Ali got a relief. The Supreme Court of the USA overturned his conviction on 28 June 1971. Now his honour and his title were restored. He was happy after five years of uncertainty.

Belinda found Ali was going around with other women and consequently losing his focus in the game. She found it insulting as his wife, and felt it would also compromise his chances of winning world titles..

After his win at the Supreme Court, Ali challenged Joe Frazier who had become the heavyweight champion during his absence from the ring. Ali had a few matches with the professionals to renew his skills before the main fight. During his legal wrangle with the US government, his boxing skills had deteriorated. The legs that gave him an advantage no longer carried him as surely around the ring; his swift reflexes were gone.

The fight with Frazier was going to be a fight of historic proportions. It was billed as the 'fight of the century'. On 8 March 1971, the fight between the two was held for the world title at Madison Square Garden in New York City. During the match, Ali's blows, which once shook the earth, did not show any magic. Frazier dominated the arena and put him on the ground after raining tough blows on his body.

Belinda was present at the venue. She wanted her husband to come out on top after the long banishment. She was disappointed with Ali's miserable performance. She thought his habit of flirting with girls had caused the loss. She shouted at the top of her voice, 'I told you so.'

Belinda later says, 'I saw how cocky he was acting before the fight.... And he was fooling around with all these girls. One night, I caught him with one of his women. I predicted then he was going to lose to Frazier.'

Belinda again worked on him to make him serious and competitive for the matches. She taunted him and made him burn. She says, 'For him to succeed, I had to bring him down in order to pick him back up.'

Belinda's dream and her constant pressure on Ali to focus and perform worked on him. She adds, 'His attitude changed after the first Frazier fight. He started listening to what I had to tell him. That is why I pushed him so hard for his fight against Foreman, which a lot of folks expected Ali to lose.'

She worked to keep him motivated for the big bouts. Before the next heavyweight fight in Zaire in 1974, she went to a carnival and brought home a customized T-shirt.

Ali saw that the front of the T-shirt bore the message, 'I love him because he is the greatest.' Then Belinda turned around, and the back read, 'George Foreman.'

'What the hell is wrong with you, woman?' Ali told her. The ploy worked. He quickly re-energized his training effort.

Ali continued taking part in heavyweight fights to return to shape and revive his skills. He fought world-class opponents and defeated them. He also fought Joe Frazier a second time and won against him, though it was not a world title match.

In 1974, he was scheduled for the Rumble in the Jungle, a heavyweight championship boxing match against George Foreman at a stadium in Kinshasa, Zaire. Foreman had become the world heavyweight champion after dethroning Frazier during a fight in Jamaica in 1973. On this tour, Ali met a model, Veronica Porche, who had come there to collect funds for charity. He was fascinated by her and asked her to meet him.

In this match, Ali defeated Foreman in the eighth round. Till then Foreman had not tasted defeat. Ali now regained the heavyweight title. After the win, he shouted, 'I told you all, all of my critics, that I was the greatest of all time.' Ali believed psychology was everything: 'What you are thinking about, you are becoming.' The US President Gerald Ford invited him to the White House to honour him after this victory in Zaire.

Ali had the next big fight waiting for him in Manila in 1975. The event was called 'Thrilla in Manila'. He was to fight heavyweight champion Joe Frazier again for the heavyweight world championship. Ali had earlier lost to Frazier in 1971. It was time to even the score. His wife,

Belinda, mocked him for losing the match and she blamed his tendency for flirting with the girls for the disaster.

Ali went to Manila. His newfound love, Veronica Porche, accompanied him, while Belinda stayed back in Chicago with their kids. During the tour, Ali introduced Veronica as a cousin, his wife's travelling companion. But the news clips showed Ali and Veronica walking arm in arm as romantic partners. She attended the presidential banquet at Malacanang Palace. President Ferdinand Marcos told Ali, 'You have a beautiful wife.' The champ replied, 'I saw your wife. You're not as dumb as you look.'

Belinda saw the footage of Ali and Porche at the banquet. She was livid. She took the first available flight to Manila with a set of 'bodyguards', and stormed into Ali's hotel suite at Manila Hilton to confront him. She tore down drapes, smashed mirrors, and scratched Ali's face.

The fight with Frazier ended in a win for Ali on 1 October 1975 after fourteen rounds. The match was one of the most brutal fights in boxing history, and it is regarded as the greatest prize fight of all time. Ali was world heavyweight champion for the third time. He says, 'Champions aren't made in the gyms. Champions are made from something they have deep inside them: a desire, a dream, a vision.'

Belinda realized his flings with women continued despite her best efforts to keep him in check. She thought she could not tolerate his dalliance with women any more. He filed for divorce on 2 September 1976 in a Chicago court. The judge finalized the petition in January 1977.

They had four children. The eldest child was Maryum Ali born in 1968, then twin daughters, Jamillah and Rasheda, born in 1971, and son Muhammad Jr, born in 1973. Belinda remarried Antar Ali in 1985 and later divorced her next husband also.

Veronica Porche, eighteen, reportedly married Ali a week before the Rumble in the Jungle fight in Kinshasa on 30 October 1974. Ali was still married to Belinda. The ceremony was performed secretly in the presence of a witness. As bigamy was illegal, the marriage was not announced to the world. Belinda did not accept that Ali had solemnized a marriage with Veronica.

Born in December 1955, Veronica was a native of Lake Charles, Louisiana. She was a model and a beauty pageant winner. She graduated from Belmont High School in Los Angeles in 1973 and enrolled at the University of Southern California.

They formally married at the Beverly Wilshire Hotel on 19 June 1977. Veronica wore a white gown with a flowing train. Ali, thirty-five, wore a cream suit. At the time of their marriage, Veronica was pregnant with their child, Laila Ali, who was born in December 1977.

Ali continued his fights and matches, though his limbs grew heavy and his speed betrayed him.

He retired from the ring in 1981. He had won the world heavyweight boxing championship three times. He had fifty-six fights in his career, and he lost only five of them. Of these, one fight was against ferocious Sonny Liston in 1964, when he was a twenty-two-year-old novice. His mother accompanied him to all his championship fights.

In his marriage with Veronica, happiness eluded him. Ali continued being friendly with women even after his third marriage. Veronica did not like him taking liberties. She has said, 'It was too much temptation for him, with women who threw themselves at him.... It didn't mean anything.

They had two children, Laila Ali and Hana Ali, from this marriage. Laila Ali went on to become a famous boxer. The two divorced in 1986 after nine years of marriage. After the divorce, Veronica earned a PhD in psychology. She appeared in television shows and acted in films.

After the divorce with Veronica, Ali married nineteen-year-old Lonnie Williams Ali on 19 November 1986. She became his fourth wife. He had met her earlier at Louisville, Kentucky, in 1963 when she was six. She was known as Yolanda Williams. Her house was the neighbourhood's social centre, where all the local children socialized.

Their house in the area was across the road from the house that Ali had brought for his parents. Lonnie's mother met Ali's mother and interacted with her regularly. Their interactions soon blossomed into friendship.. Then, Ali, twenty-one, used to come to see his mother. Ali became like a family to Lonnie.

According to Lonnie, in 1974, she felt that she was going to get married to Ali. 'I was just a kid in school, and I had things I needed to do, but I knew. I was young, but it was intuitive. The thought was like an umbrella, always over my head.' In 1982, Ali invited her to lunch during one of his visits to Louisville. In 1982, she became Ali's primary caregiver, and in return, he paid for her to attend graduate school at the University of California, Los Angeles (UCLA). Ali was forty-four at the time of marriage. She knew that Ali had been diagnosed with Parkinson's disease, a degenerative neurological condition, in 1984.

She earned an undergraduate degree in psychology at Vanderbilt College in 1978 and an MBA from UCLA in

1986. She took jobs as an employment counsellor and an accounts official.

The marriage ceremony was performed in front of a small gathering in the private home of a former mayor of Louisville, Harvey Sloane. Lonnie was twenty-nine, and Ali, forty-four. He had now shifted to Los Angeles. Lonnie worked as a financial planner and manager in Ali's life and career. Her intervention revived Ali and his fortunes, says journalist Dave Kindred. 'I think Ali would have been gone and forgotten 30 years ago, if not for Lonnie,' he adds.

Ali had holed himself up in his Los Angeles mansion and was a recluse in dire need of medical and financial attention. 'She took care of him and created a financial empire for him that made it possible for him to have a comfortable life.'

In 1992, Lonnie incorporated Greatest of All Time, Inc. (G.O.A.T. Inc) to consolidate and licence his intellectual properties for commercial purposes. She served as the vice president and treasurer of the company.

In 1996, Ali carried the Olympic torch aloft to open the Olympic games in Atlanta before a worldwide television audience estimated at 3 billion people. He remembered, 'Lighting that torch in Atlanta didn't make me nervous. Standing up to the government—that made me nervous.'

Ali died of Parkinson's disease at the age of seventy-four in a hospital in Phoenix, Arizona. Ali wished, 'I'd like to live to a hundred.' His funeral was organized in Louisville. Ali once said, 'I just wish people would love everybody else the way that they love me. It would be a better world.'

26

Immanuel Kant

Immanuel Kant is ranked with Plato and Aristotle for his contribution to philosophy. He was born on 22 April 1724 at Königsberg (in East Prussia), now part of Russia. After the Second World War, the Soviet Union took control of the territory and named it Kaliningrad. His father was a harness-maker in the city of Memel, now in Lithuania.

Kant compared himself to Copernicus and said he affected a Copernican revolution in philosophy. He tried a synthesis of continental Europe's allegiance to rational thought and British philosophy's espousal of sense-experience and thus changed the course of philosophy.

Kant never married and maintained the habits of his studious youth till old age. He was brought up by his parents in a religious environment, and he graduated from Collegium Fridericanum, Königsberg, in 1740. The same year, sixteen-year-old Kant enrolled himself at the University of Königsberg. He would stay there for the rest of his life. He studied philosophy there under an associate professor, Martin Knutzen.

He received a master's degree from the university in 1755. That year, 1755, Senat der Albertina, the governing body of the university, gave Kant the licence to lecture in the University of Königsberg. Thus, he was appointed a lecturer there. He began teaching mathematics, physics, logic, and metaphysics.

On 17 April 1770, Kant received a PhD in philosophy from the same university. That year, the university authorities appointed him professor of logic and metaphysics at the university. He said, 'Two things fill the mind with ever new and increasing admiration and awe, the oftener and the more steadily we reflect on them: the starry heavens above and the moral law within.' Now, Kant, aged forty-six, was an established scholar and an influential philosopher.

He published his work *General Natural History and Theory of the Heavens*. His fame spread across Germany.

Kant would be present at his desk in the lecture room at 7 a.m. every morning throughout his tenure as professor. Bertrand Russell has described Kant as a man of such regular habits that people used to set their watches by him as he passed their doors. He did not socialize much and lived a quiet life. He wrote until the time of his death.

Kant has given rules for happiness: something to do, someone to love, something to hope for. But there was no one in his long life of seventy-nine years whom he loved passionately and married. Kant's friend Christoph Heilsberg said, 'He felt marriage to be a desire and to be a necessity,' but he never took the final step. He came close to marrying on two occasions in his life.

The first time, a 'young, beautiful and gentle' widow fascinated him, and her beauty held his heart captive. Kant seriously thought of marrying her. However, before proposing to her, he took time to work out his source of income and to find out whether he would be able to maintain a family with children. If he was financially sound and earning enough money to meet the requirements of wife and children, he would go ahead and marry the widow. If not, he would not entertain the idea of marriage.

Before he could complete the calculation and arrive at a conclusion, the lady found a match and said farewell to Kant. She was also looking for a companion and could not keep waiting for a response from Kant. Thus, one of the greatest philosophers of the world missed the chance of marriage.

The opportunity for marriage again knocked at Immanuel Kant's door after some years. This time, a young girl, a native of the German province of Westphalia, pierced the philosopher's heart. She had come to Königsberg with a noblewoman to stay and enjoy the environ of the place. Her love filled him with its tide. He found comfort in her company and allowed people to know that he was going around with her.

However, Kant again delayed on deciding marriage with her, and the reason for the delay was the same. He had not been able to conclude whether he would be able to maintain a family with the salary and time available to him. The result was disastrous. His beloved, after dance, dinner, and song in his company returned to her home without having received his offer.

At one more time, he was disposed to marry a lady who lived in Königsberg. Her sweet voice soothed his spirit and awakened a yearning within him. He thought she would make a good companion in the journey of his life. But then his feelings and attraction for her faded after some time, and he thought she would not make a good wife. His academic activities like writing, reading, deliberations, and his perfect routine would be disrupted.

David Hume, a Scottish philosopher, published his book *A Treatise on Human Nature* in 1739. Hume argued that we can only have knowledge of things that we get through our sensory experiences, and we cannot infer anything beyond that about the real world. He says we do not get an accurate idea about things like causality and morality through our experience. If you hit a white ball with a black ball on a billiard table, the white ball will move and we believe that the black ball is the cause of white ball moving. However, we have no experience of the black ball making the white ball move. We have only experienced one event coming after the other, not of one event happening because of the other. Kant read *Hume's Treatise on Human Nature* in the late 1760s.

Hume's philosophy challenged Kant's assumptions about the nature of knowledge. Kant said that David Hume's work woke him from a 'dogmatic slumber' in which he lay comfortable with the tenets of both religion and natural philosophy.

Kant set himself to solve these problems. He isolated himself from his friends to focus on this challenge. He worked for about ten years and emerged from his silence in 1781 with the book *Critique of Pure Reason*. This work is hailed as one of the most profound contributions in the history of philosophy.

Kant argued in this book that there is a distinction between the noumenal (the world as it is in itself) and the phenomenal (the world as it appears to us). We can only have knowledge of the phenomenal world, but we can use our reason to make inferences about the noumenal world.

Kant was part of the literary society of Königsberg, and he had friends like Johann Goeschen, Konrad Jacobi, Maria Charlotta, Hippel, and others. Maria, twenty-five, a woman with thick hair, beautiful lips, and dark, glistening eyes, was married to fifty-one-year-old Konrad Jacobi. In the literary circle, she was called 'the Princess'.

Then Maria had an affair with Goeschen. After a brief courtship, she married Johann Goeschen in 1769. The affair caused a scandal in the town. Before her marriage to Goeschen, Maria had shown interest in Kant. She liked going to theatres, balls, and masquerades in his company. However, Kant could not betray the trust of his friend and her husband, Konrad Jacobi.

This scandal shocked Kant and left him without an interest in marriage. For him, Maria Charlotta became a constant reference point of what a woman could do to a man and how marriage could be ruined. Mirroring Kant's views, his friend Theodor Gottlieb von Hippel wrote in his *Essay on Marriage* (1769), 'In truth, only a fool, a knave, or a priest are capable of marriage. The last one is bound by duties, the knave hopes that his wife is unfaithful, and the fool believes that she is faithful.' Kant thus decided that he would never get married. In his lectures on anthropology, he said, 'A younger wife dominates an older husband and a younger husband an older wife.'

Kant extolled the advantages of being single. His favourite poem praised celibacy, mentioning examples of the Pope, Democritus, Thales, Descartes, and Leibnitz. A line of the poem stated, 'Permit me to say that I have no wife.'

He advised friends to marry from rational considerations rather than for the sake of affections. He shared the experience of a man who had married twice, first for the woman's wealth, the second because he loved her. The man was as happy with one as with the other. Kant thought that money outlasted beauty and all other charms.

Though Kant did not marry, he advised twenty-year-old Maria von Herbert when she was in trouble with a man. Maria was a student of Kant's philosophy. She wrote to him in 1791, 'Great Kant, as a believer calls to his God, I call to you for help … or for counsel to prepare me for death. Your writings prove that there is a future life. But as for this life, I have found nothing…. I loved someone who encompassed within himself all that is worthwhile…. I lived only for him…. I have offended this person, because of a long drawn out lie, which I have now disclosed to him … and his love vanished…. Now put yourself in my place, and either damn me or comfort me. I've read the metaphysics of morals, and the categorical imperative, and it doesn't help a bit. Answer me, I implore you.'

Kant replied to Maria, 'Your deeply felt letter comes from a heart that must have been created for the sake of virtue and honesty…. I must do as you ask, namely, put myself in your place…. I do not know whether your relationship is one of marriage or friendship, but it makes no significant difference.'

Kant told her about the difference between dishonesty and reticence and the importance of morality. He told her to wait for some time so that the anger of her beloved dissipated. Then she could transform his coldness into love.

From 1871 onwards, Kant produced many tomes. In 1783, he wrote the *Prolegomena to Any Future Metaphysics,* which was a simplified presentation of the *Critique*'s main ideas. He wrote the *Groundwork of the Metaphysic of Morals* in 1785, *Critique of Practical Reason* in 1788, and *Critique of Judgement* in 1790. He has said, 'The busier we are, the more acutely we feel that we live, the more conscious we are of life.'

When he was seventy, a friend asked him whether he was not going to marry. He told him about the advantages of marriage. The philosopher took it as a joke. The friend gave him a small pamphlet on marriage, declaring that he had published it chiefly in the hope of inducing him to marry. Kant took the pamphlet politely and paid the expense of its publication.

Kant's health was bad for a long time as he suffered from heart disease. On 12 February 1804, he died in his sleep at the age of eighty at Königsberg. He was buried at Königsberg Cathedral in the town (Kaliningrad, Russia). In 1880, his remains were moved to a chapel adjoining the north-east corner of the same cathedral.

27

Virginia Woolf

Virginia Woolf, a leading English novelist and feminist, enjoyed celebrity status in her lifetime. Born in London in 1882, she studied classics and history at King's College London from 1897 to 1901. She was part of an academic and artistic circle called the Bloomsbury Group with people like the novelist E.M. Forster, the writer Lytton Strachey, the economist John Maynard Keynes, and others. Her father, Sir Leslie Stephen, was a writer, historian, biographer, and mountaineer. Her mother died when she was thirteen, and she had a difficult and painful childhood.

Her tutor Janet Case introduced her to the women's rights movement. During her university days, she met reformers and advocates of women's higher education at King's College. She was a prolific writer, and her novels, essays, short stories, diaries, and writing style provided abundant material to feminists in the 1970s to explore the difficulties of women and challenge the existing male-dominated social order. Her works were translated into more than fifty languages. A building has been dedicated to her at the University of London.

Virginia Woolf née Stephen, eighteen, first met Leonard Woolf, twenty, while visiting her brother Thoby at Trinity College at Cambridge in 1900. Leonard, born in 1880, was a British author, civil servant, and a member of the Labour Party of Britain. His father was a barrister and Queen's Counsel.

Virginia's aunt, Caroline Stephen, organized a dinner party in July 1911, and both Virginia and Leonard were invited. Leonard was 'a tense looking young man, dark, thin, slight, long-faced, with a handsome sardonic mouth, strong blue eyes, and trembling hands'. During the interaction at the dinner party, he was fascinated by Virginia. He found Virginia and her sister Vanessa to be well-read and artistic, working to break the Victorian values and treating women as equals.

Leonard went to Sri Lanka in 1904 and joined the bureaucracy as a young civil servant. From Sri Lanka, in 1909, Leonard made an offer of marriage to her, but Virginia did not respond.

He returned to London in June 1911. He toured places and interacted with Virginia's friends at Gordon Square in London. His period of sanctioned leave from duty was over, but he did not report to his place of posting.

In September 1911, Virginia told Leonard to join her at Little Talland House in Sussex County for a long weekend. Leonard went there and spent time with her. Now they began seeing each other more frequently.

By the end of December 1911, Leonard was in love with her. In January 1912, he proposed marriage, but she said she wanted more time to consider his proposal.

Leonard asked for an extension of leave from his boss in Sri Lanka. He wanted to stay in London for another six months. However, his boss asked him to join duty on time and said that no further extension of leave was possible. Now, he had to choose between his job and the prospect of marrying Virginia. He chose the latter and resigned from the service on 25 April 1912.

However, Virginia was still not able to make up her mind. In a letter on 1 May 1912, she wrote to Leonard that she did not favour marriage. She says: 'Again, I want everything—love, children, adventure, intimacy, work.... So I go from being half in love with you ... to the extreme of wildness and aloofness. I sometimes think that if I married you, I could have everything ... and then...? As I told you brutally the other day, I feel no physical attraction in you.'

Soon, she wrote another letter in which she said: 'Leonard, I have thought over your proposal, I think we can marry.' Leonard was happy with the response. The marriage took place in St Pancras district on 10 August 1912, and they went to Spain for their honeymoon.

After the marriage, Leonard came to know about Virginia Woolf's disturbed mental state, her frequent bouts of depression, and her extreme mood swings. However, Leonard decided to take the challenge in its stride. He was a stabilizing force for her, and the couple shared a close bond.

Leonard had an interest in writing. He published his first novel, *The Village in the Jungle* (1913), which was based on his experiences in Sri Lanka. While he was on their honeymoon, he started writing another work, *The Wise Virgins*.

In 1913, Virginia had a complete nervous breakdown and made a suicide attempt by consuming barbiturates. Her biographers say this might be because of her feeling of sexual failure; she was not able to perform her conjugal duties. Leonard shifted with her to the residence of his half-brother Gerard Duckworth to take better care of her. He sat beside her and nursed her. He would persuade her to eat as she would sit before the food, lost in melancholy. Leonard would take her hand, put a fork in it, and would coax her gently, 'Darling! Please eat.'

Then she fell into a frenzy in 1915 after the start of the First World War. She was not able to maintain her academic discipline and made a second suicide attempt. However, the same year (1915), she published her first novel, *The Voyage*. Leonard consulted many doctors for her treatment. Leonard describes 1914 and 1915 as 'years which we simply lost out of our lives'.

After these episodes of acute mental disorder, her condition remained more or less stable for the next twenty-five years, till the start of the Second World War. During this period, she wrote books and made friends. Leonard read the drafts of her works and gave his opinion on them, calling them 'masterpiece', 'work of genius', and 'best work'. Leonard thought that it was not safe for her health to bear a child.

In December 1922, Virginia met Vita Sackville-West at a social gathering. The latter was a successful poet and novelist with a large volume of poetry and fiction. Writing in her diary the next day, Virginia referred to her as 'the lovely gifted aristocratic Sackville-West'. After a tentative start, their relationship turned romantic.

'Virginia's response to Vita's advances was a mix of guarded acquiescence and gentle mockery.' The relationship reached its peak during 1925–1928, and it evolved into deep friendship over the years.

In a letter to her friend Ethel Smyth in December 1925, Virginia wrote: 'The only way I keep afloat … is by working…. I stop working I feel that I am sinking down, down. And as usual, I feel that if I sink further I shall reach the truth.'

This period of Virginia's intimacy with Sackville-West proved productive for both the authors. Virginia wrote three novels: *To the Lighthouse* (1927), *Orlando* (1928), and *The Waves* (1931).

Virginia's book *Orlando*, considered a feminist classic, portrays the adventures of a poet who changes his gender from man to woman and lives for centuries, meeting the top English authors. The character of the poet was based on Vita. In this work, 'she (Virginia) explores Vita, weaves her in and out of the centuries, tosses her from one sex to the other, plays with her, dresses her in furs, lace and emeralds, teases her, flirts with her, drops a veil of mist around her.'

Deep in a relationship with Virginia, Vita Sackville-West worked to uplift her self-esteem. Vita told her, 'You should not hide yourself away from the world. You are a lively woman, graceful like a winged-fairy. Your wit shines like constellations of stars, your words sculpt shapes of hard realities. Why are you worried? Trust in the genius within you. Your writings are a product of your strength and not of weakness.'

Sackville-West guided her to switch to different kinds of intellectual activities like reading and writing.

Vita went to Tehran with her husband, a British diplomat, in 1925. She was to be away there for five years. The separation was painful for both of them. Their contact ended, but the two women remained friends till Virginia died. The relationship between the two has inspired biographies and a film in 2019.

In 1941, Virginia, fifty-nine, again fell into depression. The start of the Second World War and the destruction of her home was a trigger.

On 28 March 1941, she filled her overcoat pockets with stones and walked into River Ouse near her home Monk's House in the East Sussex village to drown herself. She left a suicide note for her husband. Leonard found the letter on a table in the drawing room. She wrote: 'Dearest, I feel certain that I am going mad again. I feel we can't go through another of these terrible times.... You have given me the greatest possible happiness. You have been in every way all that anyone could be. I don't think two people could have been happier till this terrible disease came. I can't fight it any longer.'

Leonard searched for her along the River Ouse, the nearby meadows, and a local ruin that Virginia liked to visit but could not find her anywhere. He saw her walking stick fallen along the river. He was sure that he had lost a piece of his heart.

On 18 April, the local teenagers saw a 'log' floating in the River Ouse. They realized it was Virginia's body. The body was taken out, washed, and cremated.

At the back of their house stood two elm trees. Virginia called them Leonard and Virginia. Leonard buried her ashes at their roots. He was completely broken.

28

John Maynard Keynes

A Russian star ballerina, Lydia Lopokova, thirty, who had come to London with a ballet company, left the most important economist of the age, John Maynard Keynes, thirty-eight, hurt, disarmed, and awed by her charm.

Lydia worked with Russian art director Sergei Diaghilev of the Ballets Russes company. Sergei had come to London with his troupe in 1921 to stage *The Sleeping Beauty* ballet. Lydia performed the role of the Lilac Fairy—a character of the ballet. Keynes went to see the dance, but the beauty with her crown and her sparkling dress took his breath away. Smitten by the Lilac Fairy, he came daily to the set to see the beauty who cast her spells over him. He sat in an empty box where she would notice him.

Until now, Keynes had loved men and had had passionate affairs with a few of them, though he had risked romantic entanglement with a few women also.

The chief male love of his life was Duncan Grant, a member of the Bloomsbury group, which was an influential coterie of eminent English writers, intellectuals, philosophers, and artists. Its members included Virginia Woolf, the English writer Lytton Strachey, E.M. Foster, Roger Fry, and others.

Lydia Lopokova, on the other hand, born in St Petersburg as the daughter of a Russian peasant, had matured with a few romantic affairs and was married to Randolfo Barrocchi, a tour manager of the ballet company where she worked. However, her marriage had been broken since 1919, which would work in Keynes's favour.

For four years, Keynes courted Lydia. In 1925, the queen of the ballet divorced her husband and married Keynes, forty-two, a few months later.

The British fashion magazine *Vogue* printed their picture, captioned, 'The marriage of the most brilliant of English economists with the most popular of Russian dancers makes a delightful symbol of the mutual dependence upon each other of art and science.'

The couple travelled to Sussex for their honeymoon. Lydia spoke English that few could understand and was sometimes even embarrassing. The eminent philosopher Ludwig Wittgenstein came to see and wish the couple during the honeymoon period. Lydia remarked to Wittgenstein, 'What a beautiful tree.' Wittgenstein, who had been educated at Trinity College, was shocked and asked her, 'What do you mean?' Lydia signed one of her letters addressed to Keynes as 'Your true underworld dog'.

The members of the Bloomsbury Group did not approve of Lydia. Vanessa Bell had advised Keynes not to marry her. Woolf thought Lydia had violated the boundary around Bloomsbury, and she based the character Rezia in her book *Mrs Dalloway* on Lydia. The Bloomsbury group thought Lydia was not fit to be wife of the 'father of modern theoretical macroeconomics'. John Maynard Keynes was a prodigy, a powerful government official, and an eminent economist. He was a don of Eton and Cambridge.

The Nobel laureate and English philosopher Bertrand Russell, beguiled by Keynes's intelligence, once said, 'Every time I argued with Keynes, I felt that I took my life in my hands and I seldom emerged without feeling something of a fool.'

On the other hand, here was a half-educated beauty. Lytton Strachey, a male partner of Keynes's, called her 'a half-witted canary'. However, Keynes was madly drawn to the Lilac Fairy, a character who puts the whole kingdom to sleep to delay the effects of a jilted fairy's curse.

After marriage, Keynes did not stop desiring men, but he loved Lydia increasingly. They wrote letters to each other when work or travel kept them apart.

The couple wished they could produce a poet after the marriage, but they could not become parents. Lydia was often depressed because of this handicap. Her fertility was impaired as she had suffered abortions, and Keynes, now in his mid-forties, was a heavy smoker.

In 1936, an over-worked Keynes suffered a heart attack. However, the love between the famous economist and the ballet dancer endured.

The Second World War brought heavy demands on Keynes to frame economic policies for the revival of the British economy. The work pressure exhausted him, and he died at the age of sixty-two in 1946.

Lydia believed her husband had worked himself to death for his country. She became a recluse in her house in Sussex and lived surrounded by the paintings that Keynes had bought for her. After his death, she wrote: 'And now I am so utterly alone without him. The light is gone. I grieve and weep.'

Lydia lived for another thirty-five years. She died in 1981 at the age of ninety.

29

Pablo Escobar

Maria Victoria Henao met Pablo Escobar, twenty-three, in 1973 when she was twelve. She came from a middle-class family in Envigado near Medellin, Colombia's second-largest city. Pablo was her first and only lover.

Pablo Escobar was the son of a security guard. He would move around in the locality on his new cherry-red Vespa. He passed out from high school and started his career with petty crimes like car theft. He saw Maria going to her aunt's place and was bewitched by her beauty. Once when he saw her, he stopped his Vespa and told her she looked stunning. He asked his friend Yolanda to act as a go-between. He gave her gifts, a yellow bicycle, flowers, sweets, and a Camilo Sesto music album and serenaded her with romantic balloons. Maria remembers, 'He made me feel like a fairy princess and I was convinced he was my Prince Charming.'

She says she was, however, not prepared for a physical relationship with him. 'I did not have the proper tools to understand what that intense contact meant.'

However, Maria, fourteen, began to feel 'strange', and Escobar, suspecting that she was pregnant, took her to a back-alley abortion clinic. A woman there told her to lie down. She inserted several tubes into her body, telling her to remove them when she started bleeding. 'I was in intense pain, but I could not say anything to anyone. I would just pray to God that it would be over soon.' For the next few days, she lay in bed, crippled with stomach pain and bleeding profusely.

They married a year later in 1976. The marriage ceremony was held in a church in Palmira at 6 a.m. Maria's parents did not attend the ceremony as Escobar was a criminal in their eyes. Her grandmother and her aunt attended the wedding. Escobar was happy to marry her. He gazed into her eyes and said, 'We will be together forever, my love.' Escobar wore jeans and a light blue shirt.

After the marriage ceremony, Escobar carried her across a flower-fitted patio to a decorated room on the first floor to consummate the marriage. She remembers, 'It was a night of unforgettable love that remains tattooed on my skin as one of the happiest moments of my life.... I wanted time to stand still, for the intimacy we were enjoying to last forever.'

After marriage, the routine of life—cooking food, washing the dishes, and dusting the rooms—occupied her. Escobar went out for work. She did not know what kind of work he was busy in. After some time, she came to know about the nature of his engagements, but she thought she could not leave him even if he engaged in drug peddling.

Maria pursued her education and studied at a local secondary school. During her fourth year at school, she got an indication that she was pregnant. On 24 February 1977, Maria gave birth to a baby boy at El Rosario Hospital in Medellin, and they named him Juan Pablo.

By 1976, Escobar had moved from the petty crimes of his youth like car theft to drugs. He was now working to build a drug empire, selling cocaine to the world. He built a powerful cartel in Medellin and smuggled 15 tonnes of drugs a day.

After his entry into the organized drug smuggling business, Escobar had affairs with a number of women and was often visited by girlfriends. He entertained himself with a woman for a week or two and then looked for a new one.

Maria came to know about his affairs. She says, 'Gossip about his affairs can stand and, I must admit, is deeply painful for me. I remember I used to cry all night, waiting for dawn to come.' Escobar also went to the city's nightclubs and lavished women with cash, champagne, and cocktails and invited them to parties.

On one occasion, Maria caught Escobar with women. His associate flew into the Hacienda, a large private estate owned by the don, with a plane full of women. He thought his wife would not be at home.

Maria asked him what was going on. She shouted, 'I won't stay a second longer in this place, Pablo. What you do to me is disrespectful.' Escobar said, 'Sorry, darling! The women were brought for the boys so that they could have a little fun.'

Once, the Escobar family went for dinner with friends at a farm in the Colombian countryside. During the party, there was a power failure, and it became dark. While everyone, including Maria, interacted with the guests by candlelight, Escobar disappeared to have fun with a woman. He had requested the host to cut the power so that he could have privacy during lovemaking.

Maria said that when she learnt about the women in his life, she decided to turn a blind eye to them. 'I decided not to follow him, track his phone calls, or check his shirts for lipsticks.... He who seeks shall find and I preferred not to find anything.'

In 1979, Escobar moved to Hacienda Napoles, an estate in Puerto Triunfo. It was spread out over 20 sq km and had a zoo. In this complex lived his wife, Maria, and their children. He also built an apartment camouflaged behind the stables, close to the main house. He built cabins in remote areas to which they used to escape to seek entertainment. The estate had a racing track and a bull ring.

Maria says, 'He was a great lover. I fell in love with his desire to help people and his compassion for their hardship. We would drive to places where he dreamed of building schools for the poor.'

In mid-1981, he met Wendy Chavarriaga Gil, twenty-three, at a nightclub in Medellin. She offered him a drink, and the two of them talked, danced, and eventually fell in love.

Their relationship continued for a long time. She was tall, with a swan-like neck and green eyes. She was the only woman who unravelled the bonds of Escobar's marriage.

Wendy was a rich woman who owned a home near the Medellin Country Club near the Escobars' family home.

Escobar invited her to 'La Escarcha' when his hitmen told him that a woman, who had arrived from abroad, wanted to see him for a business matter. Escobar said, 'She could see me anytime.' She came to him and sat on a maroon sofa. The meeting, which took place over a cup of coffee, lasted for 25 minutes. Escobar looked at her greenish eyes, sparkling teeth, and ruby lips. He was dazed by her beauty. The meetings became frequent, and they became intimate friends.

Maria has said, 'Pablo did not expect that his guest would arrive with a spectacular body. When he saw the woman with luminous skin and hair spun like gold, he surrendered.' Escobar spent more time with her than the rest of his women. Slowly, Wendy began to exert a subtle influence on him. She got Escobar's offices redecorated. Maria Victoria says: 'When I arrived, I was struck by the refined style of everything in the place, but mainly my husband's office; which had clearly been decorated by someone with great taste. Intuition told me that Pablo's girlfriend's hand must be there.'

He travelled with Wendy, arm in arm, through New York. The lady started taking more liberties. Maria snubbed her on some occasions, but she continued to rule Escobar's heart.

Escobar did not plan to divorce his wife; she was the mother of his children. She had given birth to Juan Pablo, six years ago, and was expecting Manuela.

One rule of the game for Escobar's girlfriends was that they would not get pregnant. However, Wendy felt she was above such rules and did not care much about such restrictions. She became pregnant. She planned to go to the USA without Escobar's consent. But if she went to the USA, she would be out of his control. She could play games and cause threats to his business interests. It was time for the final reckoning.

Learning of this, he sent his boys to call her to meet at La Escarcha.

Wendy came to his place. She was not aware of how her world had changed in the last few days. When she took a seat, a few ladies took hold of her, and a nurse injected her with a sedative.

When Wendy woke up, she saw blood on the bed and felt a sharp pain in her belly. He told her, 'I took it from you.' The baby had been aborted. She had been five months pregnant. She went to the window of the apartment to jump, but his bodyguards stopped her. Years of their relationship, golden memories, and the evenings of dance and champagne were over.

That day in 1983, Wendy swore revenge. Wendy worked on Popeye, one of Escobar's top men. He could deal a colossal loss to Escobar. She ensnared him with her charm and made love to him. Escobar came to know that his deputy had fallen for Wendy. He called Popeye and told him to go ahead with her but be a bit cautious. Escobar spied on every move of the couple.

Finally, Escobar recorded Wendy's conversation with an officer of the Colombian police to capture him—dead or alive.

Escobar summoned Popeye and played the conversation to him. He told him, 'You or her, love or death.' He ordered Popeye to execute her.

Popeye called Wendy to a restaurant in Medellin. He was under directions from Escobar to shoot her, but he couldn't pull the trigger on the twenty-eight-year-old woman. 'I loved her too much,' he said. He sent two men to do the dirty work. When the job was finished, he went to see Wendy's corpse lying in a sea of blood. He wanted to ensure that the task given by his master was done.

On learning about Wendy, Maria, his wife, said, 'The thing that hurt me the most was knowing that my husband seemed to have fallen for her hard.' Maria threatened to leave Escobar. She was sick of his relationships. But he managed Maria. She said, 'Despite his constant affairs, he managed to remain as romantic as ever ... the thoughtful husband.' From 1987 to 1993, he made it to the Forbes Billionaires list.

Veronica Valmont, a glamorous journalist, author, and a television anchor, was another of Escobar's famous friends. In 1982, Escobar saw her in a pantyhose commercial and was smitten by her. He told his men to arrange a meeting with her. His men sent an invitation to the woman, and she accepted.

She was thirty-two and one of the most famous women in South America. She claimed to be a descendant of the kings of England, and her family members included a finance minister and an army general. Her friends included Colombia's wealthiest men.

She went to Escobar's Hacienda Napoles in 1983 and interviewed him. She fell for his charm. She spent the next five years as his close friend and confidant. Her interview propelled Escobar onto the national stage. With him, Veronica experienced the high life. She had access to Escobar's jet and swanky hotels.

Escobar broke Veronica's bond with her husband using the weight of his infamy. She came to know what he had done to Wendy. She became scared and did not see him for weeks. Her contempt for him increased as he spilled more blood.

One evening, Pablo Escobar broke into her flat and grabbed the tape of his interview, currency notes, a draft of a novel she had written, and the Beretta pistol he had gifted to her.

Veronica says the reason why she became close to him was that 'he was the only rich man in Colombia who was generous with the people, in the country where the rich have never given a sandwich to the poor'.

While she hated him from inside, Escobar also decided to spurn her. He learned that the lady was friends with other men while she pretended to be close to him. That put him off.

One day, when Veronica came to Escobar's estate, the guards did not open the gates. They had orders not to allow her inside. She was shocked and returned. While she was rejected by Escobar, she realized that people in high society, her elite friends, had begun to avoid her because of her proximity with Escobar.

By the early 1980s, Pablo Escobar was a big don. His team, the Medellin cartel, was sending 80 per cent of all cocaine abroad. His drug empire generated a revenue of 70 million dollars a day.

Then Escobar ordered his hitmen to assassinate the minister of justice, Rodrigo Bonilla, thirty-seven, as he was acting tough on the drug cartel. They shot him dead in Bogota on the night of 30 April 1984. For the first time, such a senior dignitary had been killed in the county. That changed Maria's life. The government issued a warrant of arrest against Escobar and wanted an immediate clampdown on his activities.

He also assassinated Luis Carlos Galan, a Colombian politician and journalist, who contested elections for the presidency of Colombia on two occasions, during a campaign rally in 1989. The politician had denounced Pablo Escobar and the influence of the mafia in Colombian politics.

The Colombian authorities also believed that Escobar had blown up Avianca Flight 203, killing 107 persons aboard the plane, on 27 November 1989. The intention was to kill a presidential candidate, César Gaviria Trujillo, a political successor of Luis Carlos Galan. César was to take that flight to Cali, a city in south-west Colombia. For security reasons, he did not board the flight at the last moment.

By this time, Escobar was also at war with a rival drug cartel in Cali. In the 1990 general election, César was elected the president of Colombia. César, after taking the oath of office, launched a full-scale war against him.

Maria said, 'I was not able to leave him, not just out of love but also out of fear, powerlessness, and uncertainty.' She was worried that Escobar's rival would discover and silence her.

In 1991, Escobar struck a deal with the Colombian authorities for serving a five-year sentence at a prison called La Catedral, which was built on a mountain top in Medellin. He surrendered to the authorities on the promise that he would be treated leniently. He was finally put in prison.

The jail had a bar, a jacuzzi, and a waterfall. Escobar had a good time there. However, soon, the government learnt that Escobar was living in luxury and was running his drug empire from prison. He was also assassinating his opponents in the drug trade.

The government then planned to throw him in an army barracks jail. Escobar came to know about the government's intention. He slipped from there on 22 July 1992 after serving about a year as a prison sentence.

The government, with all its might, started an organized search for the drug lord, but Escobar's armed guards gave him protection. He struck back and killed informers, police personnel, rival cartel members, politicians, and the like.

The fight between him and the government's forces continued for some time. Then his opponents, security personnel, and drug gangs came together to give him a fight. They targeted his estates, strongholds, and musclemen. The combined forces of the government and his opponent proved heavy for his might, and he started receiving setbacks. His men deserted him under the heat, and he became isolated.

When the pressure became too much, he, along with his wife Maria and two children, went into hiding in a blue house in El Poblado, an area of Medellin, in August 1993. According to Maria, 'My husband and I knew that the final goodbye had come sooner than later: Our current situation was unsustainable. Death was peening at us around the corner. The blue house was to be our final hideout.... I cried and cried. I got married at 15 in the Catholic church, thinking it was for life. I was deeply in love with Pablo.'

On 18 September 1993, Escobar walked Maria into the bedroom and said, 'Sweetheart, it is time to pack everybody's suitcase. You are all going to stay in the Altos building under government protection.' That day at 11 p.m., Maria left her husband and moved out with her children: 'I understood there was no other option.

It was here; the moment of separation, of our final goodbye.'

The government agencies and cops chased him to get him to pay for his acts. His empire started crumbling, and he ran out of luck. In the end, he was left with one gunman to defend him against the might of the state.

He told his wife to leave for Germany, but the German government said they were not welcome there. The airport authorities on the Frankfurt airport runway sent them back to Bogota, the capital of Colombia.

When the flight landed in Bogota, government agencies took control of them and detained them in a hotel in the capital. Escobar came to know about their detention and became worried. He made a phone call to his son at the hotel from his hideout. He knew calling them was risky, and his location would be detected by police and the intelligence agencies. Nevertheless, he called.

Police were listening to his phone call and traced his location to Barrio Los Olivos, a neighbourhood in Medellin. They reached his hideout and saw him in a house. Escobar felt some unusual movement near his house, and while talking to his son, he said, 'Wait, I am seeing some disturbance.' He found that police commandos were at his throat.

Soon, the shoot-out started. He had just one bodyguard with him at that hour. Policemen were in and around on foot, in vehicles and in helicopter with guns. They were climbing the wall, and some were on the roof with barrels pointed towards him.

On 2 December 1993, seventy-five days after he said goodbye to his wife and children, Colombian national police killed him on a rooftop in Medellin city.

Thousands of people attended his funeral. His wife, Maria, came with their son. He was buried in the Monte Sacro Cemetery, Medellin, two days after his death.

30

Justa Grata Honoria

Valentinian III ruled the Western Roman Empire from AD 425 to 455 with its capital at Ravenna, northern Italy. He had a long tenure of thirty years as emperor, but he had a difficult time ruling his territory as his generals were vying for power, civil wars were plaguing his empire, and Vandals, Visigoths, Suebis, and the likes were invading his land.

Apart from all this, there was the political ambition of his sister Justa Grata Honoria (b. 418) and her infatuation with the empire's deadliest enemy Attila the Hun, who was waging military campaigns at the borders of Valentinian III's territory.

Honoria had been raised as a princess, as a child of destiny. Her father had bestowed the honorary title of 'Augusta' on her. She knew she was born not just to witness history, but to shape it. She had her own palace, run by a steward named Eugenius.

Honoria grew into adulthood and continued to nurse high ambitions. She was influenced by her mother and her aunt, who were powerful characters in the empire, and she wanted to wield power like her brother Valentinian III. Emperor Valentinian did not match his sister's intelligence, wit, and charm. He was inept, dim, worthless, and feeble. He had delegated much of his power to one of his top generals, Aetius. But being a woman, Honoria could not rule the empire and leave a mark in history.

To ascend the throne of the empire, Honoria required a male consort. Eugenius, the steward of the palace, was close to her and she could use him. However, that did not work.

The historian Edward Gibbon said that when the fair Honoria turned sixteen, she came to detest her status as a princess and its trappings as they stopped her from freely mixing with Eugenius. Honoria felt restless. She yielded to the impulse of nature and threw herself into the arms of her chamberlain Eugenius.

Gibbon said that while in a relationship with Eugenius, she became pregnant in AD 449. This was an embarrassment for the royals. Her brother sent her to a remote corner of Constantinople, the capital of the Eastern Roman Empire, to save the reputation of the family. Thereafter, he put Eugenius to death as a punishment for violation of trust.

Years later, Valentinian III got Honoria betrothed to a rich consul, Bassus Herculanus. Everything was fine with Bassus except that he was much older than Honoria. He was a boring personality who nursed no political ambitions. He suited Valentinian III because he was not going to pose a threat to his crown.

Valentinian III feared that if his wife Licinia Eudoxia did not produce a son and Honoria gave birth to a boy in marriage, there was every chance that Honoria's child would wear the crown of the empire after his death.

Honoria was very upset with the loss of Eugenius. Apart from that,, the consul to whom she was betrothed was a distasteful fellow. Marriage to an old man would throttle all her desires and long-held ambition. Her dream for the crown would be extinguished under the feet of such a useless man.

She looked for someone better to marry, someone who would also help her acquire power.

While Honoria was in turmoil, Attila the Hun, the ruler of the Huns, was hovering at the boundary of the Roman Empire with legions of ferocious soldiers. He was planning to extend his rule to the land of the Visigoths and would perhaps end up as the ruler of Gaul. The Huns lived beyond the Danube in Hungary and were on a rampage. They laid waste to city after city in the Balkans. Under Atilla the Hun, they were extorting wealth from the Eastern Roman Empire and threatening to ransack its capital.

Honoria thought Atilla the Hun, fifty-five, would be a perfect match for her. He was an emperor, a conqueror who could help her in her battle with her powerful brother. He could also break new ground for her to be an empress. She would be an empress of Gaul, which Atilla was invading, if not of Rome.

However, entertaining even the thought of marrying Atilla the Hun was appalling. He was ignorant, crude, and untamed, while she was the princess of the Roman empire and carried herself with grace. Nevertheless, she was burning for revenge and was blinded by her political ambition. According to Edward Gibbon, Honoria freed herself from all prejudice and offered to deliver herself into the arms of a barbarian whose language she was ignorant of, whose figure was scarcely human, and whose religion and manners she abhorred.

Honoria readied a loyal eunuch, Hyacinthus, and sent him to Attila with a plea for help. She gave the messenger a ring to hand over to the Hun ruler as proof of her faith and love. She requested Atilla to rescue her from a marriage that she did not want. The ring she sent implied that if Attila rescued her, she would become his wife.

Valentinian III had spies, but Hyacinthus was gone before they learnt of his movement. The news of Honoria's advances and invitation to Attila swept through the ranks of the court. It also reached the ears of Theodosius, the emperor of the Western Roman Empire. Honoria could have done nothing worse than this. She had disgraced the name and repute of the great Rome.

Theodosius II, the emperor of the Western Roman Empire, had a suggestion for Valentinian III. The king had just concluded a treaty with Attila and had bought peace after paying hundreds of kilograms of gold per annum as extortion. He did not want Honoria's issue to escalate and upset the whole region. His daughter was married to Valentinian III, and disturbance and instability in Valentinian III's territory had repercussions for his empire.

He told Valentinian that the best option was to hand over Honoria to Atilla and forget the whole thing. She could be sent off across the Danube, and that would be good riddance.

However, Honoria had stained the family honour and brought shame to herself and Valentinian III. If he sent his sister to Attila, he would lose face. It would be seen as an act of cowardice, and his feeble hold over the reins of the empire would be further weakened.

After a few weeks, Hyacinthus returned to Honoria and told her that he had met Attila and passed her gift and message to him. Honoria heaved a sigh of relief and waited for Atilla to make a move through which she could read his mood.

Valentinian III came to know about Hyacinthus's return. He arrested him, tortured him for details of the plan, and then beheaded him.

He also considered decapitating Honoria and closing the matter once and for all. However, his mother, Galla Placidia, a powerful lady, prevailed upon him and told him he could not kill her beloved daughter, though what she had done was disgusting.

On 28 July 450, the emperor of the Western Roman Empire, Theodosius II, fell from his horse, broke his back, and died after two days. He was fifty. He had two daughters and no son. During those days, only a male heir could succeed an emperor.

Like Valentinian III, his control over the empire was weak. He had ascended the throne as a child at the age of six.

The power behind his throne was his elder sister, Aelia Pulcheria (b. AD 398). Now that Theodosius II was dead, she had scope to exercise power and control the government. Four months after her brother's death, she married the Thracian senator Marcian in AD 450 and named him Theodosius II's successor.

Marcian's first act as emperor of the Eastern Roman Empire was to repudiate the agreement for the annual payment of 700 kg gold to be made to Attila, which Theodosius II had done with him.

Attila was preparing for a big offensive towards the west from his base, today's Hungary. He was gathering an army the likes of which the Romans had never seen. He drew men from all the tribes of his empire.

With Marcian's refusal to pay Atilla, his plan to invade territories, and cause terror in the west could crack because of shortage of fund. Atilla had his forces ready. They required money, food, clothing, and equipment. Marcian thwarted Atilla's plan. He knew Atilla's campaign against the Visigoths and then against Gaul would eventually come to haunt the Roman Empire itself.

Despite Marcian's refusal to pay money to the Huns, Atilla's embassy approached Marcian and asked for aid. Emperor Marcian replied that gold was for his friends, iron for his enemies. The most Attila could expect were gifts from the empire if he kept the peace. If he threatened war, he would meet a force more than a thunderbolt.

Attila had another option to get funds without fighting a battle. He had Honoria's ring and an invitation from Hyacinthus to come and rescue the princess. The emperor's own sister had begged him to help her. With the ring, the princess had offered herself to him in marriage. If she became his wife, a dowry would come to him from the Western Roman Empire. The size of this dowry would be large beyond imagination.

Therefore, she had to be freed and made a co-ruler of the Western Roman Empire with her brother Valentinian

III. As she had sent to him a ring, he was now betrothed to her, and it was his duty to help her.

Priscus, a Hun slave and historian, has recorded that Attila sent an envoy to Rome to tell Valentinian III that Honoria should not be wronged and should be made a co-ruler of the Western Roman Empire. If she did not receive the sceptre of sovereignty, he would sack Rome.

Valentinian III told Hun's messenger that Honoria could not become Atilla's wife as she was already given to a man. As for making her a ruler of the empire, she had no right to the sceptre since only men could rule the Roman state.

When the reply came, Attila launched an invasion on the land of the Visigoths and Gaul. Gaul was an ally of Rome, and the king of the Gauls had died recently. Romans wanted a successor who would be beholden to them. If Attila conquered Gaul, all northern Europe would be under his control, and the Roman Empire would be at his mercy.

However, this campaign was like something that Attila had never attempted before. He would have to cross mountains, rivers, and forests and cover a great distance in a flash. He would have to traverse the whole of France, over 700 km, in a month.

Attila launched the campaign, and his forces and the combined forces of the Western Roman Empire and of the Visigoths under the leadership of Aetius met on the Catalaunian Plains in France in 451. After fierce fighting, neither side claimed a decisive victory; Atilla withdrew and retired from Gaul.

After one year, Atilla returned to Valentinian III to sort out the issue arising from Honoria's proposal. He sent envoys to Rome and told Valentinian III that Honoria was his woman. He had her ring with him as proof. Everything that belonged to Honoria was his. Valentinian III had deprived her of the assets and land she had received from her father.

It was an outrageous demand. Valentinian III told the envoy to go to hell. Honoria was already married to Bassus Herculanus and was tamed from causing more damage to the empire. Still, Atilla persisted and looked for a pretext to pick a fight with Rome and invade its territory. He sent another ambassador to Valentinian III. The envoy told him, 'Attila, my master and your master, has ordered you to prepare your palace for him.'

Now, Valentinian III understood that Atilla was on his ready to invade his territory.

In AD 452, the Huns invaded Rome and sacked several cities, including Padua, Verona, and Milan. Valentinian III and his top general Aetius could do nothing to halt them. However, to the luck of the Romans, famine and pestilence raged in Italy that year. While the Roman forces failed to protect the boundaries of the empire, famine and disease pushed the Huns out of the north of Italy before they could penetrate deep south or rescue Honoria. Pope Leo the Great also intervened and requested Atilla to spare their lives.

In AD 453, before Attila the Hun could come again and raise hell, he died in his sleep on the night of his marriage to a Gothic bride named Ildico. Honoria thought God had punished Atilla for failing to keep his promise to her and taking someone other than her as a wife.

31

Joseph Stalin

In 1905, Stalin returned to Tiflis, Georgia, after serving an exile period in Serbia. He was a full-time revolutionary, and police were always on the lookout for him to prevent him from spreading disaffection against Czar Nicholas II, the ruler of Russia.

Alexander Svanidze, a confidant of Stalin, introduced Stalin, twenty-six, to his sister Ekaterine Svanidze, twenty, in 1905 at Tiflis. She was 'a placid, darkly pretty Georgian daughter of a cultured family'. Ekaterine's father, a native of Baji village in Georgia, was a railway worker. Her father was proud of Ekaterine's intelligence and beauty. She worked as a seamstress with a French national at Tiflis.

After a brief courtship, Stalin and Ekaterine got married on 15 July 1906. Stalin was an atheist and did not want any religious ceremony for the wedding, but the girl was religious and she set a condition of marriage at a church. Stalin bowed to her love and agreed to a wedding ceremony presided over by a priest at a church in Tiflis. The marriage ceremony was performed secretly in the flickering of candlelight late at night.

After the marriage, they moved from Tiflis to the oilfields of Baku, Azerbaijan, to avoid arrest by the Okhrana, the secret police of Russia. He hired a room for the family and furnished it with a bed and a few utensils. Ekaterine worked as a seamstress to put food on the table. Stalin earned no money as he devoted himself fully to underground revolutionary activities. He came home once in a while. Ekaterine became pregnant and gave birth to a son, Yakon, in Baku on 31 March 1907. Then, Ekaterine stopped working, and the family's budget was stretched thin. She had no milk in her body to nurse the young child and spent the day waiting for money and ration.

Ekaterine became ill at the new place, Baku. She lived alone and did not know people to socialize with, while Stalin remained actively engaged in revolutionary work, meeting people and telling them about the evils of the existing system. The hot weather at the new place also did not suit her. After suffering from continuous high fever, she consulted a doctor at the local hospital. The doctors diagnosed tuberculosis, a serious and deadly disease in those days. She required medicine, healthy and adequate food, and somebody to care for her and her newborn baby. But she had none of these.

Stalin loved his wife and referred to her as 'very sweet and beautiful'. She was someone who always 'melted' his heart. However, his political and revolutionary activities took precedence. He worked as a journalist and organizer for the Bolshevik party. He travelled to distant places while his beloved wife lay bedridden in a dim room, spitting blood and phlegm.

Due to his wife's bad health, he was forced to shift her to Tiflis in the autumn of 1907. Her family members lived there and could have taken care of her. But it was too late. Her condition was beyond repair. Stalin stayed with her, sat by her side, and hoped for the best. On 22 November 1907, Kato died in his arms. Stalin closed her eyes. They had been married only for sixteen months. Her death shattered him.

The funeral was held at the church in Tiflis where they had married a few months back. As Stalin stood beside Ekaterine's body during the funeral, he collapsed. People there supported him, and he regained consciousness. When her body was being put in the grave, he threw himself into the pit with the coffin.

After this loss, he turned east and reached Baku by train, leaving his eight-month-old son with his wife's sister.

Now he was free to throw himself completely in revolutionary work. However, he still carried the grief and hollowness created by his wife's departure. He felt guilty and said he had been unable to keep her happy. His comrades took his Mauser pistol from him as they feared he might shoot himself.

Stalin says, 'I realised how many things in life I hadn't appreciated. While my wife was alive, there were times I didn't return home at night. I told her when I left not to worry about me but when I got home, she would be sitting there. She would wait all night.'

Shortly after his wife's death, he was arrested and sent to Siberia to suffer in the cold desert.

After release from prison, he went to Finland to meet Lenin, the patriarch of the Bolshevik movement in Russia. Stalin also travelled to other parts of Europe, including London, to attend the communist Congresses.

He fell into the hands of the Russian police again. He was captured and sent to Solvychegodsk, a town in north Russia, as banishment from 1908 to 1912.

In 1912, he was out of exile and went to Petersburg. That year, Lenin co-opted him in the party's central committee at a conference in Prague. Thereafter, Stalin became busy with party work, but before he could contribute to party activities, in 1913, the Okhrana re-arrested him and sent him to four years exile in the distant cold north-east of Siberia.

This was a difficult time for Stalin. He wrote letters to the communist comrade Sergei Alliluyev and others, telling them about life in the frozen land and seeking money to escape from there.

He completed the exile period and came to Petersburg. By then, in February 1917, the rule of the tsar was overthrown. A provisional government governed Russia. Stalin had now more scope to tour, work, and establish himself as a top leader of the Bolsheviks.

During this time, Nadezhda Sergeyevna Alliluyeva, or Nadya, came into Stalin's life. She was the daughter of his friend and senior fellow revolutionary Sergei Alliluyev. Born on 22 September 1901 at Baku, Azerbaijan, she was raised in St Petersburg and was the youngest of the children. Sergei Alliluyev, her father, was an electrical artisan, and her mother, Olga Fedorenko, was a beautiful

Georgian woman. The family sheltered members of the Russian revolutionary group at their home. Stalin had also sought refuge in the house of this family in 1904 after one of his escapes from Siberia. Nadya knew Stalin from her childhood. Stalin, for her, was a man of charisma and character. The leader had saved her life when she was drowning in the Caspian Sea at Baku, which further raised his reputation in her eyes.

Stalin remained in touch with Nadya and her family members on and off when he was available in Baku. As a teen, Nadya joined the Bolshevik party and attended the party meetings. Stalin saw her after a gap of a few years at Vladimir Lenin's office, working as a clerk. She started assisting Stalin also in clerical work.

Stalin was forty-one and without a wife and family. Though a revolutionary moving from place to place, living on meagre resources, and in hiding, he wanted to have a family. He saw Nadya, a blooming beauty of eighteen, and proposed marriage to her. She agreed, and her parents also had no objection to this proposal. Finally, they married in February 1919. He loved the woman deeply, and it is said that while the Russian Revolution was underway, he was away sitting with his lover. For the first time in his life, Stalin had a home, a home made by his wife. She gave birth to a baby boy. In 1921, his son Yakon from Ekaterine also joined him to live with the family. Later, during the Second World War, Yakon was taken prisoner by the Germans.

In 1922, the Soviet Union was established, and Lenin became its chief. This year was important for Stalin also as he took over the charge of secretary general of the party's central committee. Lenin died after a brain stroke at the age of fifty-three in Gorki in 1924. Stalin took over the reins of the Soviet government after Lenin's death, and Nadya became the first lady of the state. Stalin was busy with work, while Nadya tried to resume her life as a secretary in the political party. Now, she was carrying another child.

Nadya felt lonely in Moscow while Stalin administered the massive Soviet state. She felt he had no time to spend with her, appreciate her mundane stories, stroll hand in hand under the soft golden sun with her, and see her joyous smiles.

As the days passed, her loneliness became unbearable. She lamented to her husband about the emptiness she felt, yet he could not give her much time because of the demands of his duty.

One Kremlin staff member said, 'A woman of strong character. She sometimes gets angry. The Master consoles her, but even he is afraid of her sometimes. Especially when the smile disappears from her face.'

Their second child was a girl born in 1926. They named her Svetlana. On one occasion, Nadya went to Leningrad with the children. Stalin told her, 'Your absence is an empty sky. Please come back.' She returned after a short break and decided to enrol herself at the Industrial Academy in 1929 to study synthetic fibres and keep herself busy. She also started taking an interest in the party activities.

In June 1930, Stalin was busy revamping the Soviet Union's economy. He wrote to her, 'I miss you so much Tatochka.... I'm as lonely as a horned owl.' She had gone to Germany in 1930 for the treatment of headaches.

Stalin further wrote, 'I'm not going out of town on business.... I'm just finishing up my work and then I'm going to go out of town to the children tomorrow ... so goodbye, don't be too long, come home sooner! My kisses! Your Joseph.'

In 1932, they went to Sochi with the children. Their son Vasya was ten and the daughter, Svetlana, five. The husband and wife fought often, and sometimes, Nadya thought of leaving Stalin.

On 8 November 1932, they were at a dinner party in Moscow to commemorate the October Revolution. Top Bolshevik leaders and their spouses were in attendance on the occasion. Stalin raise a toast for the destruction of the 'Enemies of the State'. During the party, the couple had an argument, following which Nadya rosee from the table and left the party. She went home and bolted herself in a room from the inside. In the morning, a housekeeper brought her breakfast, but when he opened her door, he found her dead. The rose she had worn in her hair was lying by the door.

Her obituary in *Pravda,* the official newspaper of the communist party, stated, 'A comrade dear to us, a person with a beautiful soul, is no more. A young woman still full of strength, a Bolshevik devoted to the Party and to the Revolution, has departed from us.'

When she was lying in her coffin, Joseph Stalin went up to the coffin to pay his last respects. As he stood there by the coffin, tears ran down his cheeks. He went up to it and said, 'I didn't take enough care of you.' He kissed her head.

The funeral was held on 12 November, and she was buried in Novodevichy Cemetery in Moscow. They had been married fourteen years.

After Nadya's death, Joseph established his daughter Svetlana as the 'lady of the house'. From her, he received unquestioning adoration. The daughter used to give him written orders! This was the man to whom no one else dared give orders. It was a game which he took seriously. She hung around her father the whole time. She wrote to him, 'Order No. 4—You must allow me to spend holidays at Lipki-one.'

32

J. Robert Oppenheimer

Jean Tatlock, a psychiatrist and physician, was the first love of 'the father of the atom bomb', J. Robert Oppenheimer. In 1936, thirty-two-year-old Oppenheimer met twenty-two-year-old Jean at the University of California, Berkeley, where he taught physics.

Jean Tatlock was born in Michigan, and her father, John Tatlock, was a professor of English at Stanford and Harvard Universities. She graduated from Vassar College, New York, and went to the University of California, Berkeley, to complete a course that would make her eligible for admission at Stanford Medical School.

Oppenheimer had rented an accommodation at the house of Mary Washburn, a scholar and daughter of a professor at UC Berkeley. Mary and Jean belonged to the same social and academic circle. She introduced Jean to Oppenheimer at her residence. The physicist was instantly attracted to her brilliance and beauty, and the two started dating. Oppenheimer had joined the University of California as a faculty member in 1929.

Jean, her sweet words, and her devastating greenish eyes soon dominated Oppenheimer's thoughts. He described her as 'a lyrical, uplifting, sensitive, yearning creature'. He proposed marriage to her twice, but she said she was not prepared for marriage. She suffered from bouts of depression, normal at times and extremely low at others. She introduced him to the metaphysical poet John Donne's poetry and delighted him by reciting his lines:

> Come live with me, and be my love,
> And we will some new pleasures prove
> Of golden sands, and crystal brooks,
> With silken lines, and silver hooks.

He gifted her roses, earrings, and blouses.

Her depression cast a shadow on Oppenheimer's mood and spirit and made his days heavy and melancholic. The relationship between the two continued till 1939, and thereafter, there was a break-up. She was not sure whether she wanted to marry the physicist. She was also attracted to women and believed that getting attracted to a person of the same sex was a sign of a mental disorder.

After studying in Berkeley, Jean travelled 300 km south and went to Stanford Medical School, California, from where she graduated in 1941 as a psychiatrist. She took an interest in Marxism and became a member of the communist party of America.

In 1939, Oppenheimer encountered Katherine Puening, twenty-nine, a German biologist of American origin. She was also a follower of Marxism and participated in communist party activities. She studied botany at the University of Pittsburgh, Pennsylvania. She had divorced her first husband, Frank Ramseyer, a Harvard graduate and Boston musician, in 1933.

She met her second husband, Joe Dallet, a handsome hard-core communist, at a New Year's Eve party in Ohio in 1933. He attended Cornell University and organized workers into a trade union in Ohio. He went to Spain in 1937 to fight in the Spanish Civil War against General Francisco Franco's fascist forces. Katherine travelled to France to join her husband in the fight, but before she could reach him, Dallet was killed on 17 October 1937.

She flew back to the USA and, in 1938, enrolled herself to study botany at the University of Pennsylvania, where she met Richard Harrison, a medical doctor from Oxford University. Harrison proposed marriage to her. She set a condition that he should allow her to pursue a doctorate at the University of California, Los Angeles. Harrison agreed, and they got married in 1938.

After the marriage with Harrison, Katherine moved to the western coast of USA with her husband and enrolled herself as a graduate student at the University of California. Oppenheimer was a faculty member at the university. She met Oppenheimer, a 'very tall, very slim, wunderkind physicist who held a dual professorship at Caltech and UC Berkeley', at a garden party in Pasadena in California in 1939. Then they met at dinner parties, dance floors, and restaurants, and developed an immense liking for each other.

As she got closer to Oppenheimer, she heart began to change. She told Harrison that it would be difficult for her to continue her relationship with him and asked for a divorce. But Harrison said no. Then she approached a court and told the court that she was not happy with Harrison and wanted to end the marriage. The court favoured her and granted her an instant divorce. She married Oppenheimer in Virginia City, Nevada, in 1940 on the day her divorce was finalized.

Later, she shared with a friend, 'I got Robert Oppenheimer to marry me in the old-fashioned way—by getting pregnant.' John, their first child, was born in May 1941, and Olivia, their second child, in December 1944. She loved riding horses and spent time racing and playing horse games.

Katherine brought discipline to Oppenheimer's life. She made him have his suits pressed and persuaded him to wear tweeds and even sport jackets in a variety of colours besides his traditional blue grey. She got him to cut his hair shorter. Oppenheimer started eating three meals a day and stopped staying up all night.

While he was married to Katherine, Oppenheimer's love for Jean was rekindled. However, a liaison with Jean was a dangerous proposal. She was a communist, and Oppenheimer presided at the centre of the US government as the director of the Manhattan Project in 1942. This project was to develop an atomic bomb to defeat Germany's Adolf Hitler and his allies in the Second World War. His office was located on a secret plateau in New Mexico in the USA. A romance with Jean Tatlock, a communist, could cost Oppenheimer his job and his reputation.

In 1943, Oppenheimer was thirty-nine and Jean Tatlock twenty-nine. Jean was now a physician and a resident in the psychiatry department at Mount Zion Hospital, University of California. She worked with troubled children.

Oppenheimer, while working on his project in New Mexico, came to the University of California, Berkeley, to recruit young scientists for his project. His attraction for Jean got the better of his rational mind, and so he decided to take a risk. Three months earlier, when he was leaving Berkeley for Los Alamos, Jean had told him that she wanted to spend time with him, but they could not meet. Now he thought it was time to fulfil her wishes. He took a train to San Francisco to meet Jean Tatlock.

He reached the railway station at 8:45 p.m. Jean was there, waiting for him with a car. He hugged the young lady, kissed her, and walked arm in arm with her. They went to a Mexican restaurant for dinner. From there, they went to her apartment and spent the night together.

A few weeks after this meeting, in the winter of 1944, Jean died. She was only twenty-nine. She had been suffering from severe clinical depression and was under treatment. One evening, her father came to meet her and knocked on her door. But there was no response. After waiting for what felt like an eternity, he broke open the door. Jean was lying submerged in a bathtub. She had written a suicide note and had left it on the table. The note read, 'I am disgusted with everything.... To those who loved me and helped me, all love and courage. I wanted to live and to give and I got paralyzed somehow.'

When Oppenheimer learnt about Jean's death, he left his office in New Mexico and wandered deep into the wilderness, grieving her departure.

After Jean Tatlock's death, Oppenheimer, then forty, met Ruth Tolman, a psychologist.

It was 1944, a time when the Second World War raged. Ruth worked with the government as a clinical psychologist. She tested the psychological stability of field agents deployed for war work. Ruth later became a faculty member at the University of California. She was then fifty-one, ten years elder to Oppenheimer and eleven years younger to her husband Richard Tolman.

Ruth's husband, Richard Tolman, was an eminent physicist at the University of California. He was also a colleague of Oppenheimer's and was contributing to the Manhattan Project as a scientific advisor. As a top American scientist, he administered the National Defense Research Committee. Anthropology stalwarts like Margaret Mead and Ruth Benedict were their family friends.

Though still married to Katherine, Oppenheimer's relationship with Ruth deepened. They often travelled and stayed together to Richard Tolman's discomfort. Psychology, which Ruth taught at the university, fascinated Oppenheimer too.

At one time, Richard Tolman bought a house in Washington. Oppenheimer and other top scientists stayed at this place when the government called them to the capital.

The Manhattan Project came to fruition on 16 July 1945 with the successful detonation of plutonium in the New Mexico Desert. Oppenheimer quoted the Gita, 'Now, I am become Death, the destroyer of worlds', on this epic development. He became a superstar the world over, a renowned American theoretical physicist.

While her husband and other scientists worked on the Manhattan Project, Katherine felt lonely and depressed at their flat in New Mexico. She hosted cocktail parties for the partners of her husband's colleagues. She loved alcohol and smoking. Later, she became an alcoholic and often suffered falls after excessive drinking.

Robert Oppenheimer's connection with Ruth Tolman faded after he got in trouble with the government and lost his post. One of the factors for falling foul of the government was Oppenheimer being in touch with Jean Tatlock and Katherine, both communists, while working on a secret war project. The communist party was believed to be a vehicle of espionage in the US, and association with the two ladies was an act of treason.

Three years after the end of the Second World War, in 1948, Ruth's husband died of a heart attack. Perhaps her closeness with Oppenheimer sat heavy on his heart.

Oppenheimer, an avid smoker, was diagnosed with throat cancer in 1966. He underwent surgery, but it was unsuccessful. Then he was given radiation treatment and chemotherapy, but that also did not work. Then, after a few months, Oppenheimer fell into a coma. He died at his home in Princeton, New Jersey, on 18 February 1967 at the age of sixty-two. His body was cremated, and his wife, Katherine Oppenheimer, took his ashes to their home in Saint John in the US Virgin Islands and scattered them into the ocean. The place is now called 'Oppenheimer Beach'.

After Oppenheimer's death, Katherine planned a trip around the world in 1972. She started from the US with Bob Serber, Robert's close friend. However, while on the tour, in October 1972, she developed clots in her lungs and died in Panama. She was planning to sail to Japan through the Panama Canal.

33

Wolfgang Pauli

Wolfgang Pauli, quantum physicist and Nobel laureate, was born in Vienna in Austria on 25 April 1900. His father taught medical chemistry at university, and his mother worked as a journalist and author. Pauli was a child prodigy. His genius earned him the title of physicists' physicist.

Pauli studied at the Ludwig-Maximilians University in Munich, Germany, and received a PhD degree in June 1921 for his work on quantum physics. At twenty-four, three years after receiving his PhD degree, he proposed ideas that would solve the fundamental problem of the structure of the atom. In 1923, he got a teaching position at the University of Hamburg, Germany, where he served till 1928. During this period, Pauli contributed to the development of the modern theory of quantum mechanics. He formulated the exclusion principle and the theory of non-relativistic spin in 1925.

From 1925 to 1928, the world of physics was undergoing a churning process, and a new physics called quantum mechanics was taking birth. The development was so remarkable that it has been called the second scientific revolution. Wolfgang Pauli was one of its pioneers, and Werner Heisenberg, Paul Dirac, Enrico Fermi, and Pascual Jordan, all aged between twenty-three and twenty-five years, were the superstars of this revolution. Pauli predicted in 1931 that conservation laws required the existence of the massless and chargeless particle, which he called neutrino. The existence of this particle was confirmed in 1956.

In 1928, while Pauli taught at the University of Hamburg, he journeyed 300 km east to Berlin to attend performances of cabaret dancers. He loved cabaret dance and sometimes indulged in alcohol and substance abuse. Here, he came across a nightclub performer, Käthe Margarethe Deppner. He fell in love with her, and without much delay, he got married to her on 23 December 1929 in Berlin.

However, Pauli had only a few days of marital bliss. The union was shaky from the start. The life of a top physicist and a nightclub dancer had nothing in common, and their tastes and routine varied. He told his friend Oskar Klein that all was not well in the marriage, and it ended in divorce after 11 months. The woman left him for a chemist.

Pauli was devastated. Some physicists were scornful of scientists working in other fields like chemistry or biology. Rutherford once said, 'All science is either physics or stamp collection.' When Pauli came to know that his wife had left him for a chemist, he realized nothing could have been worse. He remarked, 'Had she taken a bullfighter (for marriage) I would have understood—with such a man I could not compete—but a chemist—such an average chemist!' He divorced her on 26 November 1930.

In 1928, he had joined the Department of Theoretical Physics at ETH (Eidgenössische Technische Hochschule) Zurich in Switzerland as professor after his tenure at the University of Hamburg.

While Pauli worked on the serious problems of physics, his personal life underwent a series of upheavals. His mother, Bertha Schütz, committed suicide in 1927 at the age of forty-eight in reaction to his father's infidelity. His father courted a young artist, Maria Rottler, and separated from his mother. In 1928, his father married Maria, who was in her twenties. Pauli abhorred his father's decision to marry this woman and called his father's new wife 'the evil stepmother'.

The disastrous marriage and crisis in his parents' life pushed Wolfgang Pauli to the brink. He drank heavily and got into heated arguments with people. There were instances of him being thrown out of bars as he became intolerable.

Pauli descended into a psychological crisis and shared his problems with Ralph Kronig, his friend: 'I had great fear of everything concerning feeling, and therefore repressed it. This finally caused a revolt against an attitude ... that had become too one-sided.... Thereby I also became acquainted with psychic matters that I did not know before, which I want to summarize under the phrase "the soul acting on its own" or "proper activity of the soul".'

He further wrote to Ralph Kronig, 'Physics is once again at a dead end at this time. For me, at any rate, it is much too difficult, and I wish I were a film comedian or something like that and had never heard anything of physics.'

Kronig empathized with his problem. He and Pauli's father recommended that he consult Carl Jung, the noted psychoanalyst, who, along with Pauli, was a faculty at ETH, Zurich. Pauli went to Jung's lectures and read his books.

Pauli talked to Jung in January 1932 and told him about his problems. He said, 'Success in the academic world comes more easily to me than success with women. As it is the other way around with Mr Jung, he seemed to me right man to give me medical treatment.'

Jung differed with him. Jung concluded that the latter's difficulties stemmed from his troubles with women. Pauli nursed deep prejudices against women. He said, 'Women should keep out of science: the few who entered the field either did so only to find successful husbands or became transformed into unwomanly, ice-cold monsters.'

Jung referred him to his Austrian student Erna Rosenbaum, thinking that a woman would be of a greater help to him, given the kind of problem he was facing. However, Pauli was offended by Jung's approach. He expected Jung to give him personal attention and heal him, instead of referring him to his disciple.

Pauli shared his disappointment with Rosenbaum on 3 February 1932: 'I consulted Mr Jung because of certain neurotic problems which are connected with the fact that it is easier for me to achieve academic success than success with women. Since for Mr Jung the opposite seems to be the case, he appeared to me to be the appropriate man to treat me medically. To my considerable surprise Mr Jung explained to me that this was not so, and that I should absolutely have myself treated by a woman.'

Rosenbaum has been described as a 'young Austrian, pretty, foolish, always laughing'. She assured Pauli that he was at the right place. She would do her best to solve his problem and requested Pauli to come to her for a treatment session. When Pauli reported to her at her clinic in Zurich, she did an analysis of his personality. She recorded 1300 of his dreams and convinced him to appreciate non-rational thoughts. The session with her lasted for five months. Thereafter, Pauli also did three months of self-analysis.

The consultation with the psychoanalyst worked, and Pauli felt better. He thought he could handle a woman if one came into his life. He thought of marrying again.

Pauli came to know about Franziska Bertram, thirty-two, a native of Munich, in 1933. Their common friend and psychologist Adolf Guggenbühl introduced him to Franziska at his home at a party. She was then working as a manager of a Russian orchestra. After a month of interaction and dating, Pauli felt that Franziska was the kind of woman he could marry. He took her to his father and stepmother in Vienna. His father gave him the go-ahead. Finally, they got married in London on 4 April 1934, the year he had completed self-analysis and consultation with Rosenbaum. This was his first visit to London. He also cut down on drinking. Franziska lived in Vienna while Pauli worked in Zurich. They had no children.

Pauli's interaction with Jung extended beyond the treatment of his psychological crisis. The two came closer intellectually. Pauli shared a thousand dreams of his with

Jung for analysis. They delved into philosophical dialogue and co-authored a book.

While Pauli discovered the secrets of nature and endured the crises, Germany annexed Austria in 1938. This made Pauli a German citizen. Being a German citizen when the Nazis were on the rise was undesirable. He tried to obtain citizenship of Switzerland, where he taught at the university, but that did not come through.

In 1940, he received an invitation from the USA to come and lecture at the universities. He went there and worked as a professor of theoretical physics at the Institute for Advanced Study.

In 1945, Pauli received the Nobel Prize for his 1925 discovery of the exclusion principle. Einstein had recommended him for this award. He received the prize at Princeton in a special ceremony organized for him on 10 December. He returned to Zurich from the USA in 1946 and stayed there for the rest of his life. Late in 1958, Pauli fell seriously ill, and on 14 December that year, he died of cancer in room number 137 of Rotkreuzspital in Zurich.

After his death, Franciska remembered, 'He was very easily hurt and therefore would let down a curtain. He tried to live without admitting reality. And this stemmed precisely from his belief that this was possible.'

34

Stephen Hawking

Stephen Hawking, the English theoretical physicist, met Jane Wilde for the first time at a party in St Albans, a small town north of London, in 1962. Jane was an undergraduate student of languages at Westfield College, London. A college friend, Diana, introduced her to Stephen Hawking at a party. Then Hawking was studying applied mathematics and theoretical physics at Trinity Hall, Cambridge University.

After this interaction, they became friends. They met more frequently, strolled in the university campus, swayed at a dance bar, and rowed in the blue waters of the Cam River.

In 1963, shortly after meeting Jane, Hawking was diagnosed with the debilitating motor neuron disease that would gradually paralyse him and confine him to a wheelchair. Doctors made a doom-laden prognosis and gave him two more years to live. He had gone to a doctor earlier. But then the doctor told him there was nothing to worry about. He says, 'In my last year at Oxford University, I was getting clumsy, but a doctor advised me, "Just lay off the beer".'

By 1964, Hawking became depressed with his disease. The future awaiting him was scary. He drank wine and listened to Wagner for long hours at full volume. Uncertain of his future, he thought Jane should go away from his life. Why should she suffer with him? She was a butterfly meant to soar, he thought.

But Jane Wilde decided not to back off; she told him she would live and die with him. Jane remembers, 'It was too late.... I was completely under his spell, bewitched by his clear blue-grey eyes and the broad dimpled smile.'

They married in a small ceremony at the chapel of Trinity Hall in July 1965, though Hawking's parents did not approve of this marriage. Hawking was twenty-three, and his bride twenty-one. They went on their honeymoon to Suffolk, east of England, for a week.

To support his family during his studies, he joined a research fellowship at Gonville and Caius College, University of Cambridge. Seeing Hawking's health condition, Frank, Jane's father-in-law, advised the couple to have children quickly. Stephen's life was short, and it was better to have children before his life's journey came to an end.

Though the marriage did not appear to be the brightest move under the circumstances, but against all the challenges, it gave Hawking strength and 'something to live for'. 'I therefore started working for the first time in my life,' he says. Two years later, in 1967, their first child, Robert, was born, and their daughter, Lucy, in 1970.

In 1974, Stephen Hawking was elected a fellow of the Royal Society, a worldwide fellowship of scientists, and within years he was promoted to the rank of professor. The next year (1975), he got an invitation from the California Institute of Technology (Caltech) in the US to work on general relativity. He went there with Jane for a one-year residency, and thereafter, the couple returned to England.

By this time, Hawking's health condition became worse. Stephen had to use a cane to walk, and soon, he would lose his ability even to walk.

Seeing Hawking's condition, Jane felt distressed. The responsibility of raising the children compounded her misery. She had to balance a toddler on one hand and a sick husband on the other. She had to feed Stephen, give him a bath, dress him, and so on. Stephen did not want to have assistance from anyone other than Jane. She was left with 'the crushing responsibility, the emotional strain, the aching fatigue of bringing up two small children unaided at the same time as caring for a seriously disabled person who was wasting away before one's very eyes'.

Their passion for each other was extinguished. At one point, Jane felt she could not carry the burden anymore and she should commit suicide.

However, to take her mind off the trouble, Jane started spending time on her hobbies, including singing. She went to the local church in Cambridge for carol singing with her daughter on Christmas day of 1977. There, Jane met Jonathan Hellyer Jones, church choir musician. Jonathan had been widowed a few years earlier and was lonely.

Jane felt good meeting him. 'I talked as I had not in years and had the uncanny sensation that I had met a familiar friend of long acquaintance,' says Jane. Slowly, Jane Wilde and Jonathan Jones came closer, and a melody began to play between their hearts.

At that time, Stephen Hawking was busy with his scientific work, and his contribution would soon earn him international recognition, making him a celebrity. In 1979, he was elected to the Lucasian Professorship of Mathematics, a post which people like Isaac Newton and Paul Dirac had held. The same year (1979), their third child, Timothy, was born.

Though battling a monster, Stephen never mentioned his illness. It was as if it did not exist. He would never ever talk about how he felt.

Sometime later, Jonathan moved into the house where Hawking and Jane lived. He became a part of the family. Hawking accepted the relationship between Jane and her new muse. 'I would have objected but I too was expecting an early death and felt I needed someone to support the children after I was gone,' says Stephen. Jane and Jonathan went on camping trips and other vacations. Jonathan taught the children piano, helped the family bring up three children, and cared for Hawking. He became part of the extended family.

Jane did a PhD on Spanish poetry from Westfield College in 1981 to make her life meaningful. It took her twelve years to complete the degree as she was busy taking care of Stephen.

Jane loved Jonathan, but she could not leave Stephen Hawking as she felt committed to him. The couple had no alternative but to carry on. Hawking also could not move and be productive in his career without her. The children, too, required a stable life. So, they all lived in harmony.

In 1985, while he was in Switzerland for a conference, Hawking contracted pneumonia and was put on a ventilator. Doctors at the hospital thought he would not survive and offered to turn off the ventilator and end his life. However, Jane rejected the doctor's proposal. He was brought to Cambridge, and the doctors performed tracheotomy. He survived, but he could not speak. Now Stephen required 24/7 care. Jane hired Elaine Mason to help Hawking after his tracheotomy.

Elaine was married to David Mason, an engineer who helped to create Hawking's speech synthesizer. She had two sons with David. She started taking care of Hawking. She loved cooking for him and prepared curries and roast dinners. Slowly, Hawking developed feelings for Elaine Mason.

Elaine came from a dysfunctional family. Her parents did not look after her while she was a teenager. She was not in love with her husband. She married him in 1980 because he was the first man who asked for her hand. Elaine was a nurse and had worked at an orphanage in Bangladesh. So the feeling of being valued by Stephen Hawking was something special for her.

Hawking published his best seller *A Brief History of Time* in 1988. It was a book on theoretical cosmology, written for the readers who had no background in physics. The book made him a popular and internationally known scientist.

Elaine Mason divorced her husband in February 1990. Hawking told Jane that he would no longer live with her. He was moving on with Elaine. 'I became more and more unhappy about the increasingly close relationship between Jane and Jonathan. In the end, I could stand the situation no longer, and in 1990, I moved out to a flat with one of my nurses, Elaine Mason.'

After about five years of separation from Jane Wilde, in 1995, Hawking divorced her. He married Elaine Mason, thirty-four, the same year (1995) in September at the Cambridge Register Office. He commented about his new marriage, 'It's wonderful—I have married the woman I love.'

Divorced by Hawking, Jane Wilde married Jonathan Jones, her musician friend, nine months later in 1996. Jane published a book, *Music to Move the Stars*, in 1999, where she discussed her marriage with Hawking and how it was broken. Some of the issues discussed were embarrassing, but Hawking avoided making any comment on the revelations.

Everything was not smooth in the relationship between the top physicist and his new wife, Elaine. Stephen says, 'My marriage to Elaine was passionate and tempestuous. We had our ups and downs but Elaine's being a nurse saved my life on several occasions.'

One time, Hawking's children suspected that the lady had physically and emotionally abused Hawking. He was reportedly taken to a hospital in 2000 with 'cuts and bruises' he could not explain. However, the suspicion against Elaine was not proven. In January 2004, Hawking cleared the doubts, 'My wife and I love each other very much, and it is only because of her that I am alive today.'

While Stephen Hawking lived with Elaine, Jane visited him in his office and spent time talking with him about the children and grandchild.

Then a strain developed in his relationship with Elaine. His regular health crisis took an emotional toll on the lady. The couple divorced in 2007 after twelve years of marriage. 'Since the divorce I have lived alone with a housekeeper,' says Stephen.

In 2014, Hawking was living near the house of his first wife, Jane, in Cambridge, and her husband Jonathan. The three met regularly and enjoyed Sunday lunches with children.

35

Richard Feynman

Richard Feynman is one of the greatest theoretical physicists in history. He received the Nobel Prize in 1965 for his contribution to quantum electrodynamics. Freeman Dyson, a physicist, called him 'the most original mind of his generation'.

Feynman enrolled at Far Rockaway High School in New York City in 1931 when he was thirteen. His father was a sales manager, and the family lived on the outskirts of the city. His father wanted him to be a scientist and read pages of Encyclopaedia Britannica to him when he was a small boy. He taught him to notice new things and explore the world around him.

Feynman met Arline Greenbaum, thirteen, at the Rockaway school, and got lost in the depth of her beauty and charm. Their connection promised to blossom into lifelong love and friendship. They used to converse till late evening, share jokes, and walk on nearby Far Rockaway beaches in the morning sun. Her cherry lips tempted him for a kiss. The melody of her voice soothed his heart. He thought that he would marry Arline after growing up.

Feynman's performance at the school was above par. Once, he won a prize in a math competition.

Arline joined the Feynman family on a vacation. While on the tour, Feynman's father saw a lump on her neck. On return, she went to a doctor for a diagnosis. After a long investigation, in 1941, the doctor told her she was afflicted with tuberculosis. Doctors gave her two more years to live.

After graduating from school, Feynman entered the Massachusetts Institute of Technology (MIT), Cambridge, in 1935 and studied there for four years. He obtained a BSc degree in 1939.

Thereafter, he took graduate school entrance exams and got accepted to Princeton University, New Jersey. He became busy with his studies, but Arline's health continued to decline. Despite this, he got engaged to her. He wanted to get married to her undeterred by her condition. But the institution did not allow its students to marry during the period of study. It considered marriage a distraction to serious academic pursuits. Feynman received a PhD degree from Princeton in 1942. He was twenty-four.

After graduating, Feynman set his sights on marrying Arline. However, his parents were against this marital alliance as they knew Arline was going to die soon. Feynman still went ahead, despite opposition from his parents.

He wrote to her, 'I know nothing can separate us—we've stood the tests of time and our love is as glorious now as the day it was born—dearest riches have never made people great but love does it every day—we're not little people—we're giants ... I know we both have a future ahead of us—with a world of happiness—now and forever.'

A civil ceremony was performed in Arline's hospital room on Staten Island, New York City, on 29 June 1942, and the two became husband and wife. No friends or family members were present during the occasion. The young couple could not kiss each other during the ceremony as this could have led to infection with tuberculosis.

After the marriage ceremony, Feynman took Arline to Deborah Hospital in New Jersey, 100 km south of New York City, for her treatment. He visited her there from New York City every weekend. Lying on the bed, she read *The Rubaiyat* of Omar Khayyam:

> For in and out, above, about, below,
> It is nothing but a Magic Shadow-show,
> Played in a Box whose Candle is the Sun,
> Round which we Phantom Figures come and go.

During the Second World War, Germany, on the one hand, and the US leading the Allied Nations, on the other, were racing to develop nuclear bombs. In the US, the noted physicist J. Robert Oppenheimer was the leader of the team working on the Manhattan Project for the development and detonation of the first atomic bomb. In 1943, Princeton's leading physicists recruited Feynman also for the Manhattan Project at Los Alamos Laboratory in New Mexico.

At Los Alamos, Feynman was far away from Arline, who was hospitalized in New Jersey. It was difficult for him to visit her regularly. One year after reporting for the project, he had Arline brought to Albuquerque, New Mexico. The new place was lower in altitude, and it was believed that a dry climate was good to cure tuberculosis. However, she was slowly dying from the disease.

Army nurses cared for her at the new place, but they could not provide the lady with the level of care she needed. During the weekends, Feynman visited Arline at the clinic; at times, some of his friends visited her and tried to cheer her up. Feynman went to see her mostly alone, either taking a bus or hitching rides.

In the beginning, Feynman thought everything would become normal and she would be fine. Slowly, he realized that the situation was grave. His sweetheart was slipping into the abyss of death, and he could do nothing about it. To perform his official duties, he compartmentalized his feelings. While on duty, he focussed on his project, and when free, he thought about his love. They wrote love letters to each other. In his second-to-last letter to Arline, he wrote, 'My Wife, I understand at last how sick you are. I understand that this is not the time to ask you to make any effort to be less of a bother to others.... It is a time to comfort you as you wish to be comforted.... It is a time to love you in any way that you wish.... I love you, I adore you, I shall serve you without question, but with understanding.... I am your husband. I love you.'

While he and his team were busy developing the atom bomb at Los Alamos, on 16 June 1945, Feynman received a message that Arline's condition had further deteriorated. He drove to Albuquerque in a car borrowed from a colleague and reached her place. He sat with her for hours. Arline's condition worsened, and she stopped breathing as he looked at her. She was only twenty-five. The atom bomb would be detonated one month later in the barren expanse of the New Mexican Desert.

With Arline's death, Feynman, twenty-seven, was broken-hearted. He had been married for two years. He went home to Faraway Rock to be with family and friends to grieve Arline's passing. After a few days, he received a message from Hans Bethe, head of the Theory Division at Manhattan Project: 'The baby is expected on such and such a day.' Feynman understood the import of the message. He had made essential contributions to the atomic bomb project. He immediately returned to Los Alamos and found the team of scientists busy with the project work. On 16 July 1945, the nuclear detonation took place. The scientists were happy and excited and held parties. A few weeks later, the bomb would be dropped on Hiroshima and Nagasaki.

After Arline's death, Feynman was alone. He spent time reading *The Arabian Nights*. On the lookout for a woman who could fill the vacuum created by his wife's death, he dated graduate girls and flight attendants. In his autobiography *Surely You're Joking, Mr. Feynman!*, he describes how he learnt to seduce women at a bar in the summer of 1946.

He says a mentor taught him to ask a woman if she would sleep with him before buying her anything. In his book, he tells a story of how he told a woman named Ann that she was 'worse than a whore'. She had persuaded him to buy her sandwiches by telling him he could eat them at her place but then, after he bought them, said they could not eat together because another man was coming over.

Though he sought warmth in passing glances, he missed Arline badly. On 17 October 1946, he wrote a letter to the dead Arline:

D'Arline,

I adore you, sweetheart.

I know how much you like to hear that—but I don't only write it because you like it—I write it because it makes me warm all over inside to write it to you.

I find it hard to understand in my mind what it means to love you after you are dead … and I want you to love me and care for me. I want to have problems to discuss with you—I want to do little projects with you. I never thought until just now that we can do that. What should we do? We started to learn to make clothes together … Can't I do something now? No. I am alone without you and you were the 'idea-woman' and general instigator of all our wild adventures.

When you were sick you worried because you could not give me something that you wanted to and thought I needed. You needn't have worried. Just as I told you then there was no real need because I loved you in so many ways so much. And now it is clearly even more true—you can give me nothing now yet I love you so that you stand in my way of loving anyone else—but I want you to stand there. You, dead, are so much better than anyone else alive.

… I'll bet you are surprised that I don't even have a girlfriend (except you, sweetheart) after two years. But you can't help it, darling, nor can I—I don't understand it, for I have met many girls and very nice ones and I don't want to remain alone—but in two or three meetings they all seem ashes. You only are left to me. You are real.

My darling wife, I do adore you…

Rich.

After the Manhattan Project, Hans Bethe arranged for Feynman to join the physics department of Cornell University, New York, in 1945 as an assistant professor, where he would teach theoretical physics till 1950.

At Cornell University, he met Mary Louise Bell in a cafeteria in 1946. Mary, twenty-eight, was an attractive woman. She was from Kansas and had taken a degree in the history of Mexican art and textiles. She taught the history of furniture and interiors at Michigan State University. Feynman saw her dressed in a white shirt and a skirt, and was smitten by her. Lawrence Krauss, a physicist, says she was 'a platinum blonde with a penchant for high heels and tight clothes'.

Feynman has said about their relationship: 'I liked her for a while, but we used to argue a bit; finally we decided it was hopeless, and we separated.'

Feynman moved from Cornell University in 1950 to the physics department at the California Institute of Technology (Caltech), Pasadena, as a faculty member and conducted groundbreaking research in quantum electrodynamics and physics of superfluidity. He remained at Caltech for the rest of his career.

In July 1949, Feynman, thirty-one, travelled to Brazil for about six weeks in search of better weather and ambience. He was planning to go somewhere in South America, but on the suggestion of a student of physics, he chose Brazil.

He also took a sabbatical year between 1951 and 1952 and visited Brazil again and stayed there for 10 months. He delivered lectures at Centro Brasiliero de Pesquisas Friscas at Rio de Janeiro.

He joined a samba band and played drums in the carnival. He dated flight attendants and bar girls he met in the bar of the Miramar Palace Hotel. He wanted to beat bar girls at their own games.

While in Rio de Janeiro in 1951, he felt lonely. Though he met many women, he was not able to find a lady whom he could marry: 'But after a year of taking out these air hostesses and not really getting anywhere, I was frustrated.' He remembered Mary Louise Bell and the time spent with her and felt nostalgic. He wrote to her, proposing marriage. Mary saw it was a right proposal from a bright physicist teaching at Caltech. She said she was ready to tango.

Richard Feynman returned to California, and the two married in Idaho on 28 June 1952. However, they were not happy. Their priorities and temperament were different. They quarrelled frequently, and she said she was frightened by his violent temper.

Feynman continued working on theoretical problems of physics and received the Albert Einstein Award in recognition of his work in 1954 from the US Atomic Energy Commission. On the family front, the journey of their marriage veered onto a rocky path. Finally, they separated on 20 May 1956. An interlocutory decree of divorce was entered on 19 June 1956 on grounds of 'extreme cruelty'.

The divorce complaint by Mary Louise Bell read, 'He begins working calculus problems in his head as soon as he awakens. He did calculus while driving in his car, while sitting in the living room, and while lying in bed at night.' The divorce became final on 5 May 1958.

Feynman charmed women with playful words and was on the look out for a life partner again. He visited topless bars every week. One of his girlfriends walked off with his

Albert Einstein Award medal. She feigned pregnancy and extorted money from him, saying that she needed money for an abortion. When he gave the medal to her, she used that to buy furniture. Feynman felt cheated.

The US government sent Feynman, forty-two, to Geneva for Atoms for Peace Conference in September 1958. He was to present a paper there on a topic in physics. During his free time, he took a walk on the banks of the calm waters of Lake Geneva, the largest alpine lake in Europe. A beautiful young girl in a polka-dot bikini attracted his attention. She was Gweneth Howarth, twenty-three, the daughter of a jeweller and a native of Yorkshire, England. He had a casual conversation with her. 'You speak English!' He requested her to meet him again. The lady was a school librarian who loved travelling. She was in Switzerland on vacation and had taken up a job of child-caring with a family to finance her visit.

Feynman told her about himself and his life in the world of science and in California. He learnt that Howarth was being paid only US$25 a month for childcare work. He requested her to work for him and offered her US$20 a week to be his help. He requested his friend and physicist Matthew Sands, who had worked on the Manhattan Project, to act as her sponsor.

Howarth told Feynman that she already had two friends, one from Zurich and the other from Germany. Feynman told her that he was not worried and was ready to accept her as his partner. The lady decided to take up his offer and arrived in California in June 1959 to work as his maid. Gweneth found that Feynman was living with five identical pairs of shoes, a set of dark blue serge suits, and white shirts. He owned neither a radio nor a television. He kept keys, tickets, and money change always in the same pocket so that he would find them immediately when he needed them.

Richard Feynman taught her to drive a car, and the two went outside the city driving fast. He proposed marriage to her in March 1960, and they were married on 24 September 1960 at the Huntington Hotel in California. The new lady tried to make Feynman happy and his life peaceful. Feynman endeavoured to share the wonders of science with her.

A son was born to them in 1962. Feynman named him after his physicist friend Carl Anderson. They adopted a two-month-old baby girl in 1968 and named her Michelle. The family would go on regular tours to distant places. They bought a large van and would camp at exotic places and camping sites instead of staying in hotels.

Feynman, along with his colleagues Julian Schwinger and Shinichiro Tomonaga, won the Nobel Prize on 10 December 1965 for his work in quantum electrodynamics. Feynman travelled with Gweneth to Stockholm to receive the prize and enjoyed the journey. He dedicated the award to the memory of Arline.

The family had a home near the California University campus. Feynman bought another house in Baja California, Mexico, with the money he received for the Nobel Prize.

Stephen Hawking, in his autobiography, says that two principal stars of Caltech physics department in 1975 were Nobel Prize winners Richard Feynman and Murray Gell-Mann. There was great rivalry between them. At a weekly seminar, Murray said, 'I am just going to repeat some talks I gave last year.' On this, Feynman got up and walked out. Murray then said, 'Now that he is gone I can tell you what I really wanted to talk about.'

In 1985, Feynman published a book of stories of his life and career, *Surely You're Joking, Mr. Feynman,* which got listed as the national bestseller.

Feynman suffered from abdominal pains in 1978. Doctors diagnosed him with cancer and conducted a surgery. After a short span when he was relatively healthy, in 1986, doctors discovered another cancer and operated upon him. Thereafter, again after a short break, he was hospitalized in California on 3 February 1988 for kidney failure. He died on 15 February 1988 at the hospital while his wife Gweneth Howarth sat beside him.

While close to death, Feynman asked his friend and colleague Danny Hillis why he appeared sad. Hillis replied, 'Because you are going to leave us soon.' Feynman said this issue bothered him too. 'But I had told so many stories to so many people that I would not be completely gone even after my death.' His last words were, 'I'd hate to die twice. It's so boring.' Perhaps he meant to say that he had already died with Arline.

He was buried in a cemetery in California. Walter Moore, a journalist, says, 'He was a man of absolute integrity; his understanding of physics was unequalled; he was an inspired teacher; and he once lived a love story that surpasses our understanding.'

Howarth died of cancer at the age of fifty-five in 1989.

36

Sigmund Freud

Sigmund Freud, the founder of psychoanalysis, a mental health therapy, was a towering scholar and had a huge impact on 20th-century thought, comparable to that of Charles Darwin and Karl Marx.

Freud was born in Příbor, a town in Czech Republic, on 6 May 1856. His father, Jakob Freud, was a wool merchant. The family lived in a rented room in Příbor and were struggling financially when Freud was born. The town was then a part of the Austrian empire.

His father shifted to Vienna, Austria, about 300 km from Příbor, in 1860 with his wife and two children. In 1865, Freud was enrolled in a reputed school in Vienna. He was good in studies and passed the senior secondary school examination in 1873. He joined the medical school at the

University of Vienna at seventeen. He graduated from there with an MD in March 1881. He began his medical career at Vienna General Hospital as a clinical assistant immediately after that.

Freud, twenty-six, met twenty-year-old Martha Bernays, a friend of his sister Anna Freud, at his home in April 1882. He was soon in love with her. Martha's mother, Emmeline Bernays, was a widow and lived in Vienna. Her father, a wealthy merchant, had died in 1869 when she was seven. She had four siblings.

Freud started his career as a doctor and was publishing academic papers, but he was not earning money. Martha's mother did not want her daughter to marry Freud, who, in her opinion, was as poor as a church mouse.

Martha's mother, Emmeline Bernays, moved from Vienna to Wandsbek, near Hamburg, Germany, with her daughter. Her brother and sisters lived there, and they could provide her social support after her husband's death.

After Martha's departure from Vienna in 1883, Freud started writing love letters to her and visited her dozens of times till 1886, the year they got married.

Sigmund Freud wrote about 900 lengthy letters to his love Martha. Martha replied to him, her words carrying the warmth of her love. They wrote to each other about flowers, dreams, Shakespeare, and their daily activities and surroundings. Freud sent her sketches of his lodgings and told her that she was the most beautiful woman he had ever seen. In one letter, Freud expressed jealousy and forbade her from ice-skating as it involved gliding arm in arm with another man. He requested her to sever her relations with a girl who became pregnant before her marriage. He told her he would crush her religious faith and turn her into a fellow atheist..

In one letter, Martha recounted a dream in which the two of them held hands, gazed into each other's eyes, and then did something more. But she did not elaborate on what they did 'more'.

At Hamburg, Martha spent her time helping her mother and her younger sister Mona Bernays. She read books, walked down the tree-covered lanes, and visited clubs and theatres. Her interest in the arts and love for artists incensed Freud. He complained that as a scientist, he had no weapons against artists, as an artist would write a song and he would get the key to the heart of women, while the scientist would be gazing at an electron in an atom's orbit.

In 1886, Freud left the hospital and started private practice in Vienna. He specialized in 'nervous disorders'. He was on his way to becoming one of the most influential thinkers of the 20th century. In 1899, he published one of his most groundbreaking works of psychoanalysis and literature, *The Interpretation of Dreams*.

One day, Freud started from Vienna to Hamburg with a gold ring, to where Martha was living, to propose marriage to her. He had inscribed on the lid of the box a poem titled 'When my Sweetheart is Married'. The poem was about the agony of a man on a journey, who grieved at losing his love to another man. Fortunately, Freud did not lose his sweetheart, and Martha accepted his proposal for marriage.

Freud made good progress in his medical career and earned a reputation. Martha's mother saw that Freud had a promising career ahead. She gave her permission to

Martha to marry Freud. Martha moved to Vienna for the marriage ceremony.

On 13 September 1886, he married Martha Bernays in a civil function, followed by a religious ceremony a few days later. Martha's grandfather, the chief rabbi in Hamburg, presided over the ceremony. The couple had six children in eight years, all born between 1887 and 1895 in Vienna.

By this time, Freud, with his research, experiments, and writings, had emerged as an eminent scholar and authority. He was talking and writing about sex, the theory of seduction, repressed desires, neuroses, dreams, seething cauldron of desires, and the like. He was causing scandals with his writings and theories.

While Martha had a happy married life with Freud, her younger sister, Mona Bernays, was not so fortunate. In 1886, her fiancé, Isaac Goldberg, a student in the philosophy department at the University of Vienna, died of tuberculosis. After this tragedy, Mona decided to live alone and not marry. In 1896, Mona moved into Martha's house and became a permanent member of Freud's family.

Mona was a talented artist and musician. She was 'intelligent, caustic'. She provided Freud with insights into his patients' behaviour and helped him to develop his theories of psychoanalysis. She also helped the family in household chores and child rearing.

Freud was romantically drawn to Mona. The Swiss psychoanalyst Carl Gustav Jung, a disciple rival of Sigmund Freud, learnt about Freud's romantic relationship with Mona from the latter: 'She [Mona] was very much bothered by her relationship with Freud and felt guilty about it.... From her I learned that Freud was in love with her and that their relationship was indeed very intimate.'

Carl Jung further said that during a journey to America in 1909, Freud confided to him some dreams about Martha and Mona. But he abruptly ended the discussion, saying, 'I could tell you more, but I cannot risk my authority.'

But this revelation of Jung's is strongly contested by scholars and Freud's students, friends, and followers. They believed Freud was 'a scientist of flawless integrity with a reputation for rigid personal morality'.

German sociologist Franz Maciejewski of the Heidelberg University, Germany, gathered evidence about the romantic affair between the two.

Freud, forty-two, went on a vacation with Mona, thirty-three, in the Swiss Alps on 13 August 1898 for two weeks. They stayed together at an inn at Maloja village, Switzerland. Freud entered their details in the record of the inn as 'Dr Sigmund Freud and wife'. Martha, at home in Vienna, knew about the trip, but she did not know her husband was having a romance with her sister. From Maloja, Freud wrote about the beauty of the frosted glacier, lofty clouds, verdant hills, and calm lakes to his wife. He described the inn where he was lodged in a room with Mona as 'humble', though it was the second fanciest in town.

Peter Swales, a researcher, adds more details about the relationship between the two. He says Freud had a trip to Meran in Austria with Mona Bernays in 1900. Mona later spent some weeks at a health spa in Merano in the Italian Alps.

Writing to the American neurologist James Putman in 1915, Freud said, 'I stand for a much freer sexual life. However I have made little use of such freedom.'

In 1938, Freud's family, along with Mona, left Vienna due to the Nazi annexation of Austria and migrated to London.

Freud had a productive life in London. He authored another great work, *Civilization and Its Discontents,* published in 1930.

He was diagnosed with oral cancer in 1923 because of heavy smoking. He underwent thirty-four surgical procedures but did not quit smoking. He died in 1934 when his friend Max Schur gave him an overdose of morphine on his request. He was eighty-three. His body was cremated in north London. Mona Bernays died in London in 1941 and Martha in 1951.

References

1. Napoleon Bonapart

Bains, Indi, 'The truth behind the turbulent love story of Napoleon and Joséphine,' 15 November 2023, National Geographic.

BBC, 'Napoleon's other wife: who was Habsburg Archduchess Marie-Louise?' 22 November 2023, The History Extra, BBC History Magazine.

Charleston, L.J., 'Why the great love story of Napoleon and Josephine Bonaparte wasn't that great after all,' 16 March 2019, *The New Zealand Herald*.

Mark, Harrison W., 'Joséphine de Beauharnais,' Worldhistory.org.

Mcllvenna, Una, 'Napoleon and Joséphine: Their Tumultuous Love Story,' History channel, https://www.history.com/news/napoleon-josephine-bonaparte-love-story-marriage-divorce.

Melting Pot, 'Napoleon's Feisty Love Letters,' mgpt-magazine.com.

Muhlbach, Louise, 'The Empress Josephine,' 2003, www.gutenberg.org.

New York Times, 'The Napoleon Legend—A New Look,' *The New York Times*, 1964.

Public Broadcasting Service, 'The Emperor and Empress,' https://www.pbs.org/empires/napoleon/n_josephine/emperor/page_1.html.

Scraps from the Loft, 'Empress Joséphine: The Woman Who Stole Napoleon's Heart,' 2023, Scrapsfromtheloft.com.

Tarbell, Ida M., *A Life of Napoleon Bonaparte with a Sketch of Josephine, Empress of the French*, 2019, Project Gutenberg.

The Napoleon Series, *Popular History of Napoleon: Book Two Chapter One*, www.napoleon-series.org.

Truitt, Brian, 'She definitely turned him on: How Napoleon's love letters to Josephine inform a new film,' 22 November 2023, USA Today.

Wikipedia, 'Alexandre de Beauharnais.'

2. John Stuart Mill

Anil, Pratinav, 'The love life of JS Mill, the father of liberalism, caused quite the scandal,' 5 May 2023, Unherd, https://unherd.com/2023/05/the-love-life-of-js-mill/.

Gopnik, Adam, 'Right Again,' 29 September 2008, *The New Yorker*, https://www.newyorker.com/magazine/2008/10/06/right-again.

Gray, John, 'How Friedrich Hayek became fascinated with the romance of Harriet Taylor and J S Mill, 2015, *The New Statesman*, https://www.newstatesman.com/culture/2015/05/how-friedrich-hayek-became-fascinated-romance-harriet-taylor-and-j-s-mill.

Mill, John Stuart, 'John Stuart Mill and Harriet Taylor: their correspondence, friendship and subsequent marriage,' Internet Archive, https://docs.google.com/document/d/1hevskWZigF6m4wGPw5C34zlJDvYdVwCoFhiVhOStzZ4/edit?tab=t.0#heading=h.rqzo3z27nv7y.

Peart, Sandra J., 'Harriet Taylor's Partnership with John Stuart Mill,' 4 April 2024, Online Library of Liberty.

3. V.S. Naipaul

Braid, Mary, 'Naipaul reveals secrets of his sexual life,' 14 May 1994, *Independent*, https://www.independent.co.uk/news/naipaul-reveals-secrets-of-his-sexual-life-1436060.html

French, Patrick, *The World Is What It Is*, Picador, 2008.

Graham-Yooll, Andrew, 'The return of V.S. Naipaul,' 21 October 2023, *Buenos Aires Times*, https://www.batimes.com.ar/news/opinion-and-analysis/the-return-of-vs-naipaul.phtml.

Hawksley, Rupert, 'The brilliant but troubling legacy of VS Naipaul,' 13 August 2018, *The National News*.

Ramchand, Kenneth, 'VS Naipaul obituary,' 12 August 2018, *The Guardian*, https://www.theguardian.com/books/2018/aug/12/vs-naipaul-obituary.

Wikipedia, 'VS Naipaul.'

4. Amrita Pritam

Kazmi, Zehra, 'Ek Mulaqat: The unfinished love story of Amrita Pritam and Sahir Ludhianvi,' *Hindustan Times*, 2017, https://www.hindustantimes.com/art-and-culture/ek-mulaqat-the-unfinished-love-story-of-amrita-pritam-and-sahir-ludhianvi/story-quGbNGr4MrtZFsVHZmSsSO.html.

Khurana, Suanshu, 'Dear Zorbi,' 11 February 2024, *The Indian Express*.

Khurana, Suanshu, 'How Imroz's love built Amrita Pritam, as a woman and a poet,' 29 December 2023, *The Indian Express*.

Manwani, Akshay, *Sahir Ludhianvi: The People's Poet*, HarperCollins: New Delhi, 2013.

Pritam, Amrita, 'Ek Mulaqat,' in *Amrita Pritam Kagaz or Canvas*, Rajkamal Prakashan, 2010.

Pritam, Amrita, 'Raseedi Ticket,' Kitab Ghar Prakashan, 2008.

Pritam, Amrita, 'मैं तैनू फैर मलिांगी,' https://www.youtube.com/watch?v=1dDbn7X7D6o.

Pritam, Amrita, *The Revenue Stamp*, Times Group Books: New Delhi, 2015.

Rawat, Surabhi, 'Main tainu pher milangi: Amrita Pritam and Imroz's timeless love story,' 25 December 2023, Times of India. https://timesofindia.indiatimes.com/life-style/relationships/love-sex/main-tainu-pher-milangi-amrita-pritam-and-imrozs-timeless-love-story/articleshow/106270433.cms#:~:text=At%2016%2C%20Amrita%20was%20married,was%20not%20meant%20to%20last.

Trilok, Uma, *Amrita Imroz: A Love Story*, Penguin India: New Delhi, 2006.

5. Mirza Ghalib

Ghalib, rahulnegi.blogspot.com.

Verma, Pavan K., 'Ghalib: The Man,' 1989, *Times*, https://books.google.co.in/books/about/Ghalib.html?id=uwcwAQAAMAAJ&redir_esc=yet.

Wikipedia, 'Mirza Ghalib,' https://en.wikipedia.org/wiki/Ghalib.

YouTube, Mirza Ghalib television drama series, 1988.

6. Camille Claudel

Akbar, Arifa, 'How Rodin's tragic lover shaped the history of sculpture, 2012, *Independent*, https://www.independent.co.uk/arts-entertainment/art/features/

how-rodin-s-tragic-lover-shaped-the-history-of-sculpture-8026836.html.

Alberge, Dalya, 'Overshadowed by Rodin, but his lover wins acclaim at last, 2017, *The Guardian*, https://www.theguardian.com/artanddesign/2017/feb/26/camille-claudel-rodins-lover-acclaim-sculptor.

Claudel, Camille and Auguste Rodin, 'It's Complicated Zuzanna Stańska,' 12 November 2024, Daily Art Magazine, https://www.dailyartmagazine.com/love-and-despait-camille-claudel-rodin/.

Garman, Emma, 'Genius, Interrupted: The life, times, and trials of sculptor Camille Claudel, 2017, Roundtable, https://www.laphamsquarterly.org/roundtable/genius-interrupted.

Smee, Sebastian, 'Her tragic story eclipsed her art. This show restores the dazzle, 2023, *The Washington Post*, https://www.washingtonpost.com/entertainment/art/2023/11/07/camille-claudel-auguste-rodin/

Webster, Paul, 'Fame at last for Rodin's lost muse, 2003, *The Guardian*, https://www.theguardian.com/world/2003/mar/23/arts.artsnews.

7. Karl Marx

Anti-Capitalist Resistance, 'The Radical History of Hackney: The Sad Story of Fred Demuth – Marx's Son in Hackney, 2023, https://anticapitalistresistance.org/the-sad-story-of-fred-demuth-marxs-son-in-hackney/.

Ashton, Rosemary, 'Karl Marx in London,' 2028, *De Gruyter*.

BBC, Karl Marx (1818–1883), www.bbc.co.uk

Fluss, Harrison and Sam Miller, 'Jenny Marx's life of love and revolution, 2021, *Tribune*, https://docs.google.

com/document/d/1hevskWZigF6m4wGPw5C34zlJDvYdVwCoFhiVhOStzZ4/edit?tab=t.0.

Fluss, Harrison and Sam Miller, 'Jenny Marx's Life of Love and Revolution,' 2021, *Tribune Magazine*.

Larissa, Romensky, 'Housekeeper at the centre of Karl Marx's illicit affair in new play by central Victorian writer, 1 June 2016, www.abc.net.au.

Marx/Engels Archive, 'The Life and Work of Karl Marx.' https://www.marxists.org/archive/marx/bio/marx/lifeandwork.htm#:~:text=Marx%20and%20Engels%20meet%20in,lifelong%20friendship%20and%20joint%20work.&text=A%20congress%20of%20the%20League,is%20renamed%20the%20Communist%20League

Menand, Louis, 'Karl Marx, Yesterday and Today,' 3 October 2016.

Summer, Timothy Shenk, 'Love in the Time of Capital,' 2012, *Dissent Magazine*.

Wikipedia, 'Karl Marx.'

8. Margaret Mead

Brand, Stewart, 'For God's Sake, Margaret! Conversation with Gregory Bateson and Margaret Mead, *CoEvolutionary Quarterly*, June 1976, https://sites.evergreen.edu/arunchandra/wp-content/uploads/sites/395/2018/05/BatesonAndMead.pdf.

Camilla Gibb, 'Euphoria by Lily King: The colourful love life of Margaret Mead,' 2014, *The Guardian*, https://www.theguardian.com/books/2014/dec/24/euphoria-lily-king-review-margaret-mead-new-guinea.

Dobrin, Lise M. and Ira Bashkow, 'The Truth in Anthropology Does Not Travel First Class: Reo

Fortune's Fateful Encounter with Margaret Mead,' University of Nebraska Press, 2010, https://muse.jhu.edu/article/398061/summary.

Dresser, Sam, 'The life and meaning of Margaret Mead,' 2020, Essay Decode, https://www.sapiens.org/culture/mead-freeman/.

King, Charles, 'Gender Is What You Make of It: Margaret Mead, Ruth Benedict, and the Relationship That Changed Social Science, 2020, *Nautilus*, https://nautil.us/gender-is-what-you-make-of-it-237915/.

Louis Menand, 'How Cultural Anthropologists Redefined Humanity,' 2019, *The New Yorker*, https://www.newyorker.com/magazine/2019/08/26/how-cultural-anthropologists-redefined-humanity.

Mead, Margaret, *To Cherish the Life of the World: Selected Letters of Margaret Mead*, New York: Basic Books, 2006.

Popova, Maria, 'Pioneering Anthropologist Margaret Mead's Beautiful Love Letters to Her Soul Mate,' *The Marginalian*, https://www.themarginalian.org/2013/10/23/margaret-mead-ruth-benedict-love-letters/.

Stocking Jr, George W., 'Character as Culture,' 1983, *The New York Times*, https://www.nytimes.com/1983/05/22/books/character-as-culture.html

Time, 'Margaret Mead Today: Mother to the World, 1969, Time, https://time.com/archive/6634006/behavior-margaret-mead-today-mother-to-the-world/.

VoA Learning English, 'Margaret Mead, 1901–1978: One of the Most Famous Anthropologists in the World,' 2011, https://learningenglish.voanews.com/a/margaret-mead-1901-1978-one-of-the-most-famous-anthropologists-in-the-world-124869344/112571.html.

9. Edward Gibbon

Breen, T.H. 'Making History,' 2000, *The New York Times*, https://archive.nytimes.com/www.nytimes.com/books/00/05/07/reviews/000507.07breent.html?_r=1&oref=slogin.

Gibbon, Edward, 'Memoirs of My Life and Writings, 2012, Gutenberg, https://www.gutenberg.org/files/6031/6031-h/6031-h.htm

Gutenberg, 'Private Letters of Edward Gibbon (1753–1794), https://docs.google.com/document/d/1hevskWZigF6m4wGPw5C34zlJDvYdVwCoFhiVhOStzZ4/edit?tab=t.0#heading=h.o9l95i39850n

Perkins, James Breck, 'Madame Necker,' February 1888, *The Atlantic*, https://www.theatlantic.com/magazine/archive/1888/02/madame-necker/634492/

Kronenberger, Louis, 'Edward Gibbon,' Nov 1954, *The Atlantic*, https://www.theatlantic.com/magazine/archive/1954/11/edward-gibbon/642262/

10. Catherine of Aragon

History on the Net, 'Catherine of Aragon Timeline: Her Life and Times, https://www.historyonthenet.com/catherine-of-aragon-timeline

Hughes, Kathryn and Giles Tremlett, 'Catherine of Aragon: Henry's Spanish Queen,' 2010, *The Guardian*, www.theguardian.com/books/2010/oct/30/catherine-aragon-giles-tremlett-review

Mantel, Hilary, 'Anne Boleyn: witch, bitch, temptress, feminist,' 2012, *The Guardian*, https://www.theguardian.com/books/2012/may/11/hilary-mantel-on-anne-boleyn.

Real Royalty, 'Was Anne Boleyn a Victim or a Schemer? A Tale of Two Sisters,' YouTube.

11. Winston Churchill

Buckley, Tom, 'Broadway Pays Tribute to Ethel Barrymore,' 18 Dec 1979, *The New York Times*.

Churchill Archive, 'Churchill and Women highlight,' https://www.churchillarchive.com.

Churchill, Sir W.L.S. 'Autograph letter,' Christie's. https://www.christies.com.

Collins, Joseph, 'Lady Spencer□Churchill in London in 1975,' 13 Dec 1977, *The New York Times*.

International Churchill Society, 'Churchill, Major Pond, and the Lecture Tour of 1900–1901.'

International Churchill Society, 'Young Soldier Archives,' https://winstonchurchill.org.

Sempa, Francis P., 'Winston Churchill in India,' 2015, *The Diplomat*, thediplomat.com.

Seshan K.S.S., 'Where Churchill loved and lost,' 10 July 2017, *The Hindu*.

Shelden, Michael, 'Winston Churchill proposed to three society beauties in his…,' 22 Mar 2013, www.dailymail.co.uk.

Smith, David, 'Letters reveal heartbreak of young Winston,' 9 Nov 2003, *The Guardian*.

The Economic Times, 'When Churchill proposed to 3 most beautiful women of his time,' 2013, *The Economic Times*, https://economictimes.indiatimes.com/when-churchill-proposed-to-3-most-beautiful-women-of-his-time/articleshow/19165263.cms?from=mdr.

The Economist, 'How the young Winston Churchill escaped from a prisoner-of-war camp,' 24 Feb 2024, *The Economist*.

Tingle, Rory, 'Winston Churchill's first love is revealed,' 21 July 2020, Mailonline.

12. Steve Jobs

AllAboutSteveJob.com, 'Steve at Home,' https://allaboutstevejobs.com/persona/steve_at_home.

Elkind, Peter, 'When Steve Jobs' Ex-Girlfriend Asked Him to Pay $25 Million for His "Dishonorable Behavior",' *Fortune,* https://fortune.com/2015/08/06/steve-jobs-apple-girlfriend/.

Heller, Karen, 'Listening to her older records, Joan Baez hears perfection in an "unsurpassable" voice,' 2021, *Washington Post,* https://www.washingtonpost.com/entertainment/music/joan-baez-kennedy-center-honors/2021/05/11/764fdbdc-a459-11eb-a774-7b47ceb36ee8_story.html.

Heller, Karen, 'The Kennedy Center honoree redefined folk music and showed up wherever her songs and courage were needed,' 2021, *The Washington Post,* https://www.washingtonpost.com/entertainment/music/joan-baez-kennedy-center-honors/2021/05/11/764fdbdc-a459-11eb-a774-7b47ceb36ee8_story.html.

Isaacson, Walter, 'The Real Leadership Lessons of Steve Jobs,' 2012, *Harvard Business Review,* https://hbr.org/2012/04/the-real-leadership-lessons-of-steve-jobs.

Kiddle, 'Chrisann Brennan facts for kids,' Kids Encyclopedia, Factshttps://kids.kiddle.co/Chrisann_Brennan.

NY Daily News, 'The Steve Jobs Nobody Knew,' 19 Oct 2011, NY Daily News, https://web.archive.org/web/20120425233149/http://india.nydailynews.com/article/3ea39bee2a29179c3406250afd01c526/the-steve-jobs-nobody-knew.

Ranker, 'Steve Jobs's Dating and Relationship History, 2024, Ranker, https://www.ranker.com/list/steve-jobs-loves-and-hookups/celebrityhookups.

Rolling Stone, 'The Steve Jobs Nobody Knew,' 19 Oct 2011, NY Dailynews.com, https://web.archive.org/web/20120425233149/http://india.nydailynews.com/article/3ea39bee2a29179c3406250afd01c526/the-steve-jobs-nobody-knew.

Schwartz, Alexandra, 'Jennifer Egan's Travels Through Time,' 2017, *The New Yorker*, https://www.newyorker.com/magazine/2017/10/16/jennifer-egans-travels-through-time#:~:text=Egan%20and%20Jobs%20dated%20for,own%20contexts%2C%E2%80%9D%20Egan%20said.

Vanity Fair, 'Growing Up Jobs, Lisa Brennan-Jobs, 2018,' *Vanity Fair*, https://www.vanityfair.com/news/2018/08/lisa-brennan-jobs-small-fry-steve-jobs-daughter.

13. Amrita Sher-Gil

Dalmia, Yashodhra (Ed.), *Amrita Sher-Gil: Art and Life*, New Delhi: OUP, 2014.

Dutt, Nirupama, 'When Amrita Sher-Gil vowed to seduce Khushwant Singh to take revenge on his wife,' 30 Jan 2017, Scroll.in, https://scroll.in/magazine/827982/when-amrita-sher-gil-vowed-to-seduce-khushwant-singh-to-take-revenge-on-his-wife.

Hughes, Kathryn, 'The Indian Frida Kahlo,' 2013, *The Telegraph*, https://www.telegraph.co.uk/culture/10087130/The-Indian-Frida-Kahlo.html.

Mzezewa, Tariro, 'Overlooked No More: Amrita Sher-Gil, a Pioneer of Indian Art,' 2018, *New York Times*, https://www.nytimes.com/2018/06/20/obituaries/amrita-shergil-dead.html.

Wikipedia, 'Amrita Sher-Gil.'

14. Marie Curie

Gillis, Anna Maria, 'Meet Marie Curie,' 9 July 1997, *Washington Post*.

History.aip, 'A Student in Paris (1891–1897),' Marie Curie and the Science of radioactivity, https://history.aip.org/exhibits/curie/stud1.htm.

History.aip, 'Scandal and Recovery (1910–1913): The Academy Debacle,' Marie Curie and the Science of radioactivity, https://history.aip.org/exhibits/curie/scandal1.htm.

KU Libraries, 'Poland: Marie Skłodowska Curie: 100 Year Anniversary of Nobel Prize,' https://guides.lib.ku.edu/c.php?g=95123&p=618651.

Marie Curie blog, 'Marie and Pierre Curie: a marriage of true minds,' 2015, https://www.mariecurie.org.uk/blog/marie-and-pierre-curie-a-marriage-of- true-minds/48568.

Wilkie, Tom, 'The secret sex life of Marie Curie,' 13 June 1995, *Independent*.

15. Muhammad Iqbal

Anjum, Zafar, *The Life of a Poet, Philosopher and Politician*, New Delhi: Random House, 2014.

Friday Times, 'Allama Iqbal and Atiya Faizi's Untold History of Friendship and Love,' 20 July 2022, *The Friday Times*, https://thefridaytimes.com/20-Jul-2022/allama-iqbal-and-atiya-faizi-s-untold-history-of-friendship-and-love.

Iqbal Academy, 'Biography of Allama Iqbal,' Iqbal Academy Pakistan, https://www.allamaiqbal.com/biography/en/illustrated_biography03.php.

Shah, Sabir, 'Justice Javed Iqbal dies two days before his 91st birthday,' 4 October 2015, *The News*, https://www.thenews.com.pk/print/65913-justice-javed-iqbal-dies-two-days-before-his-91st-birthday.

Sheikh, Majid, 'Harking Back: Iqbal and mud from the graves of Rumi and Ataturk,' 2020, *The Dawn*. https://www.dawn.com/news/1534675.

Singh, Iqbal, *The Ardent Pilgrim: An Introduction to the Life and Works of Mohammed Iqbal*, New Delhi: OUP, 1997.

Wikepedia, 'Muhammad Iqbal.'

Zakaria, Rafia, Iqbal's Love: Iqbal's Life,' 2015, *The Dawn*, https://www.dawn.com/news/1218512.

16. Pelé (Edson Arantes do Nascimento)

BBC, 'Pele: A sporting icon who made football beautiful,' 29 Dec 2022, BBC.

Corbella, Enrique, 'Xuxa reveals the intimacies of her romance with Pele: My first sexual relationship was with him,' 14 July 2023, https://www.marca.com/en/lifestyle/2023/07/14/64b15a78ca474192688b456c.html.

Mifflin, Lawrie, 'Pelé, the Global Face of Soccer, Dies at 82,' *New York Times*, 2022, https://www.nytimes.com/.

Novitski, Joseph, 'Pele Gains a Goal: End of World Play,' *The New York Times*, 1971.

O'Sullivan, Kyle, 'Pele had so many affairs he didn't know how many kids he had—and refused to recognise one,' 23 Feb 2021, *Mirror*, UK.

Pelé, *Pele: The Autobiography*, Simon & Schuster, 2007.

Rocha, Camilo, George Ramsay, Tara John, Flora Charner, and Rodrigo Pedroso, 'Brazilian soccer legend Pelé dies at 82,' CNN, 29 Dec 2022.

Veloso, Lea, 'Pelé Was Married 3 Times Before His Death—Inside His Complicated Relationships,' 29 December 2022, Stylecaster.

Vincent, Isabel, 'Inside Pele's personal life: Three wives, six kids and more he didn't "publicly recognise",' 2023, *New York Post*, www.news.com.au.

Vincent, Isabel, 'Pelé was the world's greatest soccer player—and, apparently, lover,' 31 Dec 2022, *New York Post*.

17. Albert Einstein

Chaudhuri, Asis Kumar, 'Einstein in Love: Part 4 (Betty Neumann: Einstein's young love),' 23 Mar 2021, https://asischaudhuri.wordpress.com/2021/03/23/einstein-in-love-part-4-betty-neumann-einsteins-young-love/.

Gagnon, Pauline, 'The Forgotten Life of Einstein's First Wife,' 2016, Scientific American.

Gerrard, Nicci, 'A genius—but you wouldn't want to marry him,' 2001, *The Guardian*,

Highfield, Roger, 'Einstein's theory of fidelity,' 11 July 2006, *The Telegraph*.

Renn, Jurgen and Robert Schulmann, 'Albert Einstein, Mileva Maric: The Love Letters', 1992.

Smith, P.D., 'The man beneath the electrified halo of hair,' 25 Aug 2002, *The Guardian*.

18. Fyodor Dostoyevsky

Frank, Joseph, *Dostoevsky: The Years of Ordeal, 1850–1859*, Princeton University Press, 1983.

Popoff, Alexandra, *The Wives*, Simon & Schuster, 2013.

Russia Beyond, 'Dostoevsky: Turbulent in love as well as life,' 29 July 2015, Russia Beyond, https://www.rbth.com/literature/2015/07/29/dostoevsky_turbulent_in_love_as_well_as_life_48107.html.

Tutorial at Home, 'Turbulent Love and Life of Dostoevsky,' 2018, Tutorial at Home, https://www.tutorialathome.in/english/turbelent-love-life-dostoevsky-poets-storytellers.

19. Charles Sobhraj

Aljazeera, 'Timeline: Case of Charles Sobhraj—"Bikini Killer", "Serpent",' 23 Dec 2022, Aljazeera, https://www.aljazeera.com/news/2022/12/23/timeline-case-of-charles-sobhraj-bikini-killer-serpent.

Clarke, Julie, and Richard Neville, 'The Life and Crime of Charles Sobhraj,' *India Today*, https://www.indiatoday.in/magazine/society-and-the-arts/books/story/19791215-the-life-and-crime-of-charles-sobhraj-by-julie-clarke-richard-neville-822285-2014-02-15.

Happyscribe, '"The Hippie Trail Killer" Charles Sobhraj,' 2020, Happyscribe, https://www.happyscribe.com/public/serial-killers/the-hippie-trail-killer-charles-sobhraj-pt-f964a9f8-e420-4583-b8c2-238a4bbf8001.

India Today, 'Charles Sobhraj: One of the most accomplished murderers in the annals of modern crime,' *India Today*, https://www.indiatoday.in/magazine/crime/story/19781015-charles-sobhraj-one-of-the-most-accomplished-murderers-in-the-annals-of-modern-crime-823063-2014-03-12.

Kathmandu Post, 'Charles Sobhraj produced before Bhaktapur District Court,' 2014, *The Kathmandu Post*, https://kathmandupost.com/miscellaneous/2014/05/18/charles-sobhraj-produced-before-bhaktapur-district-court.

Maloney, Alison, 'Spitting Venom "Serpent" killer Charles Sobhraj breaks silence on his horrifying crimes in bombshell first interview since jail release,' 2024, *The Sun*, https://www.thesun.co.uk/tv/26716149/serpent-killer-charles-sobhraj-backpacker-murders/.

Pardafas, 'Nihita Biswas: The Girl Who Married "Serial Killer" Charles Sobhraj,' 23 Dec 2022, Pardafas, https://english.pardafas.com/nihita-biswas-the-girl-who-married-serial-killer-charles-sobhraj/.

Pokhare, Gaurav, 'Charles Sobhraj left Nepal—and a romantic relationship that he had developed behind bars,' 2022, onlinekhabar, https://english.onlinekhabar.com/charles-sobhraj-nihita-biswas-apart.html.

Sharma, Suparna, 'Charles Sobhraj, convicted murderer, has a new story to tell,' 25 Aug 2023, Aljazeera, https://www.aljazeera.com/features/2023/8/25/charles-sobhraj-convicted-murderer-has-a-new-story-to-tell.

Times of India, 'Charles Sobhraj ties the knot with Nihita Biswas, 9 Oct 2008, *The Times of India*, https://timesofindia.indiatimes.com/Charles_Sobhraj_weds_Nepalese_girlfriend/rssarticleshow/3577773.cms.

20. Margaret Beaufort

Brain, Jessica, 'Lady Margaret Beaufort,' 2 Mar 202, History, UK.

Brown, Rebecca Starr, 'Margaret Beaufort and the Birth of Henry Tudor,' 28 Jan 2017, rebeccastarrbrown.com.

Garden, Leah, 'The Untold Life of Royal England's Margaret Beaufort,' 28 December 2021, newlinesmag.com.

Preis, Dorothea, 'Marriage of Margaret Beaufort and Henry Stafford,' Richard III Society of NSW, www.richardiii-nsw.org.au.

Real Royalty, 'The Great Tudor Plot to Seize the Crown,' War of the Roses, https://www.youtube.com/watch?v=KdbvCtmmvAI&t=677s.

Teysko, Heather, 'Jasper Tudor: The Loyal Uncle Who Built the Tudor Dynasty,' 9 April 2016, www.englandcast.com.

Tudorchest, 'Lady Margaret Beaufort: The Queen who never was,' 21 Aug 2021, The Tudorchest, www.thetudorchest.com.

21. Nelson Mandela

BBC, 'Nelson Mandela death: The women who loved him,' 6 Dec 2013, BBC.

Daley, Suzanne, 'The Mandelas in Divorce Court: He Tells of a Broken Marriage,' 1996, *The New York Times*, https://www.nytimes.com/1996/03/19/world/the-mandelas-in-divorce-court-he-tells-of-a-broken-marriage.html.

Independent, 'Letter to lover spells trouble for Winnie,' 07 Sept 1992, *Independent*, https://www.independent.co.uk/news/world/letter-to-lover-spells-trouble-for-winnie-1549863.html.

PTI, 'Nelson Mandela once fell in love with Indian-origin woman,' 2013, One India, https://www.oneindia.com/2013/03/30/nelson-mandela-fell-in-love-with-indian-origin-woman-1182919.html.

Smith, David, 'Amina Cachalia turned down Nelson Mandela's offer of marriage, son claims,' 2013, *The Guardian*, https://www.theguardian.com/world/2013/apr/01/amina-cachalia-mandela-marriage-proposal.

Smith, David, 'Nelson and Winnie Mandela's marriage ended, but the bond was never broken,' 6 Dec 2013, *The Guardian*.

Smith, David, 'Graca Machel on Mandela: "I learned to separate the man from the myth",' 6 Dec 2013, *The Guardian*.

Wootson Jr, Cleve R., 'Winnie and Nelson Mandela's marriage survived three decades of prison—but not freedom,' 2018, *Washington Post*, https://docs.google.com/document/d/1hevskWZigF6m4wGPw5C34zlJDvYdVwCoFhiVhOStzZ4/edit?tab=t.0.

22. Bertrand Russell

Ayer, A.J., *Bertrand Russell*, University of Chicago Press, 1988.

Gorham, D., 'Dora and Bertrand Russell and Beacon Hill School,' McMaster University Library Press, 2005.

Grattan-Guinness, Ivor, *Alys Russell's Interpretation of Her Separation from Bertie*, McMaster University Library Press, 1996.

Kennedy, Maev, 'The real Lady Chatterley: Society hostess loved and parodied by Bloomsbury group,' 2006, *The*

Guardian, https://www.theguardian.com/uk/2006/oct/10/books.booksnews.

Leiter, Brian, 'Dora Russell, Bertrand's second wife,' 2014, Leiter Reports, https://leiterreports.typepad.com/blog/2014/04/dora-russell-bertrands-second-wife.html.

McDiarmid, Lucy, 'Bertrand Russell's Principia Erotica,' 15 Aug 1992, *The Washington post*, https://www.washingtonpost.com/archive/entertainment/books/1992/08/16/bertrand-russells-principia-erotica/25e368d5-5ef0-4a22-b24e-024113376759/.

Monk, Ray, *Bertrand Russell: The Ghost of Madness (1921–1970)*, Free Press, 2016.

Philosophynews, 'Ill and Shy: A Frantic Quest for Identity,' 2014, Philosophynews.com, https://philosophynews.com/what-can-be-learned-from-bertrand-russells-life-as-a-philanderer-part-iii/.

Stangroom, Jeremy, 'Unrequited Love,' The Philosophers' Magazine, https://archive.philosophersmag.com/unrequited-love/#:~:text=Fifty%20years%20after%20Russell%20dropped,our%20mutual%20life%20very%20difficult.

Whitman, Alden, 'Bertrand Russell Is Dead,' 3 Feb 1970, *The New York Times*, https://archive.nytimes.com/www.nytimes.com/books/01/04/29/specials/russell-obit.html.

Wikipedia, 'Bertrand Russell.' https://en.wikipedia.org/wiki/Bertrand_Russell.

23. Alfred Nobel

Celje, 'Širokogrudni Alfred Nobel in njegova razsipna celjska ljubezen Sofija Hess [Broad-minded Alfred

Nobel and his wasteful Celje love Sofia Hess],' 11 Oct 2018, celje.info (Retrieved 29 Feb 2020).

Celje, 'Skok, Blaž: Kako se je Alfred Nobel zaljubil v "požiralko bankovcev" iz Celja [How Alfred Nobel fell in love with a "banknote devourer" from Celje],' N1 Slovenija, Ljubljana, 2023.

Fant, Kenne, *Alfred Nobel: A Biography*, Arcade Publishing, 2014.

Frängsmyr, Tore, 'Alfred Nobel: Life and Philosophy (A Memorial Address),' 1996, The Royal Swedish Academy of Sciences, https://www.nobelprize.org/alfred-nobel/alfred-nobel-life-and-philosophy/.

Lienhard, John H., 'Von Suttner and Nobel,' Cullen College of Engineering, The Engine of Ingenuity, https://engines.egr.uh.edu/episode/1104.

Rummel, Erika (Ed,), *A Nobel Affair: The Correspondence Between Alfred Nobel and Sofie Hess*, University of Toronto Press, 2017.

Skok, Blaž, 'How Alfred Nobel fell in love with a "banknote devourer" from Celje,' 13 May 2023, Culture.

Wienbibliothek, 'Sofie Hess in Wien Geschichte,' Wienbibliothek.at (Retrieved 7 June 2023).

24. Rabindranath Tagore

Deccan Herald, 'Sanskriti Express brings back the memories of Rabindranath Tagore,' 26 Oct 2010, *Deccan Herald*.

Get Bengal, 'Rabindranath Tagore's First Love: Annapurna,' 2021, Get Bengal, https://www.getbengal.com/details/rabindranath-tagores-first-love-annapurna.

Ghosh, Ruchira, 'Kadambari Devi: Rabindranath Tagore's Literary Companion,' 6 Dec 2018.

Goyal, Shikha, 'Rabindranath Tagore Biography,' 8 May 2024, Jagran Josh.

Hindustan Times, 'Rabindranath Tagore 159th Birth Anniversary,' 8 May 2020, *Hindustan Times*.

Roy, Amit, 'Eye on England,' 7 Oct 2012, *The Telegraph*.

Scottish Centre of Tagore Studies, 'Kadambari Devi (1859–1884); Rabindranath's sister-in-law,' The Scottish Centre of Tagore Studies, https://scotstagore.org/kadambari-devi-1859-1884-rabindranaths-sister-in-law-by-christine-kupfer/#:~:text=Kadambari%20Devi%20was%20Rabindranath's%20sister,the%20time%20a-nd%20admired%20her.

Tagore, Rabindranath, 'Unending Love, All Poetry, https://allpoetry.com/Unending-Love.

Viswanathan, R., 'The complicated relationship of Tagore, Victoria Ocampo,' 2020, *The Week*, https://www.theweek.in/leisure/society/2020/05/18/complicted-relationship-tagore-victoria-ocampo.html.

25. Muhammad Ali

Alvarado, Francisco, 'Khalilah Camacho-Ali Was in Muhammad Ali's Corner Through Some of Boxing's Greatest Moments,' 2011, *Miami News Times*, https://www.miaminewtimes.com/news/khalilah-camacho-ali-was-in-muhammad-alis-corner-through-some-of-boxings-greatest-moments-6380493.

Crouse, Karen, 'Muhammad Ali Was Her First, and Greatest, Love, 2016, *The New York Times*, https://docs.google.com/document/d/1hevskWZigF6m4wGPw5C34zlJDvYdVwCoFhiVhOStzZ4/edit?tab=t.0#heading=h.jw3g9vmde7oh.

Hause, Thomas, 'Muhammad Ali,' 2024, Britannica, https://www.britannica.com/biography/Muhammad-Ali-boxer.

Josaphat, Fabienne, 'Khalilah Camacho-Ali Stood by Muhammad Ali Through Exile and Triumph,' 2024, Sugercane.

Lipsyte, Robert, 'Muhammad Ali dies at 74,' 2016, *The New York Times*, https://www.nytimes.com/2016/06/04/sports/muhammad-ali-dies.html.

Los Angeles Times, 'Everything About Sonji Roi: First Wife of Muhammad Ali,' 2005, *Los Angeles Times*.

New York Times, 'Ali Weds Miss Porche In Ceremony on Coast,' 1977, *New York Times* https://www.nytimes.com/1977/06/20/archives/ali-weds-miss-porche-in-ceremony-on-coast.html.

Peritz, Kurt, 'How Muhammad Ali's Ex-Wives Forgave His Infidelity: Cheating "Never Meant Anything to Him",' 2016, *People*.

Robertson, Linda, 'Stings like a bee: Death of beloved Muhammad Ali is felt worldwide,' 2016, *Miami Herald*, https://www.miamiherald.com/sports/fighting/article81762562.html#:~:text=On%20the%20morning%20of%20the,along%20with%20Sammy%20Davis%20Jr.

Ward, Nathan, 'A Total Eclipse of the Sonny,' 2006, American Heritage, https://web.archive.org/web/20070111061103/http://www.americanheritage.com/articles/magazine/ah/2006/5/2006_5_48.shtml.

26. Immanuel Kant

Harding, Luke, 'Kant's wild years,' 12 Feb 2004, *The Guardian*, https://www.theguardian.

com/world/2004/feb/12/highereducation.artsandhumanities.

Kuehn, Manfred, *Kant: A Biography*, Cambridge University Press, 2002.

Russell, Bertrand, *History of Western Philosophy*, Routledge Publication, 2015, https://www.amazon.in/History-Western-Philosophy-Routledge-Classics/dp/1138127043.

Wilbra, John Henry, 'The Life of Immanuel Kant,' 2016, Stuckenberg.

27. Virginia Woolf

Barnes, Elodie, 'Beyond the Legend: Virginia Woolf and Vita Sackville-West's Love Affair and Friendship,' 2022, Literary Ladies Guide, https://www.literaryladiesguide.com/literary-musings/beyond-the-legend-virginia-woolf-and-vita-sackville-wests-love-affair-friendship/.

Kephart, Beth, 'What Passes for Love: On the Marriage of Leonard and Virginia Woolf,' 2020, Literary Hub, https://lithub.com/what-passes-for-love-on-the-marriage-of-leonard-and-virginia-woolf/.

Mills, Sam, 'A Most Sensitive and Sophisticated Mind,' *The London Magazine*, https://thelondonmagazine.org/article/essay-a-most-sensitive-and-sophisticated-mind-by-sam-mills/.

Woolf, Leonard, *The Wise Virgins*, Preface, Persephone Books, 2003. More on Leonard Woolf see *Virginia Woolf: A Writer's Life* by Lyndall Gordon, https://www.lyndallgordon.net/essays/wisevirgins.html#:~:text=It%20is%20a%20truth%20widely,marriage%20on%2010%20August%201912.

28. John Maynard Keynes

Davenport-Hines, Richard, 'Seven things you may not know about John Maynard Keynes,' 2015, *The Guardian,* https://www.theguardian.com/books/2015/mar/05/seven-things-john-maynard-keynes#:~:text=His%20orientation%20was%20towards%20other,male%20love%20of%20his%20life.

Economist, 'The love song of J. Maynard Keynes,' 2021, *The Economist.*

Gray, John, 'A Point of View: What would Keynes do?' 22 July 2012, https://www.bbc.com/news/magazine-18923542.

Mackrell, Judith, 'Carrying on with L,' 2008, *The Guardian,* https://www.theguardian.com/books/2008/mar/22/dance.stage.

Mackrell, Judith, 'Niall Ferguson should know that JM Keynes's marriage was happy—with plenty of sex,' 2013, *The Guardian,* https://www.theguardian.com/stage/2013/may/06/niall-ferguson-keynes-marriage-sex.

Menand, Louis, 'Buried Treasure,' 2002, *The New Yorker,* https://www.newyorker.com/magazine/2002/01/28/buried-treasure-5.

New York Times, 'Obituary: Lord Keynes Dies of Heart Attack,' 1946, *The New York Times,* https://archive.nytimes.com/www.nytimes.com/learning/general/onthisday/bday/0605.html.

Wikepdia, 'J. Maynard Keynes.'

29. Pablo Escobar

Anderson, Jon Lee, 'The Afterlife of Pablo Escobar,' 26 Feb 2018, The New Yorker.

Birrell, Ian, 'TV reporter who fell for Pablo Escobar reveals why he's a monster,' 2018, *Daily Mail*, https://www.nzherald.co.nz/world/tv-reporter-who-fell-for-pablo-escobar-reveals-why-hes-a-monster/I5A6DA4AL6MAPPWIQH26CJCOZE/.

Bowden, Mark, 'Killing Pablo,' 29 Apr 2001, The Guardian.

Dimuro, Gina, 'Meet Virginia Vallejo, the Journalist Who Had an Affair with Pablo Escobar—and Made Him a Celebrity,' 26 Sept 2021, All That's Interesting, https://allthatsinteresting.com/virginia-vallejo.

eShe, 'The girl behind Pablo Escobar, eShe, 3 Oct 2019, https://eshe.in/2019/10/03/mrs-escobar/.

Henao, Maria Victoria, 'Why I stayed Married to Pablo Escobar,' Primer.

Henao, Victoria Eugenia, 'Pablo Escobar's wife, Victoria Eugenia Henao, on why she stayed married to the drug lord,' 10 Aug 2019, The Sunday Times.

Maloney, Alison, 'Married to a monster: Pablo Escobar got me pregnant at 14 and built a bachelor pad at our house for sex with his mistresses,' 2020, *The Sun*, https://www.the-sun.com/news/2051876/pablo-escobar-victoria-eugenia-henao-married-house-mistresses/#:~:text=%22The%20thing%20that%20hurt%20me,as%20ever%2C%22%20she%20says.

Martin, Hugo, 'Fue amante de Pablo Escobar, tuvo sexo con su sicario más sangriento por venganza y terminó asesinada,' 24 Sept 2022, Infobae, https://www.infobae.com/historias/2022/09/24/fue-amante-de-pablo-escobar-tuvo-sexo-con-su-sicario-mas-sangriento-por-venganza-y-termino-asesinada/.

Primeaux, Emily, 'Murder, money laundering and the demise of Pablo Escobar,' September/October 2020, Fraud Magazine.

Wikipedia, 'Hacienda Nápoles.'

30. Justa Grata Honoria

Bury, J.B., 'Justa Grata Honoria and Attila: The Hunnic Invasion of Gaul,' in *The Invasion of Europe by the Barbarians*, Novo Scriptorium, https://novoscriptorium.com/2021/02/16/justa-grata-honoria-and-attila-the-hunnic-invasion-of-gaul/.

Bury, J.B., *History of the Later Roman Empire*, Macmillan, 1923, https://penelope.uchicago.edu/Thayer/E/Roman/Texts/secondary/BURLAT/home.html

Gibbon, Edward, *The Decline and Fall of the Roman Empire Vol I*, New Delhi: Penguin, 2000.

Man, John, *Attila the Hun: A Barbarian King and the Fall of Rome*, Bantam Press, 2005.

31. Joseph Stalin

Fantz, Ashley, 'Love letters reveal tyrants' hearts bleed, too,' 2012, CNN World, https://docs.google.com/document/d/1hevskWZigF6m4wGPw5C34zlJDvYdVwCoFhiVhOStzZ4/edit?tab=t.0.

Hindustan Times, 'First wife softened Stalin's heart!' HT Correspondent, London, 22 Aug 2013.

Holden, Stephen, 'A Little-Known Young Bride of a Famous Soviet Monster,' 2005, *The New York Times*.

Kun, Miklos, 'Stalin: An Unknown Portrait,' New York: Central European University Press, 2003, https://archive.org/details/stalinunknownpor0000kunm

Montefiore, Simon Sebag, 'Stalin,' 2004, *The New York Times,* https://www.nytimes.com/2004/04/18/books/chapters/stalin.html.

Radzinsky, Edvard and Ėdvard Radzinskiĭ, *Stalin*, New York: Anchor Books, 1996, https://openlibrary.org/books/OL1273139M/Stalin.

32. J. Robert Oppenheimer

Burack, Emily, 'The True Story of Jean Tatlock in *Oppenheimer*,' 2023, Town and Country, https://www.townandcountrymag.com/leisure/arts-and-culture/a44642007/jean-tatlock-oppenheimer-true-story/.

Dowd, Katie, 'What really happened to Jean Tatlock, the love of Oppenheimer's life,' 2023, SFGATE, https://www.sfgate.com/sf-culture/article/oppenheimer-what-happened-to-jean-tatlock-18175867.php#:~:text=The%20thought%20tormented%20her%20%E2%80%94%20she,off%20for%20good%20in%201939.

Gonzales, Erica, 'Kitty Oppenheimer Really Did Stand Up for Her Husband at His Security Hearings,' 2023, *Elle,* https://www.elle.com/culture/movies-tv/a44613444/oppenheimer-kitty-oppenheimer-true-story-explained/.

Grebey, James, 'The Real Life Story of Kitty and Robert Oppenheimer, and the Scandalous Beginning of Their Marriage,' 2024, NBC, https://www.nbc.com/nbc-insider/the-real-life-story-of-kitty-and-robert-oppenheimer.

Meads, Kat, 'Plaster Cast, Martini Glass, Potted Orchid: The Life Of Kitty Oppenheimer,' 2023, *The Decadent Review,* https://thedecadentreview.com/corpus/

plaster-cast-martini-glass-potted-orchid-the-life-of-kitty-oppenheimer/.

Streshinsky, Shirley, 'The Day That Could Have Brought Down Robert Oppenheimer,' 2013, Huffpost, https://www.huffpost.com/entry/the-day-that-could-have-b_b_427418.

Wikipedia, 'Jean Tatlock.', https://en.wikipedia.org/wiki/Jean_Tatlock.

33. Wolfgang Pauli

Enz, Charles P., *No Time to Be Brief: Scientific Biography of Pauli*, London: OUP, 2002.

Geniuses Club, Wolfgang Pauli, Geniuses, https://geniuses.club/genius/wolfgang-pauli.

Gieser, Suzanne, 'The Innermost Kernel,' 2004, Springer.

Halpern, Paul, 'The Synchronicity of Wolfgang Pauli and Carl Jung,' 18 Nov 2020, Nautilus.

Overbye, Dennis, 'Quantum Theory Tugged, and All of Physics Unraveled,' 2000, *The New York Times*, https://www.nytimes.com/2000/12/12/science/quantum-theory-tugged-and-all-of-physics-unraveled.html.

Von Baeyer, Hans, 'Wolfgang Pauli's Journey Inward,' 2011, Everand.

34. Stephen Hawking

Adams, Tim, 'Jane Hawking: Brief history of a first wife,' 2004, *The Guardian*, https://www.theguardian.com/theobserver/2004/apr/04/features.review17.

Anderson, L.V., 'How Accurate Is the Theory of Everything?' 2014, Slate, https://slate.com/culture/2014/11/the-theory-of-everything-how-accurate-is-the-new-stephen-hawking-movie-starring-eddie-redymane.html.

Bates, Daniel, 'How Stephen Hawking's second wife Elaine was accused of abuse,' 2020, *Daily Mail*, https://www.dailymail.co.uk/news/article-8698199/Stephen-Hawkings-second-wife-Elaine-raged-guests-slave.html.

Froelich, Paula, 'Inside wheelchair-bound Lothario Stephen Hawking's improbable, steamy love life,' 2020, *New York Post*, https://nypost.com/2020/09/05/inside-lothario-stephen-hawkings-improbable-steamy-love-life/.

Hawking, Stephen, *My Brief History*, London: Bantam Press, 2013.

35. Richard Feynman

Farnam Street, 'Richard Feynman's Love Letter to His Wife, Sixteen Months After Her Death,' Farnam Street, https://fs.blog/richard-feynman-love-letter/.

FitzGerald, Edward (Trans.), *The Rubaiyat of Omar Khayyam*, Peacock Books, 2024.

Gleick, James, 'Genius: The Life and Science of Richard Feynman,' 1994, Open Road, New York, https://publicism.info/biography/genius/7.html.

Hassan, Sarah, 'No Other Love: Heart-Wrenching Letters from Richard Feynman to His Late Wife, Arline,' 2021, Sotheby's, https://www.sothebys.com/en/articles/no-other-love-heart-wrenching-letters-from-richard-feynman-to-his-late-wife-arline.

Mehra, Jagdish, 'Richard Phillips Feynman (1918–1988), 2002, The Royal Society, https://royalsocietypublishing.org/doi/pdf/10.1098/rsbm.2002.0007

Popova, Maria, 'Love After Life: Nobel-Winning Physicist Richard Feynman's Extraordinary Letter to His Departed Wife, The Marginalian, https://www.themarginalian.org/2017/10/17/richard-feynman-arline-letter/.

36. Sigmund Freud

Blumenthal, Ralph, 'Hotel Log Hints at Illicit Desire That Dr. Freud Didn't Repress,' 2006, *The New York Times*, https://www.nytimes.com/2006/12/24/world/europe/hotel-log-hints-at-illicit-desire-that-dr-freud-didnt-repress.html.

Crews, Frederick, 'How Sigmund Freud Tried to Break and Remake His Fiancée,' 2017, Literary Hub, https://docs.google.com/document/d/1hevskWZigF6m4wGPw5C34zlJDvYdVwCoFhiVhOStzZ4/edit?tab=t.0#heading=h.rll6aosu5afh.

Telegraph Obituary, 'Peter Swales, former assistant to the Rolling Stones said to have discovered Sigmund Freud's guilty secret,' 2022, The Telegraph, https://www.telegraph.co.uk/obituaries/2022/05/06/peter-swales-former-assistant-rolling-stones-said-have-discovered/.

About the Author

Asif Jalal is a published author. He has written chapters and short stories for various books. A prolific writer, he regularly contributes articles to leading national dailies such as *The Indian Express, The Times of India, The Tribune,* and *The Economic Times,* covering topics of public interest, including policing. Asif Jalal is an Indian Police Service (IPS) officer of the Himachal Pradesh cadre. He has served with the state police and various central agencies.

An alumnus of Jawaharlal Nehru University and University of Delhi, he holds degrees in sociology and law. This book was penned during his posting in Shimla, Himachal Pradesh.